Inside the Macintosh®
Communications Toolbox

Addison-Wesley Publishing Company, Inc.

Reading, Massachusetts ■ Menlo Park, California ■ New York

Don Mills, Ontario ■ Wokingham, England ■ Amsterdam ■ Bonn

Sydney ■ Singapore ■ Tokyo ■ Madrid ■ San Juan

Paris ■ Seoul ■ Milan ■ Mexico City ■ Taipei

Publications staff for Inside the Macintosh Communications Toolbox

Writer: Rob Berkowitz

Editors: Scott Smith, Becky Reece

Art Director: Tamara Whiteside

Production Editors:
Charlotte Clark, Ron Morton

Designer: Lisa Mirski

Manufacturing Supervisor:
Robin Kerns

Contents

Figures and Tables / ix

Foreword / xi

Preface / xiii

1 About the Macintosh Communications Toolbox / 1
Communications Toolbox contents / 3
Understanding routines and tools / 4
System requirements and installation / 5

2 Programming with the Macintosh Communications Toolbox / 7
Menu events / 10
   Handling menu choices / 10
   Initiating a connection / 11
   Terminating the connection / 11
   Starting to send a file / 12
   Starting to receive a file / 13
   Configuring a connection / 14
   Configuring a terminal emulation / 14
   Configuring a file transfer / 15
   Making a new session document / 16
   Closing the session document / 19
Other events / 20
   Activate events / 20
   Resume events / 20
   Update events / 21
   Keyboard events / 22
   Mouse events / 23
Main program loop / 24

3   Connection Manager / 27

About the Connection Manager / 29
    Connection channels: data, attention, and control / 30
The connection record / 31
    Connection record data structure / 31
Connection Manager routines / 35
Preparing to open a connection / 36
Custom configuration of a connection tool / 43
Interfacing with a scripting language / 47
Opening, using, and closing the connection / 48
Reading and writing data / 56
Handling events / 61
Localizing configuration strings / 63
Miscellaneous routines / 64
Completion routines / 66
Quick reference / 67

4   Terminal Manager / 75

About the Terminal Manager / 77
The terminal emulation window / 78
    The terminal emulation region / 79
    The cache region / 79
The terminal record / 80
    Terminal record data structure / 80
Terminal Manager routines / 87
Preparing for a terminal emulation / 88
Custom configuration of a terminal tool / 94
Interfacing with a scripting language / 98
Using terminal emulation routines / 99
Searching the terminal emulation buffer / 102
Manipulating selections / 104
Handling events / 105
Localizing configuration strings / 108
Miscellaneous routines / 109
Routines that must be in your application / 114
    Sample routine for sending data / 115
    Sample showing how to break a connection / 115
    Sample showing how to cache lines / 116
    Sample terminal-environment routine / 118
Quick reference / 119

5 File Transfer Manager / 127

About the File Transfer Manager / 129

The file transfer record / 130

    File transfer record data structure / 131

File Transfer Manager routines / 137

Preparing for a file transfer / 138

Custom configuration of a file transfer tool / 144

Interfacing with a scripting language / 148

Transferring files / 149

Handling events / 151

Localizing configuration strings / 153

Miscellaneous routines / 154

Routines your application provides / 156

    Sample send routine / 157

    Sample receive routine / 158

    Sample connection-environment routine / 160

Quick reference / 161

6 Communications Resource Manager / 167

About the Communications Resource Manager / 169

    Device management / 170

    Resource management / 170

The communications resource record / 171

    Communications resource record data structure / 171

Communications Resource Manager routines / 173

Resource management routines / 177

Resource-mapping routines / 180

Registering a device / 182

    Data structures / 182

Searching for serial port devices / 184

Quick reference / 185

7 Macintosh Communications Toolbox Utilities / 189

Communications Toolbox utilities / 191

Manipulating dialog item lists (DITLs) / 198

    Special ways to append items / 200

Showing AppleTalk entities: `NuLookup` and `NuPLookup` / 202

Hook and filter procedures / 206

Quick reference / 211

8   Fundamentals of Writing Your Own Tools / 215

About writing a tool / 217
The six resources / 217
    The bundle resource / 218
    The validation code resource / 219
    The setup definition code resource / 221
    The scripting language interface code resource / 226
    The localization code resource / 229
Quick reference / 231

9   Writing Connection Tools / 233

Your connection tool's main code resource / 235
Quick reference / 251

10   Writing Terminal Tools / 255

Your terminal tool's main code resource / 257
Quick reference / 273

11   Writing File Transfer Tools / 277

Your file transfer tool's main code resource / 279
Quick reference / 283

Appendix A   Guidelines for Communications Tools / 285

Design goals / 286
    Keeping your tool self-contained / 286
    Keeping your tool task-specific / 286
User interface considerations / 287
    Modeless tool operation / 288
    The standard tool-settings dialog box / 288
    Windows and status dialog boxes / 289
    Error alerts / 290
    Menus / 290
    Handling errors / 290
    Using the right words / 291
Compatibility requirements / 291
    Keyboard considerations / 291

Appendix B Communications Tools Scripting Interfaces /293

Six rules for configuration strings / 294
ADSP Tool scripting interface / 295
Apple Modem Tool scripting interface / 299
LAT Tool scripting interface / 301
Serial Tool and Serial NB Tool scripting interface / 302
Text Tool scripting interface / 303
TTY Tool scripting interface / 304
VT102 Tool scripting interface / 305
VT320 Tool scripting interface / 309
XMODEM Tool scripting interface / 313

Appendix C Useful Code Samples / 315

Using `FTExec` and `TMIdle` effectively / 316
Determining events for Communications Toolbox managers / 319
The custom tool-settings dialog box / 323
    `Choose.p` / 323
    `Choose.r` / 330
Determining whether the managers are installed / 332
Using the scripting interface / 333

Glossary / 337

Index / 339

Figures and Tables

CHAPTER 1   **About the Macintosh Communications Toolbox**

Figure 1-1   Where the Macintosh Communications Toolbox fits in / 3
Figure 1-2   How Macintosh Communications Toolbox managers interact
with applications and tools / 5

CHAPTER 3   **Connection Manager**

Figure 3-1   Data flow into and out of the Connection Manager / 29
Figure 3-2   A sample tool-settings dialog box / 41

CHAPTER 4   **Terminal Manager**

Figure 4-1   Data flow into and out of the Terminal Manager / 77
Figure 4-2   A terminal emulation window / 78
Figure 4-3   Bounds of `viewRect` and `termRect` / 84
Figure 4-4   The text selection mode `selTextNormal` / 86
Figure 4-5   The text selection mode `selTextBoxed` / 86
Figure 4-6   A sample tool-settings dialog box / 92
Figure 4-7   Additional space in the terminal emulation region / 113
Table 4-1   `TMAddSearch` search-area delimiters / 102

CHAPTER 5   **File Transfer Manager**

Figure 5-1   Data flow into and out of the File Transfer Manager / 129
Figure 5-2   A sample tool-settings dialog box / 142

CHAPTER 6   **Communications Resource Manager**

Figure 6-1   Data flow into and out of the Communications Resource
Manager / 169

CHAPTER 7   **Macintosh Communications Toobox Utilities**

Figure 7-1   Pop-up menu in its inactive and active states / 193
Figure 7-2   Pop-up menu control when system justification is
`teJustRight` / 196
Figure 7-3   Initial dialog box and to-be-appended items / 198
Figure 7-4   Dialog box after appended items are superimposed / 199
Figure 7-5   Dialog box after items are appended to the right / 199
Figure 7-6   Dialog box after items are appended to the bottom / 199

Figure 7-7   Dialog box after items are appended relative to item 2 / 200

Figure 7-8   Network look-up dialog box / 202

Table 7-1   `TMAddSearch` search-area delimiters / 205

CHAPTER 8   **Fundamentals of Writing Your Own Tool**

Table 8-1   Connection Manager messages and parameters / 232

CHAPTER 9   **Writing Connection Tools**

Table 9-1   Connection Manager messages and parameters / 253

CHAPTER 10   **Writing Terminal Tools**

Table 10-1   Terminal Manager messages and parameters / 275

CHAPTER 11   **Writing File Transfer Tools**

Table 11-1   File Transfer Manager messages and parameters / 284

APPENDIX A   **Guidelines for Communications Tools**

Figure A-1   A sample tool-settings dialog box for a connection tool / 288

Figure A-2   Example file transfer tool status dialog box / 289

Foreword

One thing I like most about being at Apple is the gifted people who make innovation the norm. Also, it's a rush to feel the energy people radiate when they believe that what they do can make a difference in the world. The creators of the Macintosh Communications Toolbox embody these ideas, which are manifest in a product that lives up to the Apple standard.

Since you are reading the foreword to an operating system reference book, you probably have more interest in the product than simply finding parameter and field descriptions. So I'll take this opportunity to tell you why the Communications Toolbox was, is, and will continue to be a good idea.

Initially conceived as a better way to engineer MacTerminal 2.0—it enabled MacTerminal to support new protocols without having to be revised—the Communications Toolbox has evolved into an integral component of our system software. By helping programmers incorporate communications features into their applications, the Communications Toolbox provides a gateway to the ever-expanding world of information.

Bill Stevens planted the seed that first sprouted in MacTerminal 2.0. Byron Han and Tom Dowdy developed the extensibility concept with the notion of communications tools. These are the guys who thought the Communications Toolbox *was* a good idea.

Now, a lot more people agree that the Communications Toolbox *is* a good idea. The system software folks think enough of the Communications Toolbox to make it a part of system software version 7.0. As evidenced by the dozens of currently shipping products that use the Communications Toolbox, a large and growing number of developers also agree. Not only are traditional communications applications (MacTerminal, for instance) supporting the Communications Toolbox, but typically desktop-bound applications are as well.

As the Communications Toolbox takes root in the inventive minds of Macintosh developers, expect to see new tools and enhancements based on developer feedback. This is how we intend to ensure the Communications Toolbox *will continue to be* a good idea. For instance, we've already announced support for ISDN and we're working on other interesting ideas.

Thanks and congratulations are appropriate here. Byron Han is, in many ways, the person most responsible for the currently shipping Communications Toolbox. Not only did Byron write abundant and fine code, he truly believed the Communications Toolbox was, and is, a good idea. In the finest Apple tradition, he lobbied, cajoled, and ultimately convinced the right Apple people. Other key members of the engineering team include Mary Chan, who developed most of the Terminal Manager and tools; Jerry Godes, who worked on all the tools in the Basic Connectivity Set; Alex Kazim, who crafted major enhancements to the human interface of the managers and tools; and Carol Lee, who produced the File Transfer Manager. While others contributed their time and talents, these are the engineers who were with the project from the beginning through the release of version 1.0. Paul Rekieta was the engineering manager, handily piloting some stormy seas.

There is a lot more to a product like the Communications Toolbox than design and coding, so I'd like to thank more stars for their commitment. Veronica Dullaghan was the product manager who weathered the project from conception to initial product ship. Rob Neville was the Quality group leader who balanced high quality standards with the weighty issue of schedules. His team included Tom Atwood, Glen Austin, Jeanne DeVoto, and Craig Hotchkiss. Mark Baumwell and James Beninghaus were the DTS mainstays who supported developers. Steve Richard and Dan Fitch provided project leadership. Rob Berkowitz provided written illumination in a first-rate document that's a key to the success of the software.

Thanks again to these talented people, and to the other contributors I've not mentioned, for an accomplishment of which they can be proud. To our developers, I sincerely hope you find the Communications Toolbox a useful addition to the Macintosh Operating System.

Buzz Dean

Director, Communications Products Development
Cupertino, California
May 1991

Preface

Inside the Macintosh Communications Toolbox provides definitive information for application software developers, communications tools developers, and hardware developers who want to use services provided by the Macintosh® Communications Toolbox. For application software developers, this document describes and shows how to use the four Communications Toolbox managers and utilities that make it easier to write communications software for the Apple® Macintosh computer. For communications tools developers, this document shows how to develop communications tools that can be used by the Communications Toolbox managers. And for hardware developers, this document shows what protocols to follow to register hardware—like internal modems or serial cards—with the Communications Toolbox Communications Resource Manager.

About this document

Chapter 1 contains an overview of the Communications Toolbox. Chapter 2 presents a sample application that uses the Communications Toolbox. The next five chapters discuss the Communications Toolbox managers and utilities, describing the routines and data structures that an application uses. Each of these chapters contains a table that lists the routines in that chapter in the order in which they are described. Chapters 3–11 conclude with "Quick References" that summarize the contents of the chapter. Chapters 8–11 show how to create a tool to add to the Communications Toolbox. While tool developers will be interested in reading these chapters, application developers may have little need to read them. Appendix A contains guidelines that communications tool developers should read to ensure that the tools they create are fully compatible with the Communications Toolbox. Appendix B describes the scripting interface for communications tools. Appendix C provides sample code solutions to common programming problems.

Inside the Macintosh Communications Toolbox is written for experienced programmers. Readers should know how to program the Macintosh and have some familiarity with communications or networking applications. To use each manager requires specific programming knowledge; suggestions on where to find more information are included at the beginning of each chapter. In addition, the next section lists resources for reference information about the technical concepts used in this document.

For more information

Refer to the following books in the Apple Technical Library and Apple Communications Library, published by Addison-Wesley, for additional information about the subjects covered in this manual:

- *Designing Cards and Drivers for the Macintosh Family*
- *Human Interface Guidelines: The Apple Desktop Interface*
- *Inside Macintosh* (Volumes I-V, X–Ref)
- *Programmer's Introduction to the Macintosh Family*
- *Technical Introduction to the Macintosh Family*
- *AppleTalk Network System Overview*
- *Inside AppleTalk*

You may also refer to the following documents from APDA® (Apple Programmers and Developers Association):

- *Software Development for International Markets: A Technical Reference*
- *Macintosh Technical Notes*

APDA offers worldwide access to a broad range of programming products, resources, and information for anyone developing on Apple platforms. You'll find the most current versions of Apple and third-party development tools, debuggers, compilers, languages, and technical references for all Apple platforms. To establish an APDA account, obtain additional ordering information, or find out about site licensing and developer training programs, please contact.

APDA
Apple Computer, Inc.
20525 Mariani Avenue, M/S 33-G
Cupertino, CA 95014-6299
1-800-282-2732 (United States)
1-800-637-0029 (Canada)
1-408-562-3910 (International)
Fax: 1-0408-562-3971
Telex: 171-576
AppleLink® address: APDA

If you provide commercial products and services, please call 1-408-974-4897 for information on the developer support programs available from Apple.

If you plan to develop Apple-compatible hardware or software products for sale through retail channels, you can get valuable support from Apple Developer Programs. Write to:

Apple Developer Programs
Apple Computer, Inc.
20525 Mariani Avenue, M/S 51-W
Cupertino, CA 95014-6299

Conventions used in this document

The following notations are used in this document to draw attention to particular items of information:

◆ *Note:*   a note that may be interesting or useful

◆ *Assembly note:*   a note of interest to assembly-language
                     programmers only

△ **Important**   a note that is particularly important

▲ **Warning**   a point that you need to be cautious about

Words that appear in the glossary are presented in **bold** typeface when first introduced in the text.

Names of routines (procedures or functions), constants, and code fragments appear in a special typeface, as in the following example:

```
PROCEDURE GetDown(andBoogie : ONEMORETIME);
```

Chapter 1 About the Macintosh Communications Toolbox

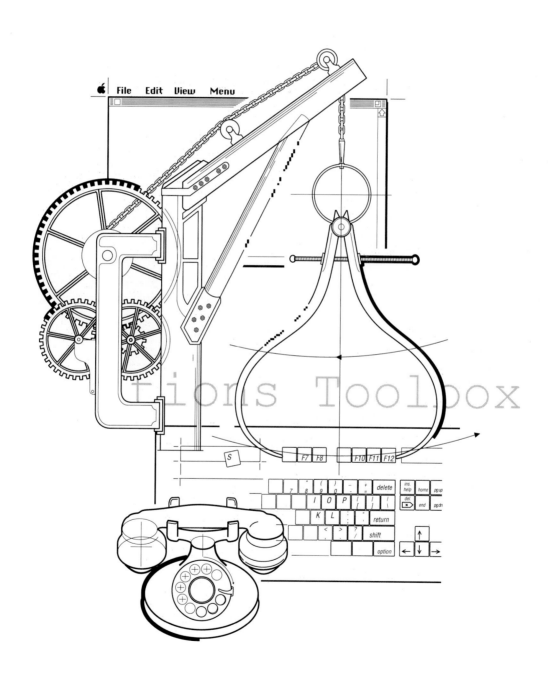

THIS CHAPTER gives you an overview of the Macintosh®
Communications Toolbox. It tells you about the managers and utilities that
are part of the Communications Toolbox, and then discusses a fundamental
concept, the difference between **routines** and tools. The last part of the
chapter provides system hardware and software requirements, and shows
how to install Communications Toolbox tools.

Communications Toolbox contents

The Communications Toolbox consists of four managers and a set of utilities. These managers and utilities are an extension to the **Macintosh Toolbox** and provide basic networking and communications services. Just as the Macintosh Toolbox makes it easier for you to develop stand-alone Macintosh applications, the Communications Toolbox helps you add networking and communications functions to applications.

Each of the managers in the Communications Toolbox handles a different aspect of networking and communications: **connection** management, **terminal emulation** management, file transfer management, and communications resource management. The managers provide routines that your application can call to indirectly interact with the operating system. *Figure 1-1* shows how the Communications Toolbox fits between your application and the operating system.

■ **Figure 1-1** Where the Macintosh Communications Toolbox fits in

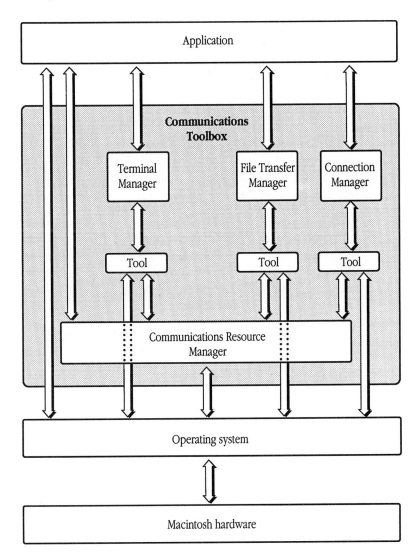

Although the managers in the Communications Toolbox handle distinctly different aspects of networking and communications, your application might need to call routines from more than one of the managers to implement a feature. For instance, in order to perform terminal emulation, in writing your program you might make use of **Connection Manager** routines to maintain the data connection, and **Terminal Manager** routines to handle the specifics of the terminal emulation.

However, your application does not have to use Communications Toolbox routines to perform all of its networking and communications tasks; for example, your application can maintain the data connection itself and use only the Terminal Manager to perform a terminal emulation. Keep in mind, though, that using Communications Toolbox routines ensures greater compatibility for your application with new tools as they become available.

Understanding routines and tools

There are two interfaces (besides the user interface) to consider when programming with the Communications Toolbox: the interface between the application and the Communications Toolbox, and the one between the Communications Toolbox and the Macintosh Operating System.

The interface between an application and the Communications Toolbox is defined by the routines in each of the managers. By calling routines, an application can request basic networking and communications services. If you are writing applications (not tools), this is the interface with which you need to be most concerned; it is discussed in Chapters 3–7.

The interface between the Communications Toolbox and the Macintosh Operating System is controlled by tools. Tools are units of code that implement the networking and communications services that your application requests. When an application calls a Communications Toolbox routine, it does so without concern for the underlying protocols. It is the job of the tool to implement basic networking and communications services according to a specific protocol. If you are writing tools (not applications), this is the interface with which you need to be most concerned; it is discussed in Chapters 8–11. Tools writers need to read at least two of these chapters: Chapter 8, which discusses concepts common to all types of tools, and one of the other chapters that deal with a specific type of tool.

Figure 1-2 shows the interaction between an application and one of the Communications Toolbox managers, in this case the Connection Manager. Notice that the application interacts with the Connection Manager, which in turn interacts with the **connection tool.** The connection tool, in turn, communicates with a driver and passes back to the application (through the manager) any relevant information. (Chapter 3 contains a complete discussion of the Connection Manager.)

■ **Figure 1-2** How Macintosh Communications Toolbox managers interact with applications and tools

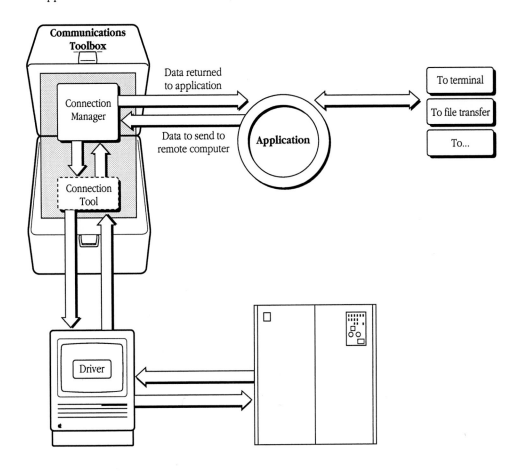

System requirements and installation

The Communications Toolbox can be run on all Macintosh computers that have at least 1 megabyte (MB) of random-access memory (RAM), Macintosh Plus (128K) read-only memory (ROM) or later, and system software 6.0.4 or a later version. Minimum disk-space requirements are two floppy disk drives, a single Apple® SuperDrive™ disk drive, or a hard disk (which is recommended).

To install the Communications Toolbox, use the Installer script on the *Communications 1* disk. If your machine will not start up using *Communications 1*, use a *Network Products Installer* disk. These disks are available from APDA® (Apple Programmers and Developers Association).

You can install communications tools by dragging the icon for each tool into the folder named *Communications Folder,* which is inside the System Folder. Your application can access tools immediately after you have installed them (you don't have to restart).

Chapter 2 **Programming with the Macintosh Communications Toolbox**

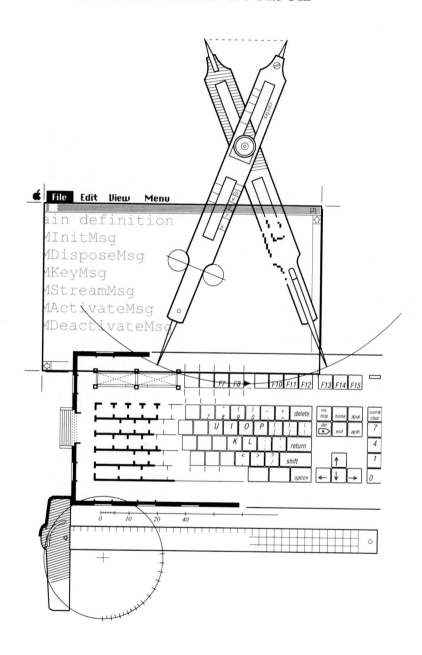

THIS CHAPTER provides an example of how applications can use the Communications Toolbox to implement communications services. The example focuses on use of the Communications Toolbox, rather than on Macintosh programming in general.

Thus, the sample code is not a complete program. It contains the parts of a program that handle communications functions; the rest of the program has been replaced with comments. This sample shows you where in an application to put the hooks to which you can attach Communications Toolbox routines.

The sample application, if it were a real, working program, would allow you to perform functions that span the three major Communications Toolbox managers: the Connection Manager, the Terminal Manager, and the **File Transfer Manager.** Specifically, the sample source code shows you how to

- open and close a connection

- send and receive files

- configure connections, terminal emulations, and file transfers

- clear the screen

- reset the terminal

The sample code is split into three sections to make it easier to understand. The first section shows how your application can deal with events that result from menu selections; the sample application contains routines that handle basic communications services, like opening a connection and sending a file. The second section shows how your application can deal with events like scrolling and mouse clicks. The last section shows the sample application's main code loop. You might find it helpful to read some of the chapters that discuss the managers before reading through the code.

Assume the following globals

```
VAR
        gTerm           : TermHandle;            { tool records }
        gFT             : FTHandle;
        gConn           : ConnHandle;
        gBuffer         : Ptr;                   { My data buffer }
        gCache          : Handle;                { 1-line cache }

        done            : BOOLEAN;               { Main Event Loop Flag }
        gStartFT        : BOOLEAN;               { Flag to start a transfer }
        gWasFT          : BOOLEAN;               { Flag set during a transfer }
```

Menu events

Handling menu choices

```
PROCEDURE DoCommand(mResult : LONGINT);
VAR
        theItem          : INTEGER;                    { menu info }
        theMenu          : INTEGER;

BEGIN
        theItem := LoWord(mResult);            { which item }
        theMenu := HiWord(mResult);            { which menu }

        { First see if the menu belonged to a tool }
        { If the tool handles it, then leave }

        IF gTerm <> NIL THEN
                IF TMMenu(gTerm, theMenu, theItem) THEN BEGIN
                        HiliteMenu(0);
                        Exit(DoCommand);               { Terminal tool handled it }
                END;

        IF gConn <> NIL THEN
                IF CMMenu(gConn, theMenu, theItem) THEN BEGIN
                        HiliteMenu(0);
                        Exit(DoCommand);               { Connection tool handled it }
                END;

        IF gFT <> NIL THEN
                IF FTMenu(gFT, theMenu, theItem) THEN BEGIN
                        HiliteMenu(0);
                        Exit(DoCommand);               { File transfer tool handled it }
                END;

        { Must be an application menu }

        (*
        Application menu handling goes here
        *)

        HiliteMenu(0);
END; { DoCommand }
```

Initiating a connection

```
PROCEDURE DoInitiate;
VAR
        theErr : CMErr;                    { Problem Flag }
        sizes  : CMBufferSizes;            { Conn tool channel sizes }
        status : CMStatFlags;              { Conn tool states }


BEGIN
        IF gConn <> NIL THEN BEGIN

                { Get the state of the connection }
                theErr := CMStatus(gConn, sizes, status);

                { If it's not already open or opening, then open it }
                { In this case, open it synchronous, no timeout }

                IF BAND(status, cmStatusOpen + cmStatusOpening) = 0 THEN
                        theErr := CMOpen(gConn, FALSE, NIL, -1);

                IF theErr <> noErr THEN
                        ;        { The tool will put up its own error alert }

        END; { Good handle }
END; { DoInitiate }
```

Terminating the connection

```
PROCEDURE DoKill;
VAR
        theErr   : CMErr;                  { Error codes }
        sizes    : BufferSizes;            { Tool channel sizes }
        status   : CMStatFlags;            { State of the connection }


BEGIN
        IF gConn <> NIL THEN BEGIN

                { Get the connection status }
                theErr := CMStatus(gConn, sizes, status );

                { Close it only if it's open or opening }
                { In this case: synchronous, no timeout }
```

```
                    IF BAND(status, cmStatusOpen + cmStatusOpening) <> 0 THEN
                            theErr := CMClose(gConn, FALSE, NIL, 0, TRUE);


                    IF theErr <> noErr THEN
                            ;           { The tool will put up its own error alert }


            END; { Good Connection }
END; { DoKill }
```

Starting to send a file

```
PROCEDURE DoSend;
VAR
            theReply : SFReply;                     { File Info }
            where    : Point;                       { upper-left corner of File dialog }
            numTypes : INTEGER;                     { File Types to display }
            typeList : SFTypeList;
            anyErr   : FTErr;                       { Error handler }


BEGIN
            IF gFT <> NIL THEN BEGIN                 { Good handle }


                    { Set location of the SFGetFile dialog }
                    SetPt(where, 100, 100);

                    { If the FT tool can only send text files, then }
                    { only display text files, else display all types }

                    { Check to see if Text Only flag is set }
                    IF BAND(gFT^^.attributes, ftTextOnly) <> 0 THEN BEGIN
                            typeList[0] := 'TEXT';
                            numTypes := 1;
                    END
                    ELSE
                            numTypes := -1;

                    SFGetFile(where, 'File to Send', NIL,
                            numTypes, typeList, NIL, theReply);


                    { Did the user hit OK or Cancel }
                    IF theReply.good THEN BEGIN


                                            { Transfer the file TO the remote }
```

```
                    anyErr := FTStart(gFT,ftTransmitting,theReply);

               IF (anyErr <> noErr) THEN
                    ;          { Handle any errors here }


          END; { Good file }


     END; { Good FTHandle }


END; { DoSend }
```

Starting to receive a file

```
PROCEDURE DoReceive;
VAR
        theReply        : SFReply;              { File Info }
        anyErr          : OSErr;                { Errors on Start }


BEGIN
     IF gFT <> NIL THEN BEGIN


               { Let the FT tool use its own default file info }
               theReply.vRefNum := 0;
               theReply.fName := '';


               { Remove the search temporarily in case it }
               { comes across during the transfer }
               (*
               Use CMRemoveSearch() to get rid of the file
               transfer auto-receive string search
               *)


               { Start receiving the file }
               { The rest gets transferred in the Idle loop }


               anyErr := FTStart(gFT,ftReceiving,theReply);


               IF (anyErr <> noErr) THEN
                       ;                { Handle error conditions }


          END; { Good Handle }


END; { DoReceive }
```

Configuring a connection

```
PROCEDURE DoConnectionConfig;
VAR
        result  : INTEGER;          { Choose went OK? }
        where   : Point;            { upper-left corner of the choose dialog }
        tempStr : Str255;

BEGIN
        { Set the dialog box as close as possible to upper-left corner of screen }
        { because the dialog box will grow down and/or to the right }

        SetPt(where, 10, 40);

        IF gConn <> NIL THEN BEGIN

                { Put up the standard tool chooser }
                result := CMChoose(gConn, where, NIL);

                (*
                Handle the result here.
                If the tool has changed, need to re-add the file
                transfer auto-receive search to the new connection tool.
                *)

        END; { Good handle }

END; { DoConnectionConfig }
```

Configuring a terminal emulation

```
PROCEDURE DoTerminalConfig;
VAR
        result : INTEGER;           { Choose went OK? }
        where  : Point;             { Upper-left corner of the choose dialog }

BEGIN
        { Set the dialog box as close as possible to top-left corner of screen }
        { because the dialog box will grow down and/or to the right }

        SetPt(where, 10, 40);

        IF gTerm <> NIL THEN BEGIN
```

```
                { Put up the standard tool chooser }
                result := TMChoose(gTerm, where, NIL);


                (*
                - Handle the result here
                *)


        END; { Good handle }


END; { DoTerminalConfig }
```

Configuring a file transfer

```
PROCEDURE DoFileTransferConfig;
VAR
        result          : INTEGER;          { User chose all right }
        where           : Point;            { upper-left corner of the dialog }
        tempString      : STR255;           { Search for FT sequence }

BEGIN
        { Set the dialog box as close as possible to top-left corner of screen }
        { because the dialog box will grow down and/or to the right }

        SetPt(where, 10, 40);

        IF gFT <> NIL THEN BEGIN

                { Put up the standard box }
                result := FTChoose(gFT, where, NIL);

                (*
                If the result = OKMajor or OKMinor, we may need to:
                    remove the old file transfer auto-receive search (if any)
                    add the new file transfer tool's auto-receive string (if any).
                *)

        END; { Good Handle }


END; { DoFileTransferConfig }
```

Making a new session document

```
PROCEDURE MakeNew;
VAR
        err                     : OSErr;             { Errors from Environ call }
        theWindow               : WindowPtr;         { Home for the terminal }
        theRect                 : Rect;              { TermRect for terminal }
        sizes                   : BufferSizes;       { Connection tool buffers }
        termEnvironment         : TermEnvironRec;
        termID,
        ftID,
        connID                  : INTEGER;           { proc IDs for the tools }
        toolName                : Str255;            { who are they? }
        tempStr                 : Str255;            { AutoReceive string for FT }

BEGIN
        { Need a home }
        theWindow := GetNewWindow(128, NIL, POINTER(-1));

        IF (theWindow = NIL) THEN BEGIN
                ;           { Handle Error }
                Exit(MakeNew);
        END;

        SetPort(theWindow);

        { Set up the termRect/viewRect for Term tool }
        theRect := theWindow^.portRect;

        { If we have scroll bars, we'll need to inset theRect }
        { to account for their widths }

        gTerm := NIL;
        gConn := NIL;
        gFT := NIL;
        gBuffer := NIL;
        gCache := NIL;

        gStartFT := FALSE;
        gWasFT := FALSE;
```

```
{ -------------------------- }
{ New terminal tool          }
{ -------------------------- }


(*
Get the terminal tool's proc ID by calling either
CRMGetIndToolName() and/or TMGetProcID()
*)


{ New Terminal tool }
gTerm := TMNew(theRect, theRect, tmSaveBeforeClear, termID,
               theWindow, @SendProc, @CacheProc, @BreakProc,
               NIL, @TermGetConnEnvirons, 0, 0);
IF (gTerm = nil) THEN BEGIN
        { Handle error }
        Exit(MakeNew);
END;



{ -------------------------- }
{ New connection tool        }
{ -------------------------- }


{ Set the desired sizes }
sizes[cmDataIn] := 1024;     { I only want data in this example }
sizes[cmDataOut] := 1024;
sizes[cmCntlIn] := 0;        { Ignore these channels }
sizes[cmCntlOut] := 0;
sizes[cmAttnIn] := 0;
sizes[cmAttnOut] := 0;


(*
Get the connection tool's proc ID by calling either
CRMGetIndToolName() and/or CMGetProcID()
*)


{ Only want the data channel }
gConn := CMNew(connID, cmData, sizes, 0, 0);


IF (gConn = nil) THEN BEGIN
        { Handle error }
        Exit(MakeNew);
END;
```

```
{ -------------------------- }
{ New file transfer tool      }
{ -------------------------- }


(*
Get the file transfer tool's proc ID by calling either
CRMGetIndToolName() and/or FTGetProcID()
*)


{ ReadProc and WriteProc are nil to let }
{ the tool handle the file input and output }

gFT := FTNew(ftID, 0, @FTsendProc, @FTreceiveProc, NIL, NIL,
            @FTGetConnEnvirons,theWindow, 0, 0);


IF (gFT = nil) THEN BEGIN
        { Handle error }
        Exit(MakeNew);
END;


(*
If the file transfer tool's auto-receive string isn't empty
then add it with CMAddSearch(gFT,theString,flags,@AutoRecCallBack)
*)


gBuffer := NewPtr(1024);        { the data buffer }
IF (gBuffer = NIL) THEN
        ; { Handle Errors }

END; { MakeNew }



{ Call Back Proc if a FT auto-receive string is found }
PROCEDURE AutoRecCallback(gConn: ConnHandle; data: Ptr; refNum: LONGINT);
BEGIN
        { We can't call FTStart() or CMRemoveSearch() here as }
        { this proc might be called from Interrupt level }

        gStartFT := TRUE;               { Set the flag to call FTStart in Idle }
END; { AutoRecCallBack }
```

Closing the session document

```
PROCEDURE DoClose(theWindow: WindowPtr);
BEGIN

        IF theWindow <> NIL THEN BEGIN
            IF gTerm <> NIL THEN
                    TMDispose(gTerm);              { Get rid of the tools }


            IF gConn <> NIL THEN
                    CMDispose(gConn);              { Tools should dispose of }
                                                   { their own windows }
            IF gFT <> NIL THEN
                    FTDispose(gFT);


            IF gBuffer <> NIL THEN                 { Get rid of my data space }
                    DisposPtr(gBuffer);


            DisposeWindow(theWindow);              { Get rid of the window }
        END; { Good Window }


END; { DoClose }
```

Other events

Activate events

```
PROCEDURE DoActivate(theEvent : EventRecord);
VAR
        theWindow      : WindowPtr;
        processed      : BOOLEAN;                        { Activate or Deactivate }


BEGIN
        theWindow := WindowPtr(theEvent.message);
        SetPort(theWindow);                              { Focus on the target }


        { Is this an activate or a deactivate }
        processed := BAND(theEvent.modifiers, activeFlag) <> 0;


        (*
        (Deactivate application stuff here
        *)


        { Tools need to adjust their menus, text selection, etc. }
        IF gTerm <> NIL THEN
                TMActivate(gTerm, processed);     { Send message to the tool }


        IF gConn <> NIL THEN
                CMActivate(gConn, processed);     { Send message to the tool }


        IF gFT <> NIL THEN
                FTActivate(gFT, processed);       { Send message to the tool }
END; { DoActivate }
```

Resume events

```
PROCEDURE DoResume(theEvent : EventRecord);
CONST
        resumeFlag = 1;


VAR
        theWindow      : WindowPtr;
        isResume       : BOOLEAN;                        { Resume/Suspend Event }
        savedPort      : GrafPtr;


BEGIN
        GetPort(savedPort);                              { Current Focus }
```

```
        theWindow := FrontWindow;               { Get the target }


{ Tools may work in background }
IF theWindow <> NIL THEN BEGIN
        SetPort(theWindow);

        isResume := BAND(theEvent.message, resumeFlag) <> 0;

        IF gTerm <> NIL THEN
                TMResume(gTerm, isResume);

        IF gConn <> NIL THEN
                CMResume(gConn, isResume);

        IF gFT <> NIL THEN
                FTResume(gFT, isResume);

        SetPort(savedPort);
    END; { if good window }
END; { DoResume }
```

Update events

```
PROCEDURE DoUpdate(theEvent:EventRecord);
VAR
        theWindow      : WindowPtr;           { The target to update }
        savedPort      : GrafPtr;             { Temporarily saved }
        savedClip      : RgnHandle;           { Clipping for the terminal }


BEGIN
        theWindow := WindowPtr(theEvent.message);

        IF theWindow <> NIL THEN BEGIN
                savedClip := NewRgn;          { Allocating for QD }

                GetPort(savedPort);           { Change the focus }
                SetPort(theWindow);

                GetClip(savedClip);           { Save the old area }
                ClipRect(theWindow^.portRect);     { Just the window }

                BeginUpdate(theWindow);
                                              { Clear the old data }
```

```
                    EraseRect(theWindow^.portRect);


                    (*

                    Update application stuff here
                    *)
                                                    { Terminal tool will redraw }
                    IF gTerm <> NIL THEN
                            TMUpdate(gTerm, theWindow^.visRgn);


                EndUpdate(theWindow);


                SetClip(savedClip);                 { Put it all back }
                DisposeRgn(savedClip);              { Clean up }


                SetPort(savedPort);
        END; { Good Window }


END; { DoUpdate }
```

Keyboard events

```
PROCEDURE DoKey(theEvent : EventRecord);
VAR
        theKey          : CHAR;             { The character hit }
        processed       : BOOLEAN;          { Did the application handle it }
        result          : LONGINT;          { value MenuKey() returns }
BEGIN
        { Get the character }
        theKey := CHAR(BAND(theEvent.message, charCodeMask));


        processed := FALSE;                         { Haven't intercepted it }


        { Was it a command equivalent }
        IF BAND(theEvent.modifiers, cmdKey) <> 0 THEN BEGIN


                result := MenuKey(theKey);          { Get the key equivalent }
                                                    { Valid menu key? }
                IF theMenu <> 0 THEN BEGIN
                        processed := TRUE;          { Application will redirect }
                        DoCommand(result);          { Calls the above routine }
                END; { Good Menu Equivalent }


        END; { Cmd-key down? }
```

```
        { If it wasn't a valid menu command then pass the event to the terminal }


        IF (gTerm <> NIL) AND NOT processed THEN
                TMKey(gTerm, theEvent);
END; { DoKey }
```

Mouse events

```
PROCEDURE DoClick(theEvent : EventRecord);
VAR
        theWindow : WindowPtr;                           { The target }


BEGIN
                                                   { Where was the click }
        thePart := FindWindow(theEvent.where, theWindow);

        CASE thePart OF
                inMenuBar: BEGIN
                                                   { Get the menu info }
                                result := MenuSelect(theEvent.where);
                                DoCommand(result);    { call above routine }
                        END;


                inGrow:      BEGIN
                             { Resize the Window, scroll bars, etc. }


                                                   { Tell the terminal }
                                TMResize(gTerm,theWindow^.portRect);
                        END;


                inContent:
                        IF gTerm <> NIL THEN BEGIN
                                (*
                                Call TMScroll() if the click was in a scroll bar
                                *)

                                TMClick(gTerm, theEvent);    { For mouse selection }
                        END;   { valid term rec }


                otherwise
                        ;        { Perform standard event action }
        END; { case }
END; { DoClick }
```

Main program loop

```
PROCEDURE MainLoop;
VAR
        theEvent        : EventRecord;          { World Happenstances }
        theWindow       : WindowPtr;            { The desired target }


BEGIN
        WHILE NOT done DO BEGIN
                DoIdle;                         { Call our idle proc once thru }

                IF WaitNextEvent(everyEvent,theEvent, 0, NIL) THEN BEGIN

                        { get the target window }
                        CASE theEvent.what OF
                                autoKey, keyDown:
                                        theWindow := FrontWindow;
                                mouseDown:
                                        IF FindWindow(theEvent.where,theWindow)=0 THEN
                                                ;
                                otherwise
                                        theWindow := WindowPtr(theEvent.message);
                        END; { case }

                        { All windows created by a tool are supposed to }
                        { have their RefCons = LONGINT(theToolHandle) }

                        (*
                        Call the tool event proc if the window is a tool
                        window. i.e. TMEvent()
                        *)

                        IF (theWindow <> NIL) THEN BEGIN
                                SetPort(theWindow);

                                CASE theEvent.what OF                    { App Window }
                                        autoKey, keyDown:
                                                { May set done to true }
                                                DoKey(theEvent);
                                        mouseDown:
                                                { May set done to true }
                                                DoClick(theEvent);
                                        updateEvt:
                                                DoUpdate(theEvent);
```

```
                                app4Evt:
                                        DoResume(theEvent);
                                activateEvt:
                                        DoActivate(theEvent);
                        END; { case }


                END; { Good Window }


        END; { WaitNextEvent }


    END; { while not done }


END; { DoMainLoop }
```

Chapter 3 Connection Manager

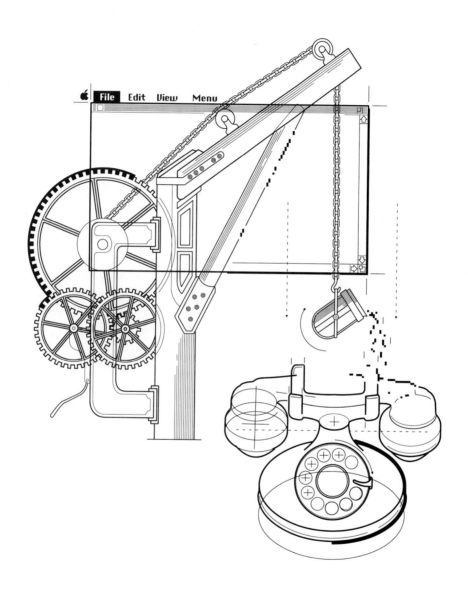

THIS CHAPTER describes the Connection Manager, the Communications Toolbox manager that allows applications to establish and maintain connections. This chapter describes some of the fundamental concepts about the Connection Manager. Then it describes the **connection record,** which is the most important data structure to the Connection Manager. Next, this chapter presents a detailed functional description of each routine provided by the Connection Manager. At the end of the chapter, you'll find a "Quick Reference" to routines, data structures, and routine selectors for programming in assembly language.

In this chapter, the term *your application* refers to the application you are writing for the Macintosh, which will implement communications services for users. Be careful not to confuse the services your application provides with the services that tools provide.

To use the Connection Manager, you need to be familiar with

- the Resource Manager (described in *Inside Macintosh,* Volumes I, IV, V)

- the Device Manager (described in *Inside Macintosh,* Volumes II, IV, V)

About the Connection Manager

By using Connection Manager routines, your application can implement basic connection services without having to take into account underlying connection protocols. Connection tools, which are discussed in Chapter 9, are responsible for implementing connection services according to specific protocols.

The Connection Manager provides a generic connection—a **channel** that carries data between your application and another computer process. The other process can be running on the same computer as your application or on any other computer.

Here's what happens inside the Connection Manager. An application makes a request of the Connection Manager when it needs a connection service, such as opening a connection. The Connection Manager then sends this request to one of the tools that it manages. The tool provides the service according to the specifics of the connection protocol that is implemented for the data connection. Once the tool has finished, it passes back to the application (through the manager) any relevant parameters and return codes.

The data is sent along the connection in a byte stream (a reliable byte stream, if the connection protocol supports error correction), rather than on a transaction-by-transaction basis. Although the Connection Manager does not provide flow control, error correction, error detection, and data encapsulation, a tool or application can provide these services.

Figure 3-1 shows the data flow into and out of the Connection Manager.

■ **Figure 3-1** Data flow into and out of the Connection Manager

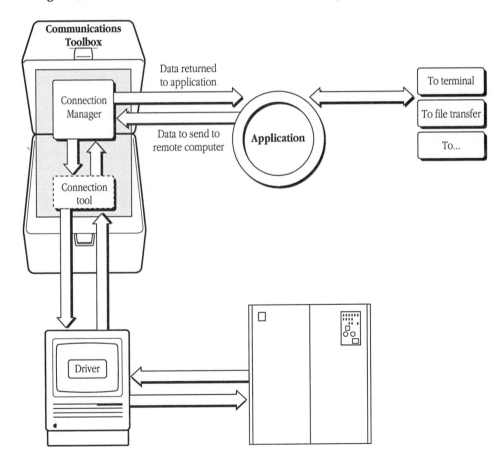

The most important data structure maintained by the Connection Manager is the connection record, which stores all the specifics about a connection. For example, the connection record might show that a connection takes place over a direct serial port connection transmitting at 9,600 bits per second (bps).

One important aspect of the connection record is that it allows for protocol-independent routines. Protocol-independent routines allow applications to use Connection Manager services without regard for the underlying communications protocols. In other words, when an application wants to read data from a remote **entity,** it tells the Connection Manager to read, and the connection tool figures out exactly how to implement a read operation on a given connection.

Another important feature of the connection record is that it lets you use multiple instances of the same tool. The same tool can be used by different processes at the same time, as in a MultiFinder® operating system environment, or by different threads in a given application.

The connection record is described in greater detail later in this chapter.

Besides providing basic connection routines, the Connection Manager includes routines that make it easy for your application to configure a connection tool, either by presenting the user with a dialog box or by interfacing directly with a scripting language. The Connection Manager also contains routines that make it easier for you to localize your applications in other languages.

You can use the Connection Manager with other Communications Toolbox managers to create a communications application with file transfer and terminal emulation capabilities. Or, you can use the Connection Manager with some other data transfer or terminal emulation service. You can also write your own connection tool for the Connection Manager to use. (This procedure is discussed in Chapters 8 and 9.) Regardless of which method you choose, your application should be able to handle different connection tools so that users can change tools and still be able to use your program.

Connection channels: data, attention, and control

When data is sent along a connection, there is a certain amount of overhead that sometimes accompanies it. This "extra" information could be a warning that the connection is about to go down or that the sending entity should slow its rate of transmitting data. Some connection protocols are designed in such a way that this sort of information can be sent simultaneously with the data stream on a channel. The Connection Manager supports up to three channels on each connection—data, attention, and control—that can be thought of as three separate lines of communication between each entity. The data channel, however, is for all protocols the primary channel for transmitting information between entities. The other two channels are used by only some connection protocols.

When you design your application, keep in mind that some protocols support all three channels, whereas others support only one (the data channel). Your application should be able to handle different connection tools in a way that allows users to change tools and still be able to use your program.

The connection record

The connection record contains information that describes a connection, as well as pointers to Connection Manager internal data structures. The Connection Manager uses this information to "translate" the protocol-independent routines used by an application into a service implemented according to a specified protocol. Most of the fields in the connection record are filled in when an application calls `CMNew`, described later in this chapter.

    Because the connection record describes how communications take place on a given connection, an application can communicate on more than one connection at the same time. All the application has to do is create a new connection record every time it initiates a new connection.

△ **Important**   Your application, in order to be compatible with future releases of the Connection Manager, should not directly manipulate the fields of the connection record (with the exception of `config` and `oldConfig`). The Connection Manager provides routines that applications and tools can use to change connection record fields. These routines are discussed later in this chapter. △

Connection record data structure

```
TYPE
        ConnHandle          =       ^ConnPtr;
        ConnPtr             =       ^ConnRecord;
        ConnRecord          =       RECORD
                procID      :       INTEGER;

                flags       :       CMRecFlags;
                errCode     :       CMErr;

                refCon      :       LONGINT;
                userData    :       LONGINT

                defProc     :       ProcPtr;

                config      :       Ptr;
                oldConfig   :       Ptr;

                reserved0   :       LONGINT;
                reserved1   :       LONGINT;
                reserved2   :       LONGINT;

                cmPrivate   :       Ptr;

                bufferArray :       CMBuffers;
                bufSizes    :       CMBufferSizes;
```

```
            mluField        :        LONGINT;

            asyncCount      :        CMBufferSizes;

      END;
```

procID

procID is the connection tool ID. This value is dynamically assigned by the Connection Manager when your application calls CMGetProcID.

flags

flags is a bit field that indicates certain specifics about a connection when the connection record is first created. The bit masks for flags are as follows:

```
TYPE
        CMRecFlags      =        LONGINT;


CONST
        cmData          =        $00000001;
        cmCntl          =        $00000002;
        cmAttn          =        $00000004;

        cmDataClean     =        $00000100;
        cmCntlClean     =        $00000200;
        cmAttnClean     =        $00000400;

        cmNoMenus       =        $00010000;
        cmQuiet         =        $00020000;
```

Your application can turn on the cmNoMenus or cmQuiet bits when it calls CMNew (discussed later in this chapter). The connection tool will set the rest of these bits.

If the tool sets the cmData, cmCntl, or cmAttn bit, your application can use a data, control, or attention channel. If the tool sets the cmDataClean, cmCntlClean, or cmAttnClean bit, your application can use a reliable (error-free, in order delivery) data, control, or attention channel.

The connection tool will not display any custom menus if your application sets the cmNoMenus bit. The connection tool will not display any status dialog boxes or error alerts if your application sets the cmQuiet bit. If your application turns the cmQuiet bit on, it is responsible for displaying status dialog boxes and error alerts that the tool would have displayed. Applications typically use these two bits to hide the connection tool from the user.

errCode

errCode contains the last error encountered by the Connection Manager. Valid error codes are as follows:

```
TYPE
        CMErr              =         OSErr;


CONST
        cmGenericError     =         -1;
        cmNoErr            =         0;
        cmRejected         =         1;
        cmFailed           =         2;
        cmTimeOut          =         3;
        cmNotOpen          =         4;
        cmNotClosed        =         5;
        cmNoRequestPending =         6;
        cmNotSupported     =         7;
        cmNoTools          =         8;
        cmUserCancel       =         9;
```

refCon

refCon is a four-byte field that your application can use.

userData

userData is a four-byte field that your application can use.

defProc

defProc is a procedure pointer to the main code resource of the connection tool that will implement the connection protocol. The connection tool's main code resource is of type `'cdef'`.

config

config is a pointer to a data block that is private to the connection tool. It can contain information such as data transfer rate or parity for direct asynchronous connections, phone numbers for modem connections, or an address for an AppleTalk® network connection; the contents vary from tool to tool.

Your application can store the contents of config to save the state of a connection in a document. The structure, size, and contents of the configuration record are set by the tool. Your application can determine the size of the configuration record by calling GetPtrSize, overwrite its contents using BlockMove, and validate the contents with CMValidate.

Your application can use CMGetConfig and CMSetConfig to manipulate fields in this record. For details, see "Interfacing with a Scripting Language," later in this chapter. Your application can save the state of the connection record by saving the string returned from CMGetConfig. Also, your application can restore the configuration of the connection record by passing a saved string to CMSetConfig.

You can find more information about config from a connection tool perspective in Chapter 8.

oldConfig

oldConfig is a pointer to a data block that is private to the connection tool and contains the most recently saved version of config. Your application is responsible for setting oldConfig when the user saves a session document.

reserved0, reserved1, and reserved2

reserved0, reserved1, and reserved2 are fields that are reserved for the Connection Manager. Your application must not use these fields.

cmPrivate

cmPrivate is a pointer to a data block that is private to the connection tool. Your application must not use this field.

bufferArray

bufferArray is a set of pointers to buffers for the data, control, and attention channels. These are the buffers that are used to read data to or write data from the entity. These buffers are allocated by the connection tool and are the exclusive property of the connection tool; your application should not use these buffers. The data type for bufferArray is CMBuffers and is defined under the description of bufSizes.

bufSizes

bufSizes contains the actual sizes of the buffers and it, too, should not be manipulated directly by an application. The data type for bufSizes is CMBufferSizes, and is defined as follows:

```
TYPE
      CMBufFields=(
            cmDataIn,
            cmDataOut
            cmCntlIn
            cmCntlOut
            cmAttnIn
            cmAttnOut
            cmRsrvIn                {Reserved for Apple}
            cmRsrvOut);             {Reserved for Apple}

      CMBuffers           =        ARRAY[CMBufFields] OF Ptr;
      CMBufferSizes       =        ARRAY[CMBufFields] OF LONGINT;
```

mluField

mluField is a pointer to a private data structure that the Connection Manager uses when searching the data stream.

asyncCount

asyncCount is used by **completion routines** to determine how many bytes were actually transmitted or received on a particular channel. Completion routines are discussed in more detail later in this chapter.

Connection Manager routines

The following sections describe the routines that tools and applications can use to access Connection Manager services. These routines are protocol independent; your application does not need to be familiar with the specifics of a particular communications protocol in order to use the connection. Your application can call three Connection Manager routines from interrupt level: CMRead, CMWrite, and CMStatus. The other routines cannot be called from interrupt level.

   Below is a listing of the routines described in this section in the order in which they are presented.

InitCM / 36
CMGetProcID / 37
CMNew / 38
CMDefault / 40
CMValidate / 40
CMChoose / 41
CMSetupPreFlight / 43
CMSetupSetup / 44
CMSetupFilter / 44
CMSetupItem / 45
CMSetupCleanup / 45
CMSetupPostFlight / 46
CMGetConfig / 47
CMSetConfig / 47
CMOpen / 48
CMClose / 49
CMAbort / 49
CMDispose / 50
CMIdle / 50
CMListen / 50
CMStatus / 51
CMAccept / 52

CMIOKill / 52
CMReset / 53
CMBreak / 53
CMGetConnEnvirons / 54
CMRead / 56
CMWrite / 58
CMAddSearch / 59
CMRemoveSearch / 60
CMClearSearch / 60
CMActivate / 61
CMResume / 61
CMMenu / 61
CMEvent / 62
CMIntlToEnglish / 63
CMEnglishToIntl / 63
CMGetToolName / 64
CMSetRefCon / 64
CMGetRefCon / 64
CMSetUserData / 65
CMGetUserData / 65
CMGetVersion / 65
CMGetCMVersion / 65

Preparing to open a connection

Before your application can open a connection, it must initialize the Connection Manager (by calling InitCM), find out the procID of the tool it requires (by calling CMGetProcID), create a connection record (by calling CMNew), and then configure the connection tool (by restoring config from a saved document; or by calling CMChoose, the connection tool custom configuration routines, or CMSetConfig).

InitCM

Initializing the Connection Manager

InitCM initializes the Connection Manager. Your application should call this routine only once, after calling the standard Macintosh Toolbox initialization routines.

▲ **Warning** Your application must initialize the **Communications Resource Manager** (by calling InitCRM) and then the Communications Toolbox Utilities (by calling InitCTBUtilities), whether or not it uses any of their calls, before it initializes the Connection Manager. ▲

Function   InitCM : CMErr;

Description   InitCM returns an operating system error code if appropriate. Your application must check for the presence of the Communications Toolbox before calling this function. Sample code under "Determining Whether the Managers are Installed" in Appendix C shows you how your application can make this check.

Result Codes cmGenericError, cmNoErr, cmNoTools.

Getting current `procID` information

Your application should call `CMGetProcID` just before creating a new connection record, to find out the `procID` of a tool.

Function

```
CMGetProcID(name: Str255): INTEGER;
```

Description

`name` specifies a connection tool. If a connection tool is available with the specified `name`, its `procID` is returned. If `name` references a nonexistent connection tool, `CMGetProcID` returns –1.

Creating a connection record

Before your application can open a connection, it must create a connection record so the Connection Manager knows what type of connection to establish. CMNew creates a new connection record; fills in the fields that it can, based upon the parameters that were passed to it; and returns a handle to the new record in ConnHandle. CMNew automatically makes two calls to CMDefault (which is described later in this chapter) to fill in config and oldConfig. The Connection Manager then loads the connection tool main code resource, moves it high in the current heap, and locks it. If an error occurs that prevents a new connection record from being created (for example, running out of memory), CMNew passes back NIL in ConnHandle.

Function

```
CMNew(procID : INTEGER; flags : CMRecFlags; desiredSizes :
CMBufferSizes; refCon : LONGINT; userData : LONGINT) : ConnHandle;
```

Description

procID is dynamically assigned by the Connection Manager to tools at run time. Applications should not store procID values in settings files. Instead, they should store tool names, which can be converted to procID values with the CMGetProcID routine. Your application should use the ID that CMGetProcID returns for procID.

flags is a bit field with the following masks:

```
CONST
        cmData          =       $00000001;
        cmCntl          =       $00000002;
        cmAttn          =       $00000004;

        cmDataClean     =       $00000100;
        cmCntlClean     =       $00000200;
        cmAttnClean     =       $00000400;

        cmNoMenus       =       $00010000;
        cmQuiet         =       $00020000;
```

flags represents a request from your application for a level of connection service. If your application sets cmNoMenus, the connection tool will not display any custom menus. If your application sets cmQuiet, the connection tool will not display any windows. Applications typically use these bits to hide the connection tool from the user.

The connection tool sets the other bits, and returns in the flags field of the connection record the level of connection service that it grants your application. The flags field is discussed in "Connection Record Data Structure," earlier in this chapter.

Apple Computer, Inc. has reserved the bits of flags not shown in this manual. Do not use them, or your code may not work in the future.

`desiredSizes` specifies buffer sizes that your application requests for its read, write, control read, control write, attention read, and attention write channels. Your application can specify the sizes that it wants when it calls `CMNew`, but the connection tool might not provide the requested sizes. To have the tool set the size of these buffers, your application should put zeros in the array. These buffers become the exclusive property of the connection tool and should not be manipulated by the application in any way. The actual buffer sizes are kept in the `bufSizes` field of the connection record.

`refCon` and `userData` are fields that your application can use.

Initializing the configuration record

CMDefault fills the specified configuration record with the default configuration specified by the connection tool. CMNew calls this procedure automatically when it fills in the config and oldConfig fields in a new connection record.

Procedure   CMDefault(VAR theConfig: Ptr; procID: INTEGER; allocate: BOOLEAN);

Description   If allocate is TRUE, the tool allocates space for theConfig in the current heap zone.

Validating the configuration record

CMValidate performs an internal consistency check on the configuration and private data records of the connection record. CMNew and CMSetConfig call this routine after they have created a new connection record, to make sure that the record contains values identical to those specified by the connection tool.

Function   CMValidate(hConn: ConnHandle): BOOLEAN;

Description   If the validation fails, the Connection Manager returns TRUE and the tool fills the configuration record with default values by calling CMDefault.

Your application can call this routine after restoring a configuration, to verify that the connection record contains the correct information, in a manner similar to that shown next.

```
BlockMove(saveConfig,hConn^^.config,GetPtrSize(hConn^^.config));
IF CMValidate(hConn) THEN BEGIN
     { validate failed }
     END
ELSE BEGIN
          { validate succeeded }
          END
```

Configuring a connection tool

An application can configure a connection tool in one of three ways. The easiest and most straightforward way is by calling the CMChoose routine. This routine presents the user with a dialog box similar to the one shown in *Figure 3-2*.

■ **Figure 3-2** A sample tool-settings dialog box

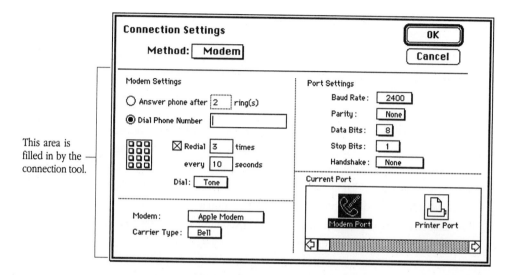

The second way an application can configure a connection tool is by presenting the user with a custom tool-settings dialog box. This method is much more difficult, and involves calling six routines. The routines are described in the next section, "Custom Configuration of a Connection Tool," and "The Custom Tool-Settings Dialog Box" in Appendix C provides example code.

The third way your application can configure a connection tool is by using the scripting language interface, described in "Interfacing With a Scripting Language," later in this chapter. This method allows your application to bypass user interface elements.

Function

```
CMChoose(VAR hConn:ConnHandle; where: Point; idleProc: ProcPtr):
INTEGER;
```

Description

where is the point, specified in global coordinates, where the upper-left corner of the dialog box should appear. It is recommended that your application place the dialog box as close as possible to the upper-left corner of the screen, because the size of the dialog box varies from tool to tool.

`idleProc` is a procedure with no parameters that the Connection Manager will automatically call every time `CMChoose` calls the setup dialog box **filter procedure.** Pass `NIL` if your application has no `idleProc`.

`CMChoose` returns one of the following values:

```
CONST
        chooseDisaster      =       -2;
        chooseFailed        =       -1;
        chooseAborted       =        0;
        chooseOKMinor       =        1;
        chooseOKMajor       =        2;
        chooseCancel        =        3;
```

`chooseDisaster` means that the `CMChoose` operation failed, destroyed the connection record, and returned `NIL` in the connection handle.

`chooseFailed` means that the `CMChoose` operation failed and the connection record was not changed.

`chooseAborted` means that the user started to change the connection while it was still open but did not commit the changes. When users try to change connection tools while the connection is still open, the Connection Manager prompts them with a dialog box that asks if they want to make the change. If the user clicks No in this dialog box, the `CMChoose` routine returns `chooseAborted`.

`chooseOKMinor` means that the user clicked OK in the dialog box but did not change the connection tool being used.

`chooseOKMajor` means that the user selected OK in the dialog box and also changed the connection tool being used. The Connection Manager then destroys the old connection handle by calling `CMDispose`. The connection is closed down, all pending read and write operations are terminated, and a new connection handle is returned in `hConn`.

`chooseCancel` means that the user clicked Cancel in the dialog box.

Custom configuration of a connection tool

Your application creates a custom tool-settings dialog box and presents it to the user by using the six Connection Manager routines: `CMSetupPreflight`, `CMSetupSetup`, `CMSetupFilter`, `CMSetupItem`, `CMSetupCleanup`, and `CMSetupPostflight`. Using these routines is more involved than calling `CMChoose`, but they provide your application with much more flexibility. Refer to the code sample in "The Custom Tool-Settings Dialog Box" in Appendix C to see how an application calls these routines.

To build a list of available connection tools, use the routine `CRMGetIndToolName`, which is described in Chapter 6.

`CMSetupPreflight`

Setting up the custom tool-settings dialog box

`CMSetupPreflight` returns a handle to a dialog item list that your application appends to the custom tool-settings dialog box. The handle comes from the connection tool. (The calling application uses `AppendDITL`, discussed in Chapter 7.) This handle is not a resource handle. Your application is responsible for disposing of the handle when done with it.

The connection tool can use `CMSetupPreflight` to allocate a block of private storage, and to store the pointer to that block in `magicCookie`. The `magicCookie` value should be passed to the other routines that are used to set up the custom tool-settings dialog box.

Function   `CMSetupPreflight(procID: INTEGER; VAR magicCookie: LONGINT): Handle;`

Description   `procID` is the ID for the connection tool that is being configured. Your application should get this value by using the `CMGetProcID` routine, discussed earlier in this chapter.

◆ *Note:* The `refcon` of the custom tool-settings dialog box should point to a data structure (shown next) in which the first two bytes are the tool `procID` and the next four bytes are `magicCookie`. `UserItem` routines, for example, may require `procID` to obtain tool resources.

```
TYPE
    chooseDLOGdata      =       RECORD
            procID      :       INTEGER
            magicCookie :       LONGINT
END;
```

Setting up custom tool-settings dialog box items

CMSetupSetup tells the connection tool to set up controls (such as radio buttons or check boxes) in the dialog item list returned by CMSetupPreflight.

Procedure

```
CMSetupSetup(procID: INTEGER; theConfig: Ptr; count: INTEGER;
theDialog: DialogPtr; VAR magicCookie: LONGINT);
```

Description

procID is the ID for the connection tool that is being configured. Your application should use the same value for procID as it passed to CMSetupPreflight.

theConfig is a pointer to a configuration record for the tool being configured.

count is the number of the first item in the dialog item list appended to the dialog box.

theDialog is the dialog box in which configuration is taking place.

magicCookie is a pointer to private storage for the connection tool.

Filtering custom tool-settings dialog box events

Your application calls CMSetupFilter as a filter procedure before it calls the standard modal dialog box filter procedure for the custom tool-settings dialog box. This routine allows connection tools to filter events in the custom tool-settings dialog box.

Function

```
CMSetupFilter(procID: INTEGER; theConfig: Ptr; count:INTEGER;
theDialog: DialogPtr; VAR theEvent: EventRecord; VAR theItem:
INTEGER; VAR magicCookie: LONGINT): BOOLEAN;
```

Description

procID is the ID for the connection tool that is being configured. Your application should use the same value for procID as it passed to CMSetupPreflight.

theConfig is a pointer to the configuration record for the tool being configured.

count is the number of the first item in the dialog item list appended to the dialog box.

theDialog is the dialog box performing the configuration.

theEvent is the event record for which filtering is to take place.

theItem can return the item clicked in the dialog box.

magicCookie is a pointer to private storage for the connection tool.

If the event passed in was handled, CMSetupFilter returns TRUE. FALSE indicates that your application should perform standard dialog box filtering.

Processing custom tool-settings dialog box events

`CMSetupItem` processes events for controls in the custom tool-settings dialog box.

Procedure

`CMSetupItem(procID: INTEGER; theConfig: Ptr; count: INTEGER; theDialog: DialogPtr; VAR theItem: INTEGER; VAR magicCookie: LONGINT);`

Description

`procID` is the ID for the connection tool being configured. Your application should use the same value for `procID` as it passed to `CMSetupPreflight`.

`theConfig` is a pointer to the configuration record for the tool being configured.

`count` is the number of the first item in the dialog item list appended to the dialog box.

`theDialog` is the dialog box performing the configuration.

`theItem` is the item clicked in the dialog box. This value can be modified and sent back.

`magicCookie` is a pointer to private storage for the connection tool.

`CMSetupCleanup`

Performing clean-up operations

`CMSetupCleanup` disposes of any storage allocated in `CMSetupPreflight` and performs other clean-up operations. If your application needs to shorten a dialog box, it should do so after calling this routine.

Procedure

`CMSetupCleanup(procID: INTEGER; theConfig: Ptr; count: INTEGER; theDialog: DialogPtr; VAR magicCookie: LONGINT);`

Description

`procID` is the ID for the connection tool that is being configured. Your application should use the same value for `procID` as it passed to `CMSetupPreflight`.

`theConfig` is a pointer to the configuration record for the tool being configured.

`count` is the number of the first item in the dialog item list appended to the dialog box.

`theDialog` is the dialog box performing the configuration.

`magicCookie` is a pointer to private storage for the connection tool.

Closing the tool file

CMSetupPostflight closes the tool file if it is not being used by any sessions.

Procedure   CMSetupPostflight(procID:INTEGER);

Description   procID is the ID for the connection tool that is being configured. Your application should use the same value for procID as it passed to CMSetupPreflight.

Interfacing with a scripting language

Your application does not have to rely on users making selections from dialog boxes in order to configure a connection tool. `CMGetConfig` and `CMSetConfig` provide the services that your application needs to interface with a scripting language.

`CMGetConfig`

Getting the configuration string

CMGetConfig gets a configuration string from the connection tool.

Function   `CMGetConfig(hConn: ConnHandle): Ptr;`

Description   `CMGetConfig` returns a null-terminated, C-style string from the connection tool containing tokens that fully describe the configuration of the connection record. For an example, see the description of the next routine. If an error occurs, `CMGetConfig` returns NIL.

It is the responsibility of your application to dispose of `Ptr`.

`CMSetConfig`

Setting the configuration with a string

CMSetConfig passes a configuration string to the connection tool.

Function   `CMSetConfig(hConn: ConnHandle; thePtr: Ptr): INTEGER;`

Description   `CMSetConfig` passes a null-terminated, C-style string (see the example string later in this section) to the connection tool for parsing. The string is pointed to by `thePtr` and must contain tokens that describe the configuration of the connection record. The string can be any length.

`CMSetConfig` ignores items it does not recognize or find relevant; such an occurrence causes the connection tool to stop parsing the string and to return the character position where the error occurred. If the connection tool successfully parses the string, it returns `cmNoErr`. If the connection tool does not successfully parse the string, it returns one of the following values: a number less than –1 to indicate an `OSErr`, –1 to indicate an unknown error, or a positive number to indicate the character position where parsing was stopped.

Individual connection tools are responsible for the parsing operation.

Sample   *A null-terminated, C-style configuration string*

```
Baud 9600 dataBits 8 Parity None StopBits 1 Port "Modem Port"
Handshake None HoldConnection False RemindDisconnect False\0
```

Opening, using, and closing the connection

Once your application has performed the required tasks described in the previous sections, it can open and use a connection.

CMOpen

Opening a connection

CMOpen attempts to open a connection, based on information contained in a connection record.

Function

CMOpen(hConn: ConnHandle; async: BOOLEAN; completor: ProcPtr; timeout: LONGINT): CMErr;

Description

hConn points to the connection record for the new connection.

async specifies whether the opening request is asynchronous. If your application makes an asynchronous request, CMOpen returns cmNoErr immediately.

completor specifies the completion routine to be called upon completion of an asynchronous open request. Completion routines are discussed in greater detail later in this chapter, in the section "Completion Routines."

timeout specifies a time period, in ticks, within which CMOpen must be completed before the connection tool returns a cmTimeOut error. For no timeout, use –1. For a single attempt to open the connection, use 0. Some connection tools ignore this parameter.

If no error occurs during the open attempt, CMOpen returns cmNoErr. CMOpen returns a negative number if an operating system error occurred, or a positive number if a Connection Manager error occurred.

Result Codes

cmGenericError, cmNoErr, cmRejected, cmFailed, cmTimeout, cmNotClosed, cmNotSupported, cmUserCancel.

Closing a connection

CMClose closes a connection that is already open or in the process of opening.

Function   CMClose(hConn: ConnHandle; async: BOOLEAN; completor: ProcPtr; timeout: LONGINT; now: BOOLEAN): CMErr;

Description   async specifies whether or not the close request is asynchronous. If your application requests an asynchronous close, CMClose returns noErr immediately.

completor specifies the completion routine to be called upon completion of an asynchronous close request. Completion routines are discussed in greater detail later in this chapter, in the section "Completion Routines."

timeout specifies a time period, in ticks, within which the close operation must be completed before the connection tool returns a cmTimeOut error. For no timeout, use –1. For a single attempt to close the connection, use 0. Some connection tools ignore this parameter.

When now is TRUE, the connection tool closes the connection immediately. When now is FALSE, the connection tool waits until all pending input and output have finished before closing the connection.

Result Codes   cmGenericError, cmNoErr, cmRejected, cmFailed, cmTimeout, cmNotOpen, cmNotSupported, cmUserCancel.

Aborting a connection

CMAbort tells the Connection Manager to stop trying to complete a pending asynchronous open request. Any open completion routines are executed. Your application can also call this routine to stop an outstanding CMListen.

Function   CMAbort(hConn: ConnHandle): CMErr;

Description   hConn specifies the connection this routine affects.

Result Codes   cmGenericError, cmNoErr, cmRejected, cmFailed, cmNotOpen, cmNoRequestPending, cmNotSupported.

Disposing of a connection record

CMDispose disposes of the connection record and all associated data structures. It is up to the connection tool to decide whether or not to wait for all pending read and write operations to complete before closing and disposing of the connection.

Procedure   CMDispose(hConn: ConnHandle);

Description   hConn specifies the connection record disposed of by this routine.

Idle procedure

Your application should call CMIdle at least once every time it goes through its main event loop, so that the connection tool can perform idle-loop tasks.

Procedure   CMIdle(hConn: ConnHandle);

Description   hConn specifies the connection for which idle-loop tasks are to be performed.

Listening for incoming connection requests

CMListen "listens" for a connection request from another entity. Your application, after it calls CMListen, should call CMStatus (which is described later in this section) to see if a connection request has been received (by checking the cmStatusIncomingCallPresent bit).

Function   CMListen(hConn: ConnHandle; async: BOOLEAN; completor: ProcPtr; timeout: LONGINT): CMErr;

Description   async specifies whether or not the opening request is asynchronous. If your application makes an asynchronous request, CMListen returns cmNoErr immediately. If your application makes a synchronous request, CMListen stays in a "listen loop" until it receives the connection request.

completor specifies the completion routine that the Connection Manager calls after it is done listening for the connection request. Completion routines are called only after asynchronous calls to CMListen. "Completion Routines," later in this chapter, discusses completion routines in more detail.

timeout specifies a time period, in ticks, within which a connection request must be received before the connection tool returns a cmTimeOut error. For no timeout, use −1. For a single listen, use 0. Some connection tools ignore this parameter.

Result Codes   cmGenericError, cmNoErr, cmRejected, cmFailed, cmTimeout, cmNotClosed, cmNotSupported, cmUserCancel.

Getting connection status information

CMStatus returns a variety of useful status information about a connection. Your application can call this routine at interrupt level.

Function CMStatus(hConn: ConnHandle; VAR sizes: CMBufferSizes; VAR flags: CMStatFlags): CMErr;

Description sizes is a variable of type CMBufferSizes that contains the number of characters to be read or written on the data, control, and attention channels. The indexes of the array are as follows:

cmDataIn, cmDataOut, cmCntlIn, cmCntlOut, cmAttnIn, cmAttnOut, cmRsrvIn, cmRsrvOut.

flags is a bit field with the following masks:

CONST

			{tool is opening connection}
cmStatusOpening	=	$00000001;	
			{connection is open}
cmStatusOpen	=	$00000002;	
			{tool is closing connection}
cmStatusClosing	=	$00000004;	
			{data present on data channel}
cmStatusDataAvail	=	$00000008;	
			{data present on cntl channel}
cmStatusCntlAvail	=	$00000010;	
			{data present on attn channel}
cmStatusAttnAvail	=	$00000020;	
			{data read pending}
cmStatusDRPend	=	$00000040;	
			{data write pending}
cmStatusDWPend	=	$00000080;	
			{cntl read pending}
cmStatusCRPend	=	$00000100;	
			{cntl write pending}
cmStatusCWPend	=	$00000200;	
			{attn read pending}
cmStatusARPend	=	$00000400;	
			{attn write pending}
cmStatusAWPend	=	$00000800;	
			{tool is breaking the connection}
cmStatusBreakPending	=	$00001000;	
			{tool is "listening" for data}
cmStatusListenPend	=	$00002000;	
			{call waiting for tool to handle}
cmStatusIncomingCallPresent	=	$00004000;	

TYPE
CMStatFlags	=	LONGINT;

Result Codes cmGenericError, cmNoErr, cmNotSupported.

Accepting or rejecting a connection request

CMAccept accepts or rejects an incoming connection request.

Function   CMAccept (hConn:ConnHandle; accept:BOOLEAN) : CMErr;

Description   Typically, an application will perform some actions after a CMListen, the results of
which determine whether to accept the request. CMAccept cannot be called from
interrupt level.

Result Codes   cmGenericError, cmNoErr, cmRejected, cmFailed, cmNoRequestPending,
cmNotSupported.

Stopping an asynchronous input/output request

CMIOKill terminates any pending input/output (I/O) requests on the specified channel.

Function   CMIOKill(hConn: ConnHandle; which: INTEGER): CMErr;

Description   which indicates the channel, and can take one of the following values:

cmDataIn, cmDataOut, cmCntlIn, cmCntlOut, cmAttnIn, cmAttnOut.

Result Codes   cmGenericError, cmNoErr, cmRejected, cmFailed, cmNotOpen,
cmNotSupported.

___

Resetting the connection

`CMReset` causes the connection to be reset. The exact state to which the connection is reset depends upon the connection protocol being implemented. The connection tool clears all local read and write buffers.

Procedure CMReset(hConn: ConnHandle);

___

Sending breaks

`CMBreak` effects a break operation upon the connection. The exact effect of this operation depends upon the tool in use.

Procedure CMBreak(hConn: ConnHandle; duration: LONGINT; async: BOOLEAN; completor: ProcPtr);

Description `duration` specifies in ticks the length of the break.

`completor` specifies the completion routine to be called upon completion of the break. Completion routines are called only after asynchronous calls to `CMBreak`. "Completion Routines," later in this chapter, discusses completion routines in more detail.

Getting the connection environment

CMGetConnEnvirons provides a means for obtaining connection environment information.

Function

CMGetConnEnvirons (hConn : ConnHandle; VAR theEnvirons : ConnEnvironRec) : CMErr;

Description

CMGetConnEnvirons returns the connection environment record in theEnvirons for the connection specified by ConnHandle. The connection tool is responsible for filling in each field of ConnEnvironRec with either a value (if it has a valid value to supply) or 0.

The structure for version 0 of the connection environment record is as follows:

```
TYPE
        ConnEnvironRecPtr      =      ^ConnEnvironRec;
        ConnEnvironRec         =      RECORD;
            version            :      INTEGER;
                                      {version of this data structure}
            baudRate           :      LONGINT;
                                      {data transfer rate}
            dataBits           :      INTEGER;
                                      {number of significant bits per byte}
            channels           :      CMChannel;
                                      {supported channels}
            swFlowControl      :      BOOLEAN;
                                      {if software flow control is in use}
            hwFlowControl      :      BOOLEAN;
                                      {if hardware flow control is in use}
            flags              :      CMFlags;
        END;
```

The version field takes on the following value:

```
CONST
        curConnEnvRecVers      =          0;
```

The flags field of the ConnEnvironRec is a bit field with the following value:

```
TYPE
        CMFlags                =          INTEGER;

CONST
        cmFlagsEOM             =          $0001;
```

Other bits of flags are reserved by Apple Computer, Inc.

channels is a bit field with the following values:

```
TYPE
     CMChannel        =        INTEGER;

CONST
     cmData           =        $00000001;
     cmCntl           =        $00000002;
     cmAttn           =        $00000004;

     cmDataClean      =        $00000100;
     cmCntlClean      =        $00000200;
     cmAttnClean      =        $00000400;
```

Other bits of channels are reserved by Apple Computer, Inc.

Result Codes   cmGenericError, cmNoErr, cmNotSupported, envVersTooBig

Reading and writing data

The Connection Manager provides routines that read from and write data to a buffer. Your application can also use the Connection Manager routine that reads data, CMRead, to search the incoming data stream for a specified pattern of bytes. Data stream searching is discussed later in this chapter in the section "CMAddSearch Adding a Data Stream Search."

CMRead

Reading data

CMRead reads data into a block of memory. Your application cannot queue multiple read requests for the same channel on the same connection. However, your application can have both a pending read and a pending write on the same channel at the same time. Your application can call this routine at interrupt level.

◆ *Note:* Your application should *not* check for an open channel prior to reading data. The connection tool might be interpreting data locally and, therefore, not need an open connection.

Function

```
CMRead(hConn: ConnHandle; theBuffer: Ptr; VAR toRead: LONGINT;
theChannel: CMChannel; async: BOOLEAN; completor: ProcPtr; timeout:
LONGINT; VAR flags: CMFlags): CMErr;
```

Description

theBuffer specifies the buffer to which the connection tool should read data.

toRead specifies the number of bytes to be read. If your application calls this routine synchronously, the connection tool returns the actual number of bytes it read in toRead. Your application can call CMStatus to see if an asynchronous read is pending. If your application calls this routine asynchronously, the asyncCount field of the connection record contains the actual number of bytes read when the connection tool calls the completion routine.

theChannel specifies the channel on which reading takes place. Acceptable values are as follows:

```
CONST
    cmData        =       $00000001;
    cmCntl        =       $00000002;
    cmAttn        =       $00000004;
```

async specifies whether or not the request is asynchronous. If an asynchronous request is made, cmNoErr is returned immediately.

`completor` specifies the completion routine to be called upon completion of an asynchronous read request. Completion routines are discussed in greater detail later in this chapter in the section "Completion Routines."

`timeout` specifies a time period, in ticks, within which the connection tool must complete the read operation. If it does not finish within the specified time, a timeout error occurs. For no timeout, use –1. If your application specifies 0, the connection tool reads as many bytes, up to `toRead` bytes, as it can in one read attempt. Some connection tools ignore this parameter.

`flags` indicates whether your application received an end-of-message indicator. If your application calls this routine asynchronously, the connection tool returns the end of message indicator in the `reserved0` field of the connection record when the completion routine is called.

```
CONST
    cmFlagsEOM    =       $0001;
```

Result Codes `cmGenericError, cmNoErr, cmRejected, cmFailed, cmTimeout, cmNotOpen, cmNoRequestPending, cmNotSupported.`

Writing data

CMWrite writes data from a block of memory. Your application cannot queue multiple write requests for the same channel on the same connection. However, your application can have both a pending read and a pending write on the same channel at the same time. Your application can call this routine at interrupt level.

◆ *Note:* Your application should *not* check for an open channel prior to writing data. The connection tool might be interpreting data locally and, therefore, not need an open connection.

Function

```
CMWrite(hConn: ConnHandle; theBuffer: Ptr; VAR toWrite: LONGINT;
theChannel: CMChannel; async: BOOLEAN; completor: ProcPtr; timeout:
LONGINT; flags: CMFlags): CMErr;
```

Description

theBuffer specifies the buffer from which the connection gets the data to write.

toWrite specifies the number of bytes to be written. If your application calls this routine synchronously, the connection tool returns the actual number of bytes it wrote in toWrite. Your application can call CMStatus to see if an asynchronous write is pending. If your application calls this routine asynchronously, the asyncCount field of the connection record contains the actual number of bytes written when the completion routine is called.

theChannel specifies the channel on which writing takes place. Acceptable values are as follows:

```
CONST
    cmData      =       $00000001;
    cmCntl      =       $00000002;
    cmAttn      =       $00000004;
```

async specifies whether or not the request is asynchronous. If your application makes an asynchronous request, CMWrite returns cmNoErr immediately.

completor specifies the completion routine to be called upon completion of an asynchronous write request. Completion routines are discussed in greater detail later in this chapter in the section "Completion Routines."

timeout specifies a time period, in ticks, within which the connection tool must complete the write operation. If it does not finish within the specified period, a timeout error occurs. For no timeout, use –1. If your application specifies 0, the connection tool writes as many bytes, up to toWrite bytes, as it can in one write attempt. Some connection tools ignore this parameter.

`flags` indicates whether the connection tool should send an end-of-message indicator. An end-of-message indicator needs to be supported by the particular communications protocol being used; if an end-of-message indicator is not supported by the connection protocol, your application should ignore this field.

```
CONST
    cmFlagsEOM      =        $0001;
```

Result Codes   `cmGenericError, cmNoErr, cmRejected, cmFailed, cmTimeout, cmNotOpen, cmNoRequestPending, cmNotSupported.`

CMAddSearch

Adding a data stream search

When an application is reading data with `CMRead`, you can have the data stream searched for one or more patterns of bytes. To perform the search, your application must pass information to the Connection Manager, such as the connection on which the data stream is coming in and the sequence of bytes for which to look. `CMAddSearch` tells the Connection Manager to perform the search, passing it search-specific information as well. Each time your application calls `CMAddSearch`, the Connection Manager searches for an additional sequence of bytes.

Function   `CMAddSearch(hConn: ConnHandle; theString: Str255; flags: CMSearchFlags; callBack: ProcPtr): LONGINT;`

Description   The value `CMAddSearch` returns is a search reference number that is used by the `CMRemoveSearch` routine (described later in this section). If `CMAddSearch` returns –1, the connection tool did not successfully add the search. Your application uses the search reference number to distinguish among different searches that may be occurring simultaneously on the same connection.

`flags` is a field that describes the search to be performed. The appropriate values are as follows:

```
TYPE
    CMSearchFlags        =        INTEGER;


CONST
    cmSearchSevenBit     =        $0001;
```

If `cmSearchSevenBit` is on, the Connection Manager matches only the low 7 bits of a character; otherwise, it matches all 8 bits. The other bits of `flags` are reserved by Apple Computer, Inc.

`callBack` is a pointer to a routine the Connection Manager will call during `CMRead` in the event that the connection tool finds a match. The calling conventions for the callback procedure are given in the next section.

What to do when there's a match

The Connection Manager will pass control to a search call-back procedure in the event that the connection tool finds a match in the incoming data stream. This routine may be called at interrupt level.

Procedure   `MySearchCallBack(hConn: ConnHandle; matchPtr: Ptr; refNum: LONGINT);`

Description   `matchPtr` points to the last matched character in the read buffer.

`MySearchCallBack` uses the search reference number `CMAddSearch` returns.

◆   *Note:* The Connection Manager calls `MySearchCallBack` when a read is completed, and therefore might be called at interrupt level. If your application makes asynchronous calls, `MySearchCallBack` has the same restrictions as the standard Device Manager completion routines.

CMRemoveSearch

Stopping a data stream search

`CMRemoveSearch` removes the search with the specified reference number for the specified connection record. This routine cannot be called at interrupt level (making it impossible for `MySearchCallBack` to call this routine).

Procedure   `CMRemoveSearch(hConn: ConnHandle; refNum: LONGINT);`

Description   `refnum` is the search reference number returned by `CMAddSearch`.

CMClearSearch

Clearing all data stream searches

`CMClearSearch` removes all searches associated with the specified connection record.

Procedure   `CMClearSearch(hConn: ConnHandle);`

Description   `CMClearSearch` cannot be called from interrupt level.

Handling events

The Connection Manager event-processing routines provide useful extensions to the Macintosh Toolbox Event Manager. This section explains the four routines the Connection Manager provides. See "Other Events" in Chapter 2 for sample code showing how an application can determine if an event needs to be handled by one of these routines.

`CMActivate`

Activate events

`CMActivate` processes an activate or deactivate event (for instance, installing or removing a custom tool menu) for a window associated with the connection.

Procedure   `CMActivate(hConn: ConnHandle; activate: BOOLEAN);`

Description   If `activate` is `TRUE`, the connection tool processes the activate event. Otherwise, it processes a deactivate event.

`CMResume`

Resume events

`CMResume` processes a resume or suspend event for a window associated with the connection.

Procedure   `CMResume(hConn: ConnHandle; resume: BOOLEAN);`

Description   If `resume` is `TRUE`, the connection tool processes a resume event. Otherwise, it processes a suspend event.

`CMMenu`

Menu events

Your application must call `CMMenu` when the user chooses an item from a menu that is installed by the connection tool.

Function   `CMMenu(hConn: ConnHandle; menuID: INTEGER; item: INTEGER): BOOLEAN;`

Description   `CMMenu` returns `FALSE` if the connection tool did not handle the menu event. `CMMenu` returns `TRUE` if the connection tool did handle the menu event.

Other events

When your application receives an event, it should check whether the `refcon` of the window is a tool's `ConnHandle`. Such an event occurs, for example, when the user clicks a button in a dialog box displayed by the connection tool. If it does belong to a connection tool's window, your application can call `CMEvent`.

Procedure

`CMEvent(hConn: ConnHandle; theEvent: EventRecord);`

Description

A window (or dialog box) created by a connection tool has a connection record handle stored in the `refCon` field for `windowRecord`.

Localizing configuration strings

The Communications Toolbox provides two routines that make it easier to localize configuration strings.

CMIntlToEnglish

Translating into English

CMIntlToEnglish converts a configuration string, which is pointed to by inputPtr, to an American English configuration string pointed to by outputPtr.

Function

```
CMIntlToEnglish(hConn: ConnHandle; inputPtr: Ptr; VAR outputPtr: Ptr;
language: INTEGER): OSErr;
```

Description

The function returns an operating system error code if any internal errors occur.

The connection tool allocates space for outputPtr. Your application is responsible for disposing of the pointer with DisposPtr when done with it.

language specifies the language from which the string is to be converted. Valid values for this field are shown in the description of the Script Manager in *Inside Macintosh*, Volume V. If the language specified is not supported, this routine returns cmNoErr, but outputPtr is NIL.

CMEnglishToIntl

Translating from English

CMEnglishToIntl converts an American English configuration string, which is pointed to by inputPtr, to a configuration string pointed to by outputPtr.

Function

```
CMEnglishToIntl(hConn: ConnHandle; inputPtr: Ptr; VAR outputPtr: Ptr;
language: INTEGER): OSErr;
```

Description

The function returns an operating system error code if any internal errors occur.

The connection tool allocates space for outputPtr; your application is responsible for disposing of the pointer with DisposPtr when done with it.

language specifies the language to which the string is to be converted. Valid values for this field are shown in the description of the Script Manager in *Inside Macintosh*, Volume V. If the language specified is not supported, cmNoErr is still returned, but outputPtr is NIL.

Miscellaneous routines

The routines described in this section perform a variety of tasks.

CMGetToolName

Getting the name of a tool

CMGetToolName returns in name the name of the tool specified by procID.

Procedure   CMGetToolName(procID: INTEGER; VAR name: Str255);

Description   If procID references a connection tool that does not exist, the Connection Manager sets name to an empty string.

CMSetRefCon

Setting the connection record's reference constant

CMSetRefCon sets the connection record's refCon field to the specified value. It is very important that your application use this routine to change the value of the reference constant, instead of changing it directly.

Procedure   CMSetRefCon(hConn: ConnHandle; refCon : LONGINT);

CMGetRefCon

Getting the connection record's reference constant

CMGetRefCon returns the connection record's reference constant.

Function   CMGetRefCon(hConn: ConnHandle) : LONGINT;

Setting the `userData` field

`CMSetUserData` sets the connection record's `userData` field to the specified value. It is very important that your application use this routine to change the value of the `userData` field, instead of changing it directly.

Procedure   `CMSetUserData(hConn: ConnHandle; userData: LONGINT);`

Getting the `userData` field

`CMGetUserData` returns the connection record's `userData` field.

Function   `CMGetUserData(hConn: ConnHandle): LONGINT;`

Getting `'vers'` resource information

`CMGetVersion` returns a handle to a relocatable block, which contains the information in the connection tool's `'vers'` resource with ID=1. Your application is responsible for disposing of the handle when done with it.

◆ *Note:* The handle returned is *not* a resource handle.

Function   `CMGetVersion(hConn:ConnHandle): Handle;`

Getting the Connection Manager version number

`CMGetCMVersion` returns the version number of the Connection Manager.

Function   `CMGetCMVersion: INTEGER;`

Description   The version number of the Connection Manager described in this document is:
```
CONST
    curCMVersion  =     1;
```

Completion routines

This section describes the syntax and conventions that apply to completion routines in your application.

Writing a completion routine

Completion routines have the same restrictions as do standard Device Manager completion routines. For example, your routines should not allocate memory. See the Device Manager chapters in *Inside Macintosh* for more information.

Procedure   `MyCompletion(hConn: ConnHandle);`

Description   When the Connection Manager calls `MyCompletion`, the `errCode` field of the connection record contains the appropriate error code. The `asyncCount` field of the connection record contains the actual number of bytes read or written. Because the `errCode` field of the connection record is used by all of the Connection Manager routines, it contains the error code for the asynchronous operation only during execution of `MyCompletion`.

Quick reference

This section provides a reference to Connection Manager routines and data structures. At the end of this section is a listing of routine selectors for programming in assembly language.

Routines

Connection Manager routines	See page
CMAbort(hConn: ConnHandle): CMErr;	49
CMAccept(hConn: ConnHandle; accept:BOOLEAN): CMErr;	52
CMActivate(hConn: ConnHandle; activate: BOOLEAN);	61
CMAddSearch(hConn: ConnHandle; theString: Str255; flags: CMSearchFlags; callBack: ProcPtr): LONGINT;	59
CMBreak(hConn: ConnHandle; duration: LONGINT; async: BOOLEAN; completor: ProcPtr);	53
CMChoose(VAR hConn:ConnHandle; where: Point; idleProc: ProcPtr): INTEGER;	41
CMClearSearch(hConn: ConnHandle);	60
CMClose(hConn: ConnHandle; async: BOOLEAN; completor: ProcPtr; timeout: LONGINT; now: BOOLEAN): CMErr;	49
CMDefault(VAR theConfig: Ptr; procID: INTEGER; allocate: BOOLEAN);	40
CMDispose(hConn: ConnHandle);	50
CMEnglishToIntl(hConn: ConnHandle; inputPtr: Ptr; VAR outputPtr: Ptr; language: INTEGER): OSErr;	63
CMEvent(hConn: ConnHandle; theEvent: EventRecord);	62
CMGetCMVersion: INTEGER;	65
CMGetConfig(hConn: ConnHandle): Ptr;	47
CMGetConnEnvirons (hConn : ConnHandle; VAR theEnvirons : ConnEnvironRec) : CMErr;	54
CMGetToolName(procID: INTEGER; VAR name: Str255);	64
CMGetProcID(name: Str255): INTEGER;	37
CMGetRefCon(hConn: ConnHandle): LONGINT;	64
CMGetUserData(hConn: ConnHandle): LONGINT;	65
CMGetVersion(hConn: ConnHandle): Handle;	65
CMIdle(hConn: ConnHandle);	50
CMIntlToEnglish(hConn: ConnHandle; inputPtr: Ptr; VAR outputPtr: Ptr; language: INTEGER): OSErr;	63

Connection Manager routines	**See page**
CMIOKill(hConn: ConnHandle; which: INTEGER): CMErr;	*52*
CMListen(hConn: ConnHandle; async: BOOLEAN; completor: ProcPtr; timeout: LONGINT): CMErr;	*50*
CMMenu(hConn: ConnHandle; menuID: INTEGER; item: INTEGER): BOOLEAN;	*61*
CMNew(procID : INTEGER; flags : CMRecFlags; desiredSizes : CMBufferSizes; refCon : LONGINT; userData : LONGINT) : ConnHandle;	*38*
CMOpen(hConn: ConnHandle; async: BOOLEAN; completor: ProcPtr; timeout: LONGINT): CMErr;	*48*
CMRead(hConn: ConnHandle; theBuffer: Ptr; VAR toRead: LONGINT; theChannel: CMChannel; async: BOOLEAN; completor: ProcPtr; timeout: LONGINT; VAR flags: CMFlags): CMErr;	*56*
CMRemoveSearch(hConn: ConnHandle; refNum: LONGINT);	*60*
CMReset(hConn: ConnHandle);	*53*
CMResume(hConn: ConnHandle; resume: BOOLEAN);	*61*
CMSetConfig(hConn: ConnHandle; thePtr: Ptr): INTEGER;	*47*
CMSetRefCon(hConn: ConnHandle; refCon: LONGINT);	*64*
CMSetupCleanup(procID: INTEGER; theConfig: Ptr; count: INTEGER; theDialog: DialogPtr; VAR magicCookie: LONGINT);	*45*
CMSetupFilter(procID: INTEGER; theConfig: Ptr; count:INTEGER; theDialog: DialogPtr; VAR theEvent: EventRecord; VAR theItem: INTEGER; VAR magicCookie: LONGINT): BOOLEAN;	*44*
CMSetupItem(procID: INTEGER; theConfig: Ptr; count: INTEGER; theDialog: DialogPtr; VAR theItem: INTEGER; VAR magicCookie: LONGINT);	*45*
CMSetupPostflight(procID:INTEGER);	*46*
CMSetupPreflight(procID: INTEGER; VAR magicCookie: LONGINT): Handle;	*43*
CMSetupSetup(procID: INTEGER; theConfig: Ptr; count: INTEGER; theDialog: DialogPtr; VAR magicCookie: LONGINT);	*44*
CMSetUserData(hConn: ConnHandle; userData: LONGINT);	*65*
CMStatus(hConn: ConnHandle; VAR sizes: CMBufferSizes; VAR flags: CMStatFlags): CMErr;	*51*
CMValidate(hConn: ConnHandle): BOOLEAN;	*40*

Connection Manager routines			*See page*
CMWrite(hConn: ConnHandle; theBuffer: Ptr; VAR toWrite: LONGINT; theChannel: CMChannel; async: BOOLEAN; completor: ProcPtr; timeout: LONGINT; flags: CMFlags): CMErr;			*58*
InitCM : CMErr;			*36*

Routines in your application			*See page*
MySearchCallBack(hConn: ConnHandle; matchPtr: Ptr; refNum: LONGINT);			*60*
MyCompletion(hConn: ConnHandle);			*66*

Connection Record

```
TYPE
        ConnHandle          =       ^ConnPtr;
        ConnPtr             =       ^ConnRecord;
        ConnRecord          =       RECORD
                procID              :       INTEGER;

                flags               :       CMRecFlags;
                errCode             :       CMErr;

                refCon              :       LONGINT;
                userData            :       LONGINT

                defProc             :       ProcPtr;

                config              :       Ptr;
                oldConfig           :       Ptr;

                reserved0           :       LONGINT;
                reserved1           :       LONGINT;
                reserved2           :       LONGINT;

                cmPrivate           :       Ptr;

                bufferArray         :       CMBuffers;
                bufSizes            :       CMBufferSizes;

                mluField            :       LONGINT;

                asyncCount          :       CMBufferSizes;

        END;
```

Constants and data types

```
TYPE
        CMBufFields=(
                cmDataIn,
                cmDataOut
                cmCntlIn
                cmCntlOut
                cmAttnIn
                cmAttnOut
                cmRsrvIn
                cmRsrvOut);


        CMBuffers           =       ARRAY[CMBufFields] OF Ptr;
        CMBufferSizes       =       ARRAY[CMBufFields] OF LONGINT;
```

Connection Environment Record

```
TYPE
        ConnEnvironRecPtr       :       ^ConnEnvironRec;
        ConnEnvironRec          :       RECORD;
            version             :       INTEGER;
            baudRate            :       LONGINT;
            dataBits            :       INTEGER;
            channels            :       CMChannel;
            swFlowControl       :       BOOLEAN;
            hwFlowControl       :       BOOLEAN;
            flags               :       CMFlags;
        END;
```

```
TYPE
        CMFlags         =       INTEGER;

CONST
        cmFlagsEOM      =       1;


TYPE
        CMChannel: INTEGER;
```

```
CONST
        cmData          =       $00000001;
        cmCntl          =       $00000002;
        cmAttn          =       $00000004;

        cmDataClean     =       $00000100;
        cmCntlClean     =       $00000200;
        cmAttnClean     =       $00000400;

        cmNoMenus       =       $00010000;
        cmQuiet         =       $00020000;
```

Version constants

```
CONST
        curConnEnvRecVers       =       0;

        curCMVersion            =       1;
```

Connection record flags bit masks

```
TYPE
        CMRecFlags      =       LONGINT;


CONST
        cmData          =       $00000001;
        cmCntl          =       $00000002;
        cmAttn          =       $00000004;

        cmDataClean     =       $00000100;
        cmCntlClean     =       $00000200;
        cmAttnClean     =       $00000400;

        cmNoMenus       =       $00010000;
        cmQuiet         =       $00020000;
```

Search flags

```
TYPE
        CMSearchFlags           =       INTEGER;


CONST
        cmSearchSevenBit        =       $0001;
```

Values returned by CMChoose

```
CONST
        chooseDisaster      =   -2;
        chooseFailed        =   -1;
        chooseAborted       =    0;
        chooseOKMinor       =    1;
        chooseOKMajor       =    2;
        chooseCancel        =    3;
```

Connection status flags

```
TYPE
        CMStatFlags              =   LONGINT;

CONST
        cmStatusOpening              =   $00000001;   {tool is opening connection}
        cmStatusOpen                 =   $00000002;   {connection is open}
        cmStatusClosing              =   $00000004;   {tool is closing connection}
        cmStatusDataAvail            =   $00000008;   {data present on data channel}
        cmStatusCntlAvail            =   $00000010;   {data present on cntl channel}
        cmStatusAttnAvail            =   $00000020;   {data present on attn channel}

        cmStatusDRPend               =   $00000040;   {data read pending}
        cmStatusDWPend               =   $00000080;   {data write pending}
        cmStatusCRPend               =   $00000100;   {cntl read pending}
        cmStatusCWPend               =   $00000200;   {cntl write pending}
        cmStatusARPend               =   $00000400;   {attn read pending}
        cmStatusAWPend               =   $00000800;   {attn write pending}

        cmStatusBreakPending         =   $00001000;   {tool is breaking the connection}
        cmStatusListenPend           =   $00002000;   {tool is "listening" for data}
        cmStatusIncomingCallPresent  =   $00004000;   {call waiting for tool to handle}
```

Errors

```
TYPE
        CMErr            =   OSErr;

CONST
        cmGenericError       =   -1;
        cmNoErr              =    0;
        cmRejected           =    1;
        cmFailed             =    2;
        cmTimeOut            =    3;
        cmNotOpen            =    4;
        cmNotClosed          =    5;
        cmNoRequestPending   =    6;
        cmNotSupported       =    7;
        cmNoTools            =    8;
        cmUserCancel         =    9;
```

Connection Manager routine selectors

◆ *Assembly note:* Your application can access Communications Toolbox routines through a Macintosh Operating System trap. To call a routine, your application pushes the appropriate parameters onto the stack and invokes the trap macro that has the same name as the routine, preceded by an underscore. When expanded, these macros place the routine selector onto the stack, set A0 to point to the selector, and invoke the trap _CommToolboxDispatch ($A08B). Upon returning from the trap, the trap macro pops the routine selector off the stack and places the return value into D0. It is your application's responsibility to clean up the stack by removing the parameters that were pushed onto the stack prior to invoking the trap macro.

CMAbort	.EQU	271		CMIOKill	.EQU	297
CMAccept	.EQU	269		CMListen	.EQU	268
CMActivate	.EQU	275		CMMenu	.EQU	277
CMAddSearch	.EQU	294		CMNew	.EQU	264
CMBreak	.EQU	293		CMOpen	.EQU	267
CMChoose	.EQU	292		CMRead	.EQU	273
CMClearSearch	.EQU	296		CMRemoveSearch	.EQU	295
CMClose	.EQU	270		CMReset	.EQU	278
CMDefault	.EQU	280		CMResume	.EQU	276
CMDispose	.EQU	265		CMSetConfig	.EQU	285
CMEnglishToIntl	.EQU	287		CMSetRefCon	.EQU	258
CMEvent	.EQU	298		CMSetupCleanup	.EQU	283
CMGetCMVersion	.EQU	289		CMSetupFilter	.EQU	290
CMGetConfig	.EQU	284		CMSetupItem	.EQU	282
CMGetConnEnvirons	.EQU	300		CMSetupPostflight	.EQU	299
CMGetProcID	.EQU	263		CMSetupPreflight	.EQU	291
CMGetRefCon	.EQU	259		CMSetupSetup	.EQU	281
CMGetToolName	.EQU	262		CMSetUserData	.EQU	260
CMGetUserData	.EQU	261		CMStatus	.EQU	272
CMGetVersion	.EQU	288		CMValidate	.EQU	279
CMIdle	.EQU	266		CMWrite	.EQU	274
CMIntlToEnglish	.EQU	286		InitCM	.EQU	257

Chapter 4 **Terminal Manager**

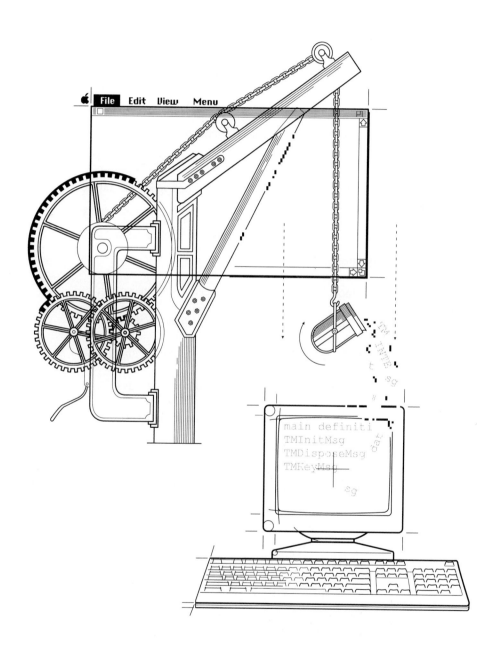

THIS CHAPTER describes the Terminal Manager, the Communications Toolbox manager that allows applications to perform terminal emulation independent of a specific type of terminal. This chapter begins by describing fundamental concepts about the Terminal Manager. It goes on to describe the **terminal emulation window** and the data structure most important to the Terminal Manager, the **terminal record.** Next, this chapter presents a detailed functional description of each routine provided by the Terminal Manager. It then describes the routines that need to be in your application. At the end of the chapter, you'll find a quick reference to routines, data structures, and routine selectors for programming in assembly language.

In this chapter, the term *your application* refers to the application you are writing for the Macintosh, which will implement communications services for users. Be careful not to confuse the services your application provides with the services that tools provide.

To use **terminal tools** in an application, you need to be familiar with

- the Resource Manager (described in *Inside Macintosh,* Volumes I, IV, V)

- the QuickDraw™ application (described in *Inside Macintosh,* Volumes I, V)

- the Event Manager (described in *Inside Macintosh,* Volumes I, IV, V)

- the Scrap Manager (described in *Inside Macintosh,* Volume I)

- the Dialog Manager (described in *Inside Macintosh,* Volumes I, IV, V)

- the Connection Manager (described in Chapter 3 of this document)

About the Terminal Manager

By using Terminal Manager routines, your application can implement a terminal emulation without having to take into account the characteristics of any one type of terminal. Terminal tools, which are discussed in Chapter 10, are responsible for implementing the characteristics of specific terminal types.

The Terminal Manager provides a generic terminal emulation that is best described with an example. Suppose your application needs to tell a mainframe at the other end of an existing data connection that the user has typed the letter *a*. Your application detects that the user has pressed a key, and passes this event on to the Terminal Manager by calling the `TMKey routine`. The Terminal Manager passes this event on to a previously selected terminal tool. The terminal tool figures out the appropriate value to transmit for *a* and sends it out on the data connection. This example, of course, is a very simple one. But it is meant to give you a general feel for what goes on inside the Terminal Manager. The rest of this chapter goes into much more detail.

Figure 4-1 shows the data flow into and out of the Terminal Manager.

■ **Figure 4-1** Data flow into and out of the Terminal Manager

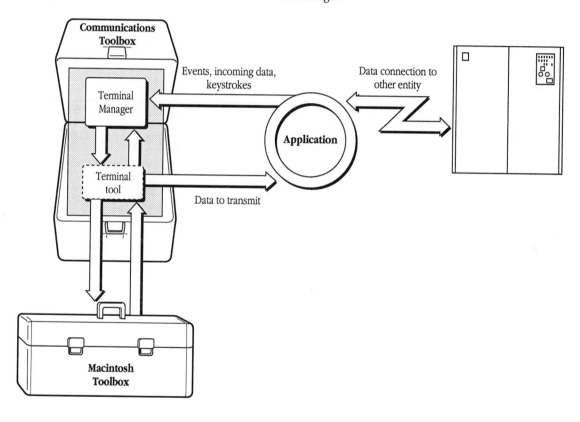

The most important data structure maintained by the Terminal Manager is the terminal record, which is where all the specifics of a terminal emulation are stored. For example, the terminal record might show that your application is emulating a VT320™ terminal, and that the Terminal Manager should try to cache the terminal window before clearing it.

One important aspect of the terminal record is that it allows you to write routines independent of specific terminal characteristics. For instance, when an application wants to transmit a keystroke to a host computer, it tells the Terminal Manager to transmit the keystroke, and the terminal tool figures out exactly how to transmit the keystroke for a specific type of terminal.

Another important aspect of the terminal record is that it allows for multiple instances of the same tool. This means that the same tool can be used by different processes at the same time, as in a MultiFinder environment, or by different threads in a given application. The terminal record is described in greater detail later in this chapter.

Besides providing access to basic terminal emulation services, the Terminal Manager includes routines that make it easy for your application to configure a terminal tool, either by presenting the user with a dialog box or by interfacing directly with a scripting language. The Terminal Manager also contains routines that make it easier for you to localize your applications in other languages.

You can use the Terminal Manager in conjunction with other Communications Toolbox managers to create a communications application with basic connection, terminal emulation, and file transfer capabilities. Or, you can use the Terminal Manager with some other connection service or file transfer service instead of the Connection Manager and File Transfer Manager. You can also write your own terminal tool for the Terminal Manager to use (this procedure is discussed in Chapters 8 and 10). Regardless of which method you choose, your application should be able to handle different terminal tools so that users can change tools and still be able to use your program.

The terminal emulation window

The Terminal Manager provides terminal tools with a terminal emulation window. In addition to title bar, scroll bars, and other standard user interface elements, the terminal emulation window has two major parts: the **terminal emulation region** and the **cache region.** *Figure 4-2* shows these parts.

■ **Figure 4-2** A terminal emulation window

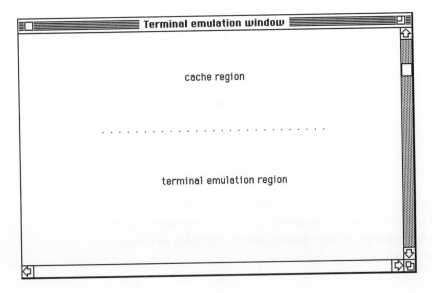

The terminal emulation region

The terminal emulation region is the area of the terminal window in which the terminal tool displays data in a manner that emulates a specific terminal. Terminal tools use a **terminal emulation buffer** to store the data displayed in the terminal emulation region. Your application and the terminal tools exchange this data through a `TermDataBlock`, which is an extensible data structure that handles text and graphics information. For text terminals, the `TermDataBlock` describes a line of text in the terminal emulation region. For graphics terminals, the `TermDataBlock` describes a picture in the terminal emulation region. The format of `TermDataBlock` is as follows:

```
TYPE
        TermDataBlockH          =       ^TermDataPtr;
        TermDataBlockPtr        =       ^TermDataBlock;
        TermDataBlock           =       RECORD
                flags           :       TMTermTypes;
                theData         :       Handle;
                auxData         :       Handle;
                reserved        :       LONGINT;
        END;
```

`flags` describes the data in the `TermDataBlock`. Valid values are: `TMTextTerminal` and `TMGraphicsTerminal`.

`theData` is a handle to data, which is text characters for text terminals and a QuickDraw picture for graphics terminals. Your application can get the size of `theData` by calling `GetHandleSize(theData)`.

`auxData` and `reserved` are reserved by Apple Computer, Inc. Do not use them or your application may not work in the future.

The cache region

The cache region is an optional area in the window, which your application can use to display data that scrolls off the top of the terminal emulation region. Because terminal tools do not maintain this area of the terminal emulation window, your application must provide all the necessary code if you want a cache region.

The terminal record

The terminal record contains information that describes a terminal emulation, as well as pointers to Terminal Manager internal data structures. The Terminal Manager uses this information to "translate" the protocol-independent routines used by an application or tool into a service implemented according to a specified terminal emulation. Most of the fields in the terminal record are filled in when an application calls TMNew, described later in this chapter.

Because the context for a given terminal emulation is maintained in a terminal record, an application can maintain more than one terminal emulation at the same time. All the application has to do is create a new terminal record every time it initiates a terminal emulation.

△ **Important**　Your application, in order to be compatible with future releases of the Terminal Manager, should not directly manipulate the fields of the terminal record (with the exception of config and oldConfig). The Terminal Manager provides routines that applications and tools can use to change terminal record fields. These routines are discussed later in this chapter. △

Terminal record data structure

```
TYPE
        TermHandle          =           ^TermPointer;
        TermPointer         =           ^TermRecord;
        TermRecord          =           RECORD
            procID          =           INTEGER


            flags           :           TMFlags;
            errCode         :           TMErr;

            refCon          :           LONGINT;
            userData        :           LONGINT;

            defProc         :           ProcPtr;

            config          :           Ptr;
            oldConfig       :           Ptr;

            environsProc    :           ProcPtr;
            reserved1       :           LONGINT;
            reserved2       :           LONGINT;
```

```
            tmPrivate        :         Ptr;

            sendProc         :         ProcPtr;
            breakProc        :         ProcPtr;
            cacheProc        :         ProcPtr;
            clikLoop         :         ProcPtr;


            owner            :         WindowPtr;
            termRect         :         Rect;
            viewRect         :         Rect;
            visRect          :         Rect;

            lastIdle         :         LONGINT;

            selection        :         TMSelection;
            selType          :         TMSelTypes;

            mluField         :         LONGINT;
        END;
```

procID

procID is the terminal tool ID. This value is dynamically assigned by the Terminal Manager when your application calls TMGetProcID.

flags

flags is a bit field with the following masks:

```
CONST
        tmInvisible         =         $00000001;
        tmSaveBeforeClear   =         $00000002;
        tmNoMenus           =         $00000004;
        tmAutoScroll        =         $00000008;

TYPE
        TMFlags             :         LONGINT;
```

If your application sets tmInvisible, the Terminal Manager maintains a terminal emulation but does not display it. Your application can use the terminal emulation and cache region to create some other presentation service, instead of a terminal emulation.

If your application sets tmSaveBeforeClear, the terminal tool will try to cache the entire terminal emulation region in response to any clear-screen operation. Clear-screen operations are generated from a user's request, a clear-screen character sequence, or a terminal-reset character sequence.

If your application sets tmNoMenus, the terminal tool will not put up any custom menus.

If your application sets tmAutoScroll, the terminal tool will automatically scroll the terminal emulation window (if necessary) while the user is highlighting a selection.

errCode

The Terminal Manager does not use `errCode`; it is included in this version (version 1.0) of the terminal record for reasons of historical preservation. Your application must not use this field.

refCon

`refCon` is a `LONGINT` that your application can use.

userData

`userData` is a `LONGINT` that your application can use.

defProc

`defProc` is a pointer to the main code resource of the terminal tool that will implement the specifics of the terminal emulation. The terminal tool's main code resource is of type `'tdef'`.

config

`config` is a pointer to a data block that is private to the terminal tool.

Your application can store the contents of `config` to save the state of a terminal in a document. The structure, size, and contents of the configuration record are set by the tool. Your application can determine the size of the configuration record by calling `GetPtrSize`, overwrite its contents using `BlockMove`, and validate the contents with `TMValidate`.

Your application can use `TMGetConfig` and `TMSetConfig` to manipulate fields in this record. For details, read "Interfacing with a Scripting Language," later in this chapter. Your application can save the state of the terminal record by saving the string `TMGetConfig` returns. Also, your application can restore the configuration of the terminal record by passing a saved string to `TMSetConfig`.

You can find a description of `config` from a terminal tool perspective in Chapter 8.

oldConfig

`oldConfig` is a pointer to a data block that is private to the terminal tool and contains the most recently saved version of `config`. Your application is responsible for setting `oldConfig` when the user saves a session document.

environsProc

`environsProc` is a pointer to a routine in your application that the terminal tool can call to obtain a record describing the connection environment. A more detailed description of `environsProc` appears later in this chapter in "Routines That Must Be in Your Application."

reserved1 and reserved2

`reserved1` and `reserved2` are reserved for the Terminal Manager. Your application must not use this field.

tmPrivate

`tmPrivate` is a pointer to a data block that is private to the terminal tool. Your application must not use this field.

sendProc

`sendProc` is a pointer to a routine your application calls when it needs to send data to another application. A more detailed description of `sendProc` appears later in this chapter in "Routines That Must Be in Your Application."

breakProc

`breakProc` is a pointer to a routine in your application that performs a break operation. The effect the break has depends on the terminal emulation being used. A more detailed description of `breakProc` appears later in this chapter in "Routines That Must Be in Your Application."

cacheProc

`cacheProc` is a pointer to a routine in your application that saves lines that scroll off the top of the terminal emulation region. The terminal tool also uses this routine to save the terminal screen before a clear-screen operation (if the `TMSaveBeforeClear` bit is set in the `flags` field of the terminal record). A more detailed description of `cacheProc` appears later in this chapter in "Routines That Must Be in Your Application."

clikLoop

`clikLoop` is a pointer to a routine in your application that handles mouse clicks. The terminal tool calls the click loop repeatedly when the user is clicking or dragging an object. A more detailed description of this routine appears later in this chapter in "Routines That Must Be in Your Application."

owner

`owner` is a pointer to the grafPort in which your application displays the terminal emulation.

termRect

`termRect` is the portRect of the current window, minus the scroll bars. This portRect represents the boundaries of the terminal emulation region. *Figure 4-3* shows how `termRect` relates to the terminal emulation window.

◆ *Note:* Your application can display the terminal emulation region in an area that is smaller than `termRect`, but it must not display the combination of the cache region and terminal emulation region in an area larger than `termRect`.

`viewRect`

`viewRect` is a rectangle, measured in pixels, that represents the screen of an actual terminal. For some terminal types—for instance, Teletype or VT102™—`viewRect` has 24 lines and 80 columns. The dimensions of `viewRect` remain constant except when elements such as a tab ruler or status bar appear in the terminal emulation window, or when the size of the display font changes. The relationship of `termRect` to `viewRect` determines how much of `viewRect` is visible in the terminal emulation window.

Figure 4-3 shows how `viewRect` relates to the terminal emulation window.

■ **Figure 4-3** Bounds of `viewRect` and `termRect`

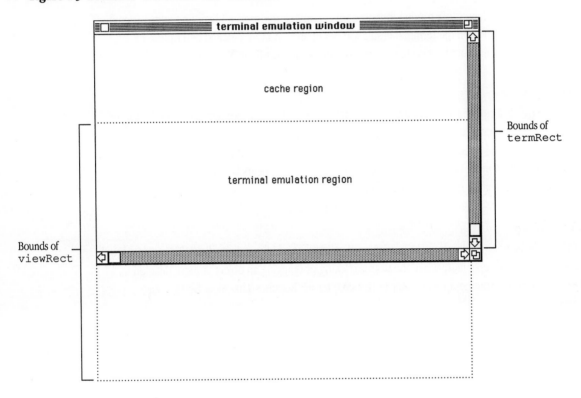

`visRect`

`visRect` is a rectangle that represents the currently visible rows and columns in the terminal emulation region (for text terminals). Numbering of rows and columns begins with the number 1.

`visRect.top` is the top visible line, and `visRect.left` is the leftmost visible column in the terminal emulation region. `visRect.bottom` is the bottom visible line, and `visRect.right` is the rightmost visible column in the terminal region. These values are used by the application to determine scroll-bar values.

lastIdle

`lastIdle` is the last time, in ticks, that the idle procedure was called for the specified terminal record.

selection

`selection` is a data structure that describes the extent of the current selection in the terminal emulation window. Since `selection` can describe either a rectangle or a region, it describes the selection in one of two kinds of data structures: a `Rect` or a `RgnHandle`. The format of the `TMSelection` data structure is as follows:

```
TYPE
        TMSelection                     =       RECORD
                CASE INTEGER OF
                1:      (
                        selRect         :       Rect;
                        );
                2:      (
                        selRgnHandle    :       RgnHandle;
                        filler          :       LONGINT;
                        );
                END;
```

`selRect` is of type `Rect` and describes the rectangle that has been selected. On a text terminal, it contains the row/column pairs, with counting beginning at 1. On a graphics terminal, it contains pixel coordinates, with (1,1) being the `topLeft` corner of the terminal region.

On a graphics terminal, if the selection is a MacPaint® program-style lasso, `selection` is a `selRgnHandle` that represents the selection region.

selType

`selType` is a field that further describes a selection; it indicates the highlighting mode that is used to show the selection. Valid values are as follows:

```
CONST
        selTextNormal           =       $0001;
        selTextBoxed            =       $0002;
        selGraphicsMarquee      =       $0004;
        selGraphicsLasso        =       $0008;

TYPE

        TMSelTypes              =       INTEGER;
```

Figure 4-4 and *Figure 4-5* show that even though two selections may have the same coordinates, different values for `selType` yield different highlighting results. *Figure 4-4* shows the text selection mode `selTextNormal`. *Figure 4-5* shows a text selection in `selTextBoxed` mode.

■ **Figure 4-4** The text selection mode `selTextNormal`

■ **Figure 4-5** The text selection mode `selTextBoxed`

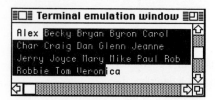

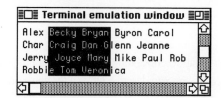

`selGraphicsMarquee` is a standard rectangular MacPaint-style marquee. `selGraphicsLasso` is a standard MacPaint-style lasso. Your application uses these types of highlighting with graphics terminals.

`mluField`

`mluField` is a `LONGINT` that terminal tools use. Your application does not need to be concerned with this field.

Terminal Manager routines

The sections describe the routines that tools and applications can use to access Terminal Manager services. Your application cannot call these routines from interrupt level.

Below is a listing of the routines described in this section in the order in which they are presented.

InitTM / 88
TMGetProcID / 88
TMNew / 89
TMDefault / 91
TMValidate / 91
TMChoose / 92
TMSetupPreFlight / 94
TMSetupSetup / 95
TMSetupFilter / 95
TMSetupItem / 96
TMSetupCleanup / 96
TMSetupPostflight / 97
TMGetConfig / 98
TMSetConfig / 98
TMStream / 99
TMPaint / 99
TMIdle / 99
TMGetLine / 100
TMScroll / 100
TMClear / 100
TMReset / 101
TMResize / 101
TMDispose / 101
TMAddSearch / 102
TMRemoveSearch / 103

TMClearSearch / 103
TMSetSelection / 104
TMGetSelect / 104
TMActivate / 105
TMResume / 105
TMMenu / 105
TMClick / 106
TMKey / 106
TMUpdate / 106
TMEvent / 107
TMIntlToEnglish / 108
TMEnglishToIntl / 108
TMGetToolName / 109
TMSetRefCon / 109
TMGetRefCon / 109
TMSetUserData / 110
TMGetUserData / 110
TMGetVersion / 110
TMGetTMVersion / 110
TMGetCursor / 111
TMDoTermKey / 111
TMCountTermKeys / 112
TMGetIndTermKey / 112
TMGetTermEnvirons / 112

Preparing for a terminal emulation

Before your application can start a terminal emulation, it must initialize the Terminal Manager (by calling `InitTM`), find out the `procID` of the tool it requires (by calling `TMGetProcID`), create a terminal record (by calling `TMNew`), and then configure the terminal tool (by restoring `config` from a saved document; or by calling `TMChoose`, the terminal tool custom configuration routines, or `TMSetConfig`).

`InitTM`

Initializing the Terminal Manager

`InitTM` initializes the Terminal Manager. Your application should call this routine after it calls the standard Macintosh Toolbox initialization routines.

▲ **Warning** Your application must initialize the Communications Resource Manager (by calling `InitCRM`) and then the Communications Toolbox Utilities (by calling `InitCTBUtilities`), whether or not it uses any of their calls, before it initializes the Terminal Manager. ▲

Function   `InitTM: TMErr;`

Description   `InitTM` returns an operating system error code if appropriate.

Your application must check for the presence of the Communications Toolbox before calling this function. Sample code under "Determining Whether the Managers are Installed" in Appendix C shows you how your application can make this check.

Result Codes   `tmGenericError, tmNoErr, tmNoTools`

`TMGetProcID`

Getting current `procID` information

Your application should call `TMGetProcID` just before creating a new terminal record, to find out the `procID` of a tool.

Function   `TMGetProcID(name: Str255): INTEGER;`

Description   `name` specifies a terminal tool. If a terminal tool is available with the specified name, its `procID` is returned. If `name` references a nonexistent terminal tool, `TMGetProcID` returns –1.

Creating a terminal record

Once the Terminal Manager has been initialized, your application needs to call `TMNew` to create a terminal record to describe the terminal emulation that is to take place. `TMNew` creates a new terminal record, fills in the fields it can, based on the parameters that were passed to it, and returns a handle to the new record in `TermHandle`. `TMNew` automatically makes two calls to `TMDefault` (which is described later in this chapter) to fill in `config` and `oldConfig`. The Terminal Manager then loads the terminal tool's main definition procedure, moves it high in the current heap, and locks it. If an error occurs that prevents a new terminal record from being created (for example, running out of memory), `TMNew` passes back `NIL` in `TermHandle`.

Your application must set the current port to the terminal window before it calls `TMNew`.

Function

```
TMNew(termRect: Rect; viewRect: Rect; flags: TMFlags; procID:
INTEGER; owner: WindowPtr; sendProc: ProcPtr; cacheProc: ProcPtr;
breakProc: ProcPtr; clikLoop: ProcPtr; environsProc: ProcPtr; refCon:
LONGINT; userData: LONGINT): TermHandle;
```

Description

`termRect` is a rectangle in local coordinates that represents the boundaries of the terminal emulation region. Your application initially sets this value by passing it as a parameter to `TMNew`.

`viewRect` is a subset of `termRect`, which the terminal tool can actually write into. Your application initially sets this value by passing it as a parameter to `TMNew`, but the terminal tool may resize it.

`flags` is a bit field with the following masks:

```
CONST
      tmInvisible           =      $00000001;
      tmSaveBeforeClear     =      $00000002;
      tmNoMenus             =      $00000004;
      tmAutoScroll          =      $00000008;
```

`flags` represents a request from your application for a level of service.

Apple Computer, Inc. has reserved the bits of `flags` that are not shown in this document. Do not use them, or your code may not work in the future.

If your application sets `tmInvisible`, the Terminal Manager maintains a terminal emulation but does not display it. Your application can use the terminal emulation and cache regions to create some other presentation service instead of a terminal emulation.

If your application sets `tmSaveBeforeClear`, the terminal tool attempts to cache the entire terminal emulation region in response to any clear-screen operation. Clear-screen operations are generated from either a user's request, a clear-screen character sequence, or a terminal-reset character sequence.

If your application sets `tmNoMenus`, the terminal tool does not display any custom menus.

If your application sets `tmAutoScroll`, the terminal tool automatically scrolls the terminal emulation window (if necessary) while the user highlights a selection.

`procID` values are dynamically assigned by the Terminal Manager to tools at run time. Applications should not store `procID` values in "settings" files. Instead, they should store tool names, which can be converted to `procID` values with `TMGetProcID`. Use the `ID` that `TMGetProcID` returns for `procID`.

`owner` is a pointer to the window in which your application is displaying the terminal emulation. If `tmInvisible` is `FALSE`, owner should be a grafPort that the terminal tool has control over.

`sendProc` is a pointer to a routine the terminal tool calls when it needs to send data on a connection. A more detailed description of `sendProc` appears later in this chapter, in the section "Routines That Must Be in Your Application."

`cacheProc` is a pointer to a routine in your application that saves lines that scroll off the top of the terminal emulation region. This routine also saves the terminal screen before a clear-screen operation (if `TMSaveBeforeClear` is set). If your application does not have a `cacheProc`, specify `NIL` in this field. A more detailed description of `cacheProc` appears later in this chapter in the section "Routines That Must Be in Your Application."

`breakProc` is a pointer to a routine in your application that performs some sort of break operation. The effect the break has depends upon the terminal emulation tool that your application is using. A more detailed description of `breakProc` appears later in this chapter in the section "Routines That Must Be in Your Application."

`clikLoop` is a pointer to a routine in your application that is called when the mouse button is held down. The terminal tool calls the click loop repeatedly when users are clicking and dragging the mouse. A more detailed description of `clikLoop` appears later in this chapter, in the section "Routines That Must Be in Your Application." Specify `NIL` in this field if your application has no `clikLoop` procedure.

`environsProc` is a pointer to a routine that the terminal tool calls when it requires information about the connection. See "Connection Manager Routines" in Chapter 3 for information about the `CMGetConnEnvirons` routine.

`userData` and `refCon` are fields your application can use.

Initializing the terminal record

TMDefault fills the configuration record pointed to by theConfig with the default configuration, which is specified by the terminal tool with the given procID. TMNew calls this procedure automatically when it fills in the config and oldConfig fields in a new terminal record.

Procedure   TMDefault(VAR theConfig: Ptr; procID: INTEGER; allocate: BOOLEAN);

Description   If allocate is TRUE, the tool allocates space for theConfig in the current heap zone.

TMValidate

Validating the terminal record

TMValidate performs an internal consistency check on the configuration and private data records of the terminal record. TMNew and TMSetConfig call this routine after they have created a new terminal record, to make sure that the record contains values identical to those specified by the terminal tool.

Function   TMValidate(hTerm: TermHandle): BOOLEAN;

Description   If the validation fails, the Terminal Manager returns TRUE and the terminal tool fills the configuration record with default values by calling TMDefault.

Your application can call this routine after restoring a configuration, to verify that the terminal record contains the correct information, in a manner similar to that shown next.

```
BlockMove(saveConfig,hTerm.config,GetPtrSize(hTerm^^.config));
IF TMValidate(hTerm) THEN BEGIN
      {validate failed}
      END
      ELSE BEGIN
              {validate succeeded}
              END
```

Configuring a terminal tool

An application can configure a terminal tool in one of three ways. The easiest and most straightforward way is by calling the TMChoose routine. This routine presents the user with a dialog box similar to the one shown in *Figure 4-6.*

■ **Figure 4-6** A sample tool-settings dialog box

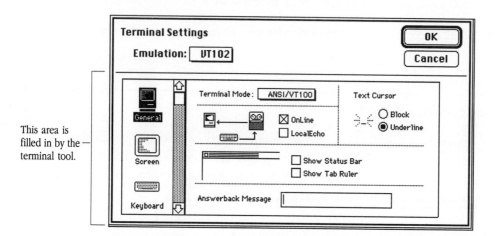

This area is filled in by the terminal tool.

The second way an application can configure a terminal tool is by presenting the user with a custom tool-settings dialog box. This method is much more difficult and involves calling six routines. The routines are described in the next section, "Custom Configuration of a Terminal Tool," and "The Custom Tool-Settings Dialog Box" in Appendix C provides example code

The third way your application can configure a terminal tool is by using the scripting language interface, described in "Interfacing with a Scripting Language," later in this chapter. This method allows your application to bypass user interface elements.

Function

```
TMChoose(VAR hTerm: TermHandle; where: Point; idleProc: ProcPtr):
INTEGER;
```

Description

where is the point specified in global coordinates, where the upper-left corner of the dialog box should appear. It is recommended that your application place the dialog box as close to the upper-left corner of the screen as possible because the size of the dialog box varies from tool to tool.

idleProc is a procedure with no parameters that the Terminal Manager will automatically call every time TMChoose loops through the setup dialog box filter procedure. Pass NIL if your application has no idleProc.

`TMChoose` returns one of the following values:

```
CONST
    chooseDisaster     =       -2;
    chooseFailed       =       -1;
    chooseOKMinor      =        1;
    chooseOKMajor      =        2;
    chooseCancel       =        3;
```

`chooseDisaster` means that the `TMChoose` operation failed, destroyed the terminal record, and returned `NIL` in the terminal handle.

`chooseFailed` means that the `TMChoose` operation failed and the terminal record was not changed.

`chooseOKMinor` means that the user clicked OK in the dialog box, but did not change the terminal tool being used.

`chooseOKMajor` means that the user clicked OK in the dialog box and also changed the terminal tool being used. The Terminal Manager then destroys the old terminal handle by calling `TMDispose`, and returns a new terminal handle in `hTerm`.

`chooseCancel` means that the user clicked Cancel in the dialog box.

Custom configuration of a terminal tool

Your application creates a custom tool-settings dialog box and presents it to the user by using six Terminal Manager routines: TMSetupPreflight, TMSetupSetup, TMSetupFilter, TMSetupItem, TMSetupCleanup, and TMSetupPostflight. Using these routines is a bit more involved than calling TMChoose, but they provide your application with much more flexibility. Refer to the code sample in "The Custom Tool-Settings Dialog Box" in Appendix C to see how an application calls these routines.

   To build a list of available terminal tools, use the routine CRMGetIndToolName, described in Chapter 6.

TMSetupPreflight

Setting up the custom tool-settings dialog box

TMSetupPreflight returns a handle to a dialog item list that your application appends to the tool-settings dialog box. The handle comes from the terminal tool. (The calling application uses AppendDITL, which is discussed in Chapter 7.) This handle is not a resource handle. Your application is responsible for disposing of the handle when done with it.

   The terminal tool can use TMSetupPreflight to allocate a block of private storage, and to store the pointer to that block in magicCookie. magicCookie should be passed to the other routines that are used to set up the custom tool-settings dialog box.

Function   TMSetupPreflight(procID: INTEGER; VAR magicCookie: LONGINT): Handle;

Description   procID is the ID for the terminal tool that is being configured. Your application should get this value by using the TMGetProcID routine, which is discussed earlier in this chapter.

   ◆ *Note:* The refcon of the custom tool-settings dialog box should point to a data structure (an example of which is shown next) in which the first two bytes are the tool procID and the next four bytes are magicCookie. UserItem routines, for example, may require procID to obtain tool resources.

```
TYPE
     chooseDLOGdata      =        RECORD
          procID         :        INTEGER
          magicCookie    :        LONGINT
END;
```

Setting up the custom tool-settings dialog box items

TMSetupSetup tells the terminal tool to set up controls (like radio buttons or check boxes) in the dialog item list returned by TMSetupPreflight.

Procedure   TMSetupSetup(procID: INTEGER; theConfig: Ptr; count: INTEGER; theDialog: DialogPtr; VAR magicCookie: LONGINT);

Description   procID is the ID for the terminal tool being configured. Your application should use the same value for procID as it passed to TMSetupPreflight.

theConfig is a pointer to a configuration record for the tool being configured.

count is the number of the first item in the dialog item list appended to the dialog box.

theDialog is the dialog box in which configuration is taking place.

magicCookie is a pointer to private storage for the terminal tool.

Filtering custom tool-settings dialog box events

Your application calls TMSetupFilter as a filter procedure before it calls the standard modal dialog box filter procedure for the custom tool-settings dialog box. This routine allows terminal tools to filter events in the custom tool-settings dialog box.

Function   TMSetupFilter(procID: INTEGER; theConfig: Ptr; count:INTEGER; theDialog: DialogPtr; VAR theEvent: EventRecord; VAR theItem: INTEGER; VAR magicCookie: LONGINT): BOOLEAN;

Description   procID is the ID for the terminal tool that is being configured. Your application should use the same value for procID as it passed to TMSetupPreflight.

theConfig is the pointer to the configuration record for the tool being configured.

count is the number of the first item in the dialog item list appended to the dialog box.

theDialog is the dialog box performing the configuration.

theEvent is the event record for which filtering is to take place.

theItem can return the item clicked in the dialog box.

magicCookie is a pointer to private storage for the terminal tool.

If the event passed in was handled, TMSetupFilter returns TRUE. Otherwise, FALSE indicates that your application should perform standard dialog box filtering.

Processing custom tool-settings dialog box events

TMSetupItem processes events for controls in the custom tool-settings dialog box.

Procedure TMSetupItem(procID: INTEGER; theConfig: Ptr; count: INTEGER; theDialog: DialogPtr; VAR theItem: INTEGER; VAR magicCookie: LONGINT);

Description procID is the ID for the terminal tool being configured. Your application should use the same value for procID as it passed to TMSetupPreflight.

theConfig is a pointer to the configuration record for the tool being configured.

count is the number of the first item in the dialog item list appended to the dialog box.

theDialog is the dialog box performing the configuration.

theItem is the item clicked in the dialog box. This value can be modified and sent back.

magicCookie is a pointer to private storage for the terminal tool.

TMSetupCleanup

Performing clean-up operations

TMSetupCleanup disposes of any storage allocated in TMSetupPreflight and performs other clean-up operations. If your application needs to shorten a dialog box, it should do so after calling this routine.

Procedure TMSetupCleanup(procID: INTEGER; theConfig: Ptr; count: INTEGER; theDialog: DialogPtr; VAR magicCookie: LONGINT);

Description procID is the ID for the terminal tool that is being configured. Your application should use the same value for procID as it passed to TMSetupPreflight.

theConfig is a pointer to the configuration record for the tool being configured.

count is the number of the first item in the dialog item list appended to the dialog box.

theDialog is the dialog box performing the configuration.

magicCookie is a pointer to private storage for the terminal tool.

Closing the tool file

TMSetupPostflight closes the tool file if it is not being used by any session.

Procedure

TMSetupPostflight (procID:INTEGER);

Description

procID is the ID for the terminal tool that is being configured. Your application should use the same value for procID as it passed to TMSetupPreflight.

Interfacing with a scripting language

Your application does not have to rely on users making selections from dialog boxes in order to configure a terminal tool. `TMGetConfig` and `TMSetConfig` provide the services that your application needs to interface with a scripting language.

Getting the configuration string

`TMGetConfig` gets a configuration string from the terminal tool.

Function   `TMGetConfig(hTerm: TermHandle): Ptr;`

Description   `TMGetConfig` returns a null-terminated, C-style string from the terminal tool containing tokens that fully describe the configuration of the terminal record. For an example, see the description of the next routine. If an error occurs, `TMGetConfig` returns `NIL`.

It is the responsibility of your application to dispose of `Ptr`.

Setting the configuration with a string

`TMSetConfig` passes a configuration string to the terminal tool.

Function   `TMSetConfig(hTerm: TermHandle; thePtr: Ptr): INTEGER;`

Description   `TMSetConfig` passes a null-terminated, C-style string (see the example string later in this section) to the terminal tool for parsing. The string is pointed to by `thePtr` and must contain tokens that describe the configuration of the terminal record. The string can be any length.

`TMSetConfig` ignores items it does not recognize or find relevant; such an occurrence causes the terminal tool to stop parsing the string and to return the character position where the error occurred. If the terminal tool successfully parses the string, it returns `tmNoErr`. If the terminal tool does not successfully parse the string, it returns one of the following values: a number less than –1 to indicate an `OSErr`, –1 to indicate an unknown error, or a positive number to indicate the character position where parsing was stopped.

Individual terminal tools are responsible for the parsing operation.

Sample   *A null-terminated, C-style configuration string*

```
FontSize 9 Width 80 Cursor Underline Online True LocalEcho False
AutoRepeat True RepeatControls False AutoWrap False NewLine False
SmoothScroll False Transparent False SwapBSDelete False\0
```

Using terminal emulation routines

Once your application has performed the required tasks described in the previous sections, it can use the routines described next to perform terminal emulations.

Putting data into the terminal

Your application should use `TMStream` to give the terminal tool data to write into the terminal emulation buffer.

Function　　　`TMStream(hTerm: TermHandle; theBuffer: Ptr; theLength: LONGINT; flags: CMFlags): LONGINT;`

Description　　`TMStream` returns the number of bytes that it processed.

`theBuffer` is the data that is either to be placed in the terminal emulation buffer or processed by the terminal tool. Typically the data `theBuffer` points to has been provided by the connection tool your application is using.

`CMFlags` is described under the description of `CMRead` in Chapter 3.

Drawing part of the terminal emulation region

`TMPaint` draws the data in `theTermData` into the rectangle `theRect`, which is in local window coordinates.

Procedure　　`TMPaint(hTerm: TermHandle; theTermData:TermDataBlock; theRect: Rect);`

Description　　`theTermData.theData` must be a handle to a block on the heap.

Providing necessary idle time

Your application should call `TMIdle` at least once every time it goes through its main event loop, so that the terminal tool can perform idle-loop tasks (like blinking the cursor or searching the terminal emulation buffer).

Procedure　　`TMIdle(hTerm: TermHandle);`

Description　　`hTerm` specifies the terminal for which idle-loop tasks are to be performed.

Getting lines from the terminal emulation buffer

TMGetLine returns a line from the terminal emulation buffer.

Procedure

```
TMGetLine(hTerm: TermHandle; lineNo: INTEGER; VAR
theTermData:TermDataBlock);
```

Description

lineNo specifies the line number of a line of data in the terminal emulation buffer. (Line numbering in the buffer begins with 1.)

Your application must allocate theTermData.theData with a length of 0. For example, theTermData.theData:=NewHandle(0). The terminal tool copies the text into theTermData.theData, and increases the size of the handle if necessary. Your application is responsible for disposing of theTermData.theData.

Scrolling the terminal emulation region

TMScroll causes the terminal emulation region to scroll horizontally, vertically, or both.

Procedure

```
TMScroll(hTerm: TermHandle; dH, dV: INTEGER);
```

Description

dH and dV specify the number of pixels to scroll horizontally and vertically. If your application specifies positive values for dH and dV, the terminal emulation region scrolls down and to the right. If your application specifies negative values, the terminal emulation region scrolls up and to the left.

Clearing the terminal emulation region

TMClear causes the terminal to clear the display screen and to place the cursor in the home position. Nothing is transmitted to the remote computer.

Procedure

```
TMClear(hTerm: TermHandle);
```

Description

If the tmSaveBeforeClear flag is on in the terminal record, the terminal tool caches the data that is cleared from the terminal emulation region.

Resetting the terminal

When your application calls TMReset, the terminal tool puts the specified terminal into a state that appears as if the terminal had just been turned on. In actuality, the screen representation structure and internal state tables (if the tool has any) are reset to the values specified by the terminal tool, and the configuration record for the terminal is reset to its last saved state.

Procedure   TMReset(hTerm: TermHandle);

Description   If the tmSaveBeforeClear flag is on in the terminal record, the terminal tool caches the data that is cleared from the terminal emulation region prior to resetting the terminal.

Resizing the terminal region

TMResize resizes the terminal emulation region to the coordinates specified in newTermRect.

Procedure   TMResize(hTerm: TermHandle; newTermRect: Rect);

Description   newTermRect specifies bounds of the new termRect. The terminal tool automatically resizes the value of viewRect.

Disposing of a terminal record

TMDispose disposes of the terminal record and all associated data structures and controls.

Procedure   TMDispose(hTerm: TermHandle);

△   **Important**   Your application must call TMDispose before disposing of the terminal emulation window with DisposeWindow. Since DisposeWindow clears all controls in the control list, a subsequent call to TMDispose may cause problems. △

Searching the terminal emulation buffer

A terminal tool can search the terminal emulation buffer any time your application requires it to, but typically a tool will perform a search during your application's idle procedure. To tell a tool to search for a specified string, your application calls the `TMAddSearch` routine. To tell the terminal tool to stop performing a search, your application calls `TMRemoveSearch`. To tell the terminal tool to stop all searches, your application calls `TMClearSearch`.

`TMAddSearch`

Adding a data stream search

`TMAddSearch` tells the terminal tool to search for a specified string.

Function

```
TMAddSearch(hTerm: TermHandle; theString: Str255; where: Rect;
searchType: TMSearchTypes; callBack: ProcPtr): INTEGER;
```

Description

If the search was successfully added, this function returns the reference number assigned to the search. If the search was not successfully added, `TMAddSearch` returns –1. The tool searches for `theString` in the area specified by `where` and within the selection specified by `searchType`.

`where` is a rectangle that contains two row/column pairs, with row and column numbers starting at 1.

By specifying a –1 as a value in the row/column pairs, your application can limit the search to one row, one column, or the intersection of one row and one column. *Table 4-1* shows how your application can use –1 as a search-area delimiter.

■ **Table 4-1** `TMAddSearch` search-area delimiters

Area to search	Row/column pair to use
rectangle bounded by n,m,o,p	$(n,m)\,(o,p)$
row n, any column	$(n,-1)\,(-1,-1)$
any row, column m	$(-1,m)\,(-1,-1)$
rows n through o (inclusive), any column	$(n,-1)\,(o,-1)$
column m through p (inclusive), any row	$(-1,m)\,(-1,p)$
anywhere (any row, any column)	$(-1,-1)\,(-1,-1)$

Your application should pass in `searchType` the sum of three values that describes the search: `searchNoDiacrit` (to ignore diacritical marks), `searchNoCase` (to ignore case), and one of the constants that describes the selection.

Valid values are as follows:

```
TYPE
     TMSearchTypes          =        INTEGER;

CONST
{  search modifiers  }
     searchNoDiacrit        =        $0100;
     searchNoCase           =        $0200;

{ constants that describe the selection }
     selTextNormal          =        $0001;
     selTextBoxed           =        $0002;
     selGraphicsMarquee     =        $0004;
     selGraphicsLasso       =        $0008;
```

`callBack` is a procedure that the tool automatically calls when it finds a match. `callBack` must be supplied by your application, and is described later in this chapter in the section "Routines That Must Be in Your Application."

TMRemoveSearch

Stopping a data stream search

TMRemoveSearch stops the search specified by `refNum`.

Procedure   `TMRemoveSearch(hTerm: TermHandle; refNum: INTEGER);`

Description   This routine cannot be called at interrupt level, but can be called by `MyCallBack`. (`MyCallBack` is discussed later in this chapter under "Routines That Must Be in Your Application.")

TMClearSearch

Clearing all data stream searches

TMClearSearch stops all searches associated with the specified terminal record.

Procedure   `TMClearSearch(hTerm: TermHandle);`

Description   `hTerm` specifies the terminal record. TMClearSearch cannot be called from interrupt level.

Manipulating selections

The Terminal Manager provides two routines that make it easier for your application to manipulate selections in the terminal emulation window. TMSetSelection highlights a selection, and TMGetSelect retrieves the data in the selection.

TMSetSelection

Setting and highlighting selections

TMSetSelection makes theSelection the current selection.

Procedure   TMSetSelection(hTerm: TermHandle; theSelection: TMSelection; selType: TMSelTypes);

Description   selType determines the type of highlighting for the selection. Valid values are:

```
TYPE
    TMSelTypes          =          INTEGER;

CONST
    selTextNormal       =          $0001;
    selTextBoxed        =          $0002;
    selGraphicsMarquee  =          $0004;
    selGraphicsLasso    =          $0008;
```

TMGetSelect

Getting data from a selection

TMGetSelect returns either the number of bytes in the selection, or an appropriate operating system error code.

Function   TMGetSelect(hTerm: TermHandle; theData: Handle; VAR theType: ResType): LONGINT;

Description   If nothing is selected, TMGetSelect returns 0. Otherwise, it returns the size of the selected data.

theData must be a handle to a block of size 0. TMGetSelect will resize this block as necessary.

theType specifies the type of data this routine returns. If theType is TEXT, theData is a handle to textual data. theType and theData may be passed directly to the Scrap Manager.

Handling events

The Terminal Manager event-processing routines provide useful extensions to the Macintosh Toolbox Event Manager. This section explains the seven routines that the Terminal Manager provides. See "Other Events" in Chapter 2 for sample code showing how an application can determine if an event needs to be handled by one of these routines.

TMActivate

Activate events

TMActivate processes an activate or deactivate event (for instance, installing or removing a custom tool menu) for a window associated with the terminal tool.

Procedure   TMActivate(hTerm: TermHandle; activate: BOOLEAN);

Description   If activate is TRUE, the terminal tool processes an activate event. Otherwise, it processes a deactivate event.

TMResume

Resume events

TMResume processes a resume or suspend event for a terminal window. Resume and suspend events are processed only if a tool has a custom menu to install or remove from the menu bar.

Procedure   TMResume(hTerm: TermHandle; resume: BOOLEAN);

Description   If resume is TRUE, then the terminal processes a resume event. Otherwise, it processes a suspend event.

TMMenu

Menu events

Your application must call TMMenu when the user chooses an item from a menu that is installed by the terminal tool.

Function   TMMenu(hTerm: TermHandle; menuID: INTEGER; item: INTEGER): BOOLEAN;

Description   TMMenu returns FALSE if the terminal tool did not handle the menu event. TMMenu returns TRUE if the terminal tool did handle the menu event.

Mouse events

TMClick processes a mouseDown event in the terminal emulation region. The routine pointed to by myclikLoop, discussed later in this chapter in the section "Routines That Must Be in Your Application," is called repeatedly by TMClick.

Procedure   TMClick(hTerm: TermHandle; theEvent: EventRecord);

Keyboard events

TMKey processes a keyDown or autoKey event. The terminal tool translates the keystroke into a sequence of bytes. The terminal tool then calls your application's sendProc routine (discussed later in this chapter under "Routines That Must Be in Your Application.") to transmit this sequence of bytes.

Procedure   TMKey(hTerm: TermHandle; theEvent: EventRecord);

Description   Your application can create its own event record for specific keyboard events by filling in the event record with the character code and –1 for the key code in the message field.

Update events

Your application will typically call TMUpdate between BeginUpdate and EndUpdate.

Procedure   TMUpdate(hTerm: TermHandle; visRgn: RgnHandle);

Description   visRgn specifies the region to be updated.

Other events

When your application receives an event, it should check whether the `refcon` of the window is a tool's `hTerm`. Such an event occurs, for example, when the user clicks a button in a dialog box displayed by the terminal tool. If it does belong to a terminal tool's window, your application can call `TMEvent`.

Procedure

`TMEvent(hTerm: TermHandle; theEvent: EventRecord);`

Description

A window (or dialog box) created by a terminal tool has a terminal record handle stored in the `refCon` field for `windowRecord`.

Localizing configuration strings

The Communications Toolbox provides two routines that make it easier to localize configuration strings.

TMIntlToEnglish

Translating into English

TMIntlToEnglish converts a configuration string, which is pointed to by inputPtr, to an American English configuration string pointed to by outputPtr.

Function

```
TMIntlToEnglish(hTerm: TermHandle; inputPtr: Ptr; VAR outputPtr: Ptr;
language: INTEGER): OSErr;
```

Description

The function returns an operating system error code if any internal errors occur.

The terminal tool allocates space for outputPtr. Your application should dispose of this pointer when done with it.

language specifies the language from which the string is to be converted. Valid values for this field are shown in the description of the Script Manager in *Inside Macintosh,* Volume V. If the language specified is not supported, this routine returns tmNoErr, but outputPtr is NIL.

TMEnglishToIntl

Translating from English

TMEnglishToIntl converts an American English configuration string, which is pointed to by inputPtr, to a configuration string pointed to by outputPtr.

Function

```
TMEnglishToIntl(hTerm: TermHandle; inputPtr: Ptr; VAR outputPtr: Ptr;
language: INTEGER): OSErr;
```

Description

The function returns an operating system error code if any internal errors occur.

The terminal tool allocates space for outputPtr. Your application is responsible for disposing of the pointer with DisposPtr when done with it.

language specifies the language to which the string is to be converted. Valid values for this field are shown in the description of the Script Manager in *Inside Macintosh,* Volume V. If the language specified is not supported, tmNoErr is still returned, but outputPtr is NIL.

Miscellaneous routines

The routines described in this section perform a variety of tasks.

`TMGetToolName`

Getting the name of a tool

`TMGetToolName` returns in `name` the name of the tool specified by `procID`.

Procedure `TMGetToolName(procID: INTEGER; VAR name: Str255);`

Description If `procID` references a terminal tool that does not exist, the Terminal Manager sets `name` to an empty string.

`TMSetRefCon`

Setting the terminal tool's reference constant

`TMSetRefCon` sets the terminal record's `refCon` to the specified value. It is very important that your application use this routine to change the value of the reference constant, instead of changing it directly.

Procedure `TMSetRefCon(hTerm: TermHandle; refCon: LONGINT);`

`TMGetRefCon`

Getting the terminal tool's reference constant

`TMGetRefCon` returns the terminal record's reference constant.

Function `TMGetRefCon(hTerm: TermHandle): LONGINT;`

Setting the `userData` field

`TMSetUserData` sets the terminal record's `userData` field to the value specified by `userData`. It is very important that your application use this routine to change the value of the `userData` field, instead of changing it directly.

Procedure   `TMSetUserData(hTerm: TermHandle; userData: LONGINT);`

Getting the `userData` field

`TMGetUserData` returns the terminal record's `userData` field.

Function   `TMGetUserData(hTerm: TermHandle): LONGINT;`

Getting `'vers'` resource information

`TMGetVersion` returns a handle to a relocatable block that contains the information that is in the terminal tool's `'vers'` resource with ID=1. Your application is responsible for disposing of the handle when done with it.

◆ *Note:* The handle returned is *not* a resource handle.

Function   `TMGetVersion(hTerm: TermHandle): Handle;`

Getting the Terminal Manager version number

`TMGetTMVersion` returns the version number of the Terminal Manager.

Function   `TMGetTMVersion: INTEGER;`

Description   The version number of the Terminal Manager described in this document is:

```
CONST
    curTMVersion  =       1;
```

Getting the current cursor position

`TMGetCursor` returns the current position of the cursor. Numbering of rows and columns begins with 1.

Function

`TMGetCursor(hTerm: TermHandle; cursType: TMCursorTypes): Point;`

Description

Valid values for `cursType` are as follows:

```
CONST
     cursorText           =        1;
     cursorGraphics       =        2;

TYPE

     TMCursorTypes        =        INTEGER;
```

For `cursorText`, the position returned is in row/column format, and for `cursorGraphics` the position is in pixel coordinates.

Emulating a special terminal key

`TMDoTermKey` emulates a special terminal key specified by `theKey`.

Function

`TMDoTermKey(hTerm: TermHandle; theKey: Str255): BOOLEAN;`

Description

If the terminal tool does not understand the key specified by `theKey`, this routine returns `FALSE`. Otherwise, if the key specified is processed, this routine returns `TRUE`.

For information about the terminal keys supported by a terminal tool, refer to that tool's documentation.

This example shows how an application can use `TMDoTermKey` to emulate the user's pressing a PF1 key:

```
IF TMDoTermKey(hTerm, 'PF1') THEN
     BEGIN
     END;
```

Counting special terminal keys

TMCountTermKeys returns the number of special terminal keys that the terminal tool supports.

Function   TMCountTermKeys(hTerm) : INTEGER;

Description   TMCountTermKeys returns 0 if the terminal tool supports no special terminal keys.

Getting a terminal key

TMGetIndTermKey returns the name of a specified key.

Procedure   TMGetIndTermKey(hTerm:TermHandle; id:INTEGER; VAR theKey:Str255);

Description   TMGetIndTermKey returns in theKey the terminal key specified by id. If id specifies a key that does not exist, this routine returns an empty string.

Getting general terminal tool information

TMGetTermEnvirons returns theEnvirons, which reflects the internal conditions of the terminal tool. The caller of this routine must fill in the version field of theEnvirons before calling TMGetTermEnvirons.

Function   TMGetTermEnvirons(hTerm: TermHandle; VAR theEnvirons: TermEnvironRec) : TMErr;

Description   This routine returns tmNoErr, envVersTooBig, or an operating system error code. The fields in theEnvirons are as follows:

```
TYPE
    TermEnvironPtr      =      ^TermEnvironRec;
    TermEnvironRec      =      RECORD
        version         :      INTEGER;
        termType        :      TMTermTypes;
        textRows        :      INTEGER;
        textCols        :      INTEGER;
        cellSize        :      Point;
        graphicSize     :      Rect;
        slop            :      Point;
        auxSpace        :      Rect;
    END;
```

`version` is the version number of the requested **terminal environment record,** which is `curTermEnvRecVers` in this release of the Terminal Manager. The caller of the routine must fill in this field before calling `TMGetTermEnvirons`.

`termType` is the type of terminal. `termType` can contain one or both of the following values:

```
CONST
     tmTextTerminal          =       $0001;
     tmGraphicsTerminal      =       $0002;
     curTermEnvRecVers       =       0;

TYPE
     TMTermTypes             =       INTEGER;
```

`textRows` is the number of rows in the terminal emulation region. The first row is row number 1.

`textCols` is the number of columns in the terminal emulation region. The first column is column number 1.

`cellSize` is the height and width of each cell.

`graphicSize` is the size of the default rectangle of the graphics terminal tool measured in pixels.

`slop` is the border of the terminal emulation region.

`auxSpace` is a rectangle that specifies any additional space that is required at the top, bottom, right, or left of the terminal emulation region, as shown in *Figure 4-7.*

■ **Figure 4-7** Additional space in the terminal emulation region

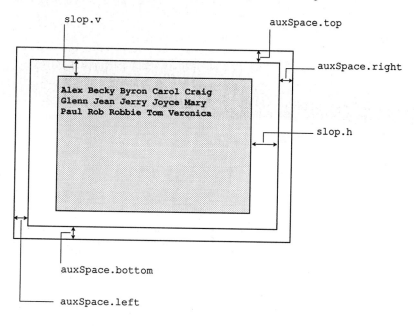

Result Codes   `tmGenericError, tmNoErr, tmNotSupported, envVersTooBig.`

Routines that must be in your application

Terminal tools do not provide all the code necessary to perform terminal emulations; your application must also provide some code (or at least pointers to code provided by other managers). This section describes the routines that must be in your application, which give the terminal tool important information about

- how to send data on the connection

- what to do with lines that scroll out of the terminal emulation region

- what to do when a specified string is found in the terminal emulation buffer

- what to do when the user wants to effect a break on the terminal

- what to do when the user is dragging the mouse in the terminal emulation region

- what the connection environment is like

MySendProc

Sending data out along the connection

When a tool needs to send data to another entity, it looks to your application to provide MySendProc. MySendProc may simply be the routine that the Connection Manager uses to send data (as is the case in the next example), or it can be a routine that you have written.

Function

MySendProc (thePtr: Ptr; theSize: LONGINT; refCon: LONGINT; flags: CMFlags): LONGINT;

Description

thePtr is a pointer to the data to be sent.

theSize is the number of characters to be sent.

refCon is the reference constant field for sending terminal's terminal.

MySendProc returns the actual number of characters sent.

flags indicates whether the connection tool should send an end-of-message indicator. An end-of-message indicator needs to be supported by the particular communications protocol being used; if an end-of-message indicator is not supported by the connection protocol, your application should ignore this field.

Sample routine for sending data

```
FUNCTION MySendProc(thePtr: Ptr;theSize: LONGINT;
                    refcon: LONGINT;flags: INTEGER): LONGINT;
VAR
      theErr : CMErr;                         { Any errors }

BEGIN
      MySendProc := 0;                        { Assume the worst }

      IF gConn <> NIL THEN BEGIN

            { DO NOT check to see if the connection is first open before sending }
            { as the tool might be handling the data locally }

                                          { Send the data }
            theErr := CMWrite(gConn,thePtr,theSize,cmData,FALSE,NIL,0,flags);

            IF (theErr = noErr) THEN
                  MySendProc := theSize       { If ok, we sent all }
            ELSE
                  ;                           { Handle errors }
      END; { Good Connection }

END; { MySendProc }
```

MyBreakProc

Sending a break

Your application needs to contain information about how to send a break on a
connection. Although it can contain the code that performs the break operation, your
application can also point to a connection tool routine that performs the break. This
section gives an example.

Procedure   `MyBreakProc(duration: LONGINT; refCon: LONGINT);`

Description   `duration` specifies, in ticks, how long the break should last.

`refCon` is the reference constant field of the terminal record.

Sample showing how to break a connection

```
PROCEDURE MyBreakProc(duration: LONGINT; refcon : LONGINT);
BEGIN
      { Here we choose to issue a synchronous break }
      IF gConn <> NIL THEN
            CMBreak(gConn, duration, FALSE, NIL);
END; { MyBreakProc }
```

Caching lines from the terminal region

Your application can cache lines that scroll off the top of the terminal emulation region and, if desired, display them in the terminal emulation window. If you want your application to display these lines, you have to provide the necessary code. If you do not want your application to display these lines, then your application should specify NIL for MyCacheProc when it calls TMNew.

Function

```
MyCacheProc(refCon: LONGINT; theTermData:TermDataBlock): LONGINT;
```

Description

MyCacheProc must return tmNoErr if no error occurred during processing. Otherwise, it should return an appropriate error code.

refCon is the reference constant for the terminal record.

theTermData is a data structure of type TermDataBlock:

```
TYPE
        TermDataBlockH          =       ^TermDataPtr;
        TermDataBlockPtr        =       ^TermDataBlock;
        TermDataBlock           =       RECORD
                flags           :       TMTermTypes;
                theData         :       Handle;
                auxData         :       Handle;
                reserved        :       LONGINT;
        END;
```

theTerm.theData is a handle to a block on the heap. Your application can calculate the size of this block with GetHandleSize. Your application must copy any data it needs because theTermData belongs to the terminal tool and may not exist after MyCacheProc has finished. Your application can use HandToHand to copy the data.

Sample showing how to cache lines

```
FUNCTION MyCacheProc (refcon : LONGINT; theTermData : TermDataBlock ) : LONGINT;
VAR
        sizeCached      : LONGINT;

BEGIN
        { Check for data integrity }
        IF (theTermData.theData = NIL) THEN BEGIN
                MyCacheProc := -1;
                EXIT(MyCacheProc);
        END; { Bad Data }

        { Cache either graphics or text }
        HLock(theTermData.theData);

        { Get rid of the old cached data }
        IF (gCache <> NIL) THEN
```

```
        DisposHandle(gCache);

    { make a copy of new text }
    gCache := theTermData.theData;
    IF (HandToHand(gCache) <> noErr) THEN BEGIN
        gCache := NIL;                  (* Handle errors *)
        sizeCached := -1;
    END
    ELSE
        sizeCached := GetHandleSize(gCache);

    HUnlock(theTermData.theData);

    IF (theTermData.flags = tmGraphicsTerminal) THEN BEGIN
        { theTermData.theData is a handle to a QD Picture }
        (*
        Could save it as PICT
        *)
    END { cache graphics }
    ELSE IF (theTermData.flags = tmTextTerminal) THEN BEGIN
        { theTermData.theData is a handle to text }

        (*
        Could write it out to the data fork
        *)
    END; { cache text }
    MyCacheProc := sizeCached;
END; { MyCacheProc }
```

MyCallBack
_____

Responding to a matched search parameter

Your application can selectively filter data in the terminal emulation buffer by making use of a search call-back procedure. Since a tool will automatically call MyCallBack when it finds a match to the search string, your application can respond in any way that you want it to.

Procedure   MyCallBack(hTerm: TermHandle; refNum: INTEGER; foundRect: Rect);

Description   refNum is the reference number associated with a particular search. Reference numbers are assigned by the Terminal Manager when a search is added to a terminal record with the TMAddSearch routine.

foundRect describes in row/column format where the match was found, with row and column numbers starting at 1.

Responding to mouse clicks

This routine is called when the user is dragging the mouse in the terminal emulation window. Initially, your application should process a mouse-down event by calling `TMClick`, which in turn calls this routine.

Function   `MyClikLoop(refCon: LONGINT): BOOLEAN;`

Description   This routine returns `TRUE` when the mouse is clicked within the cache region. Otherwise, it returns `FALSE`.

Getting connection environment information

To get information about the connection environment, the terminal tool calls a routine in your application, `MyEnvironsProc`.

Function   `MyEnvironsProc(refCon: LONGINT; VAR theEnvirons: ConnEnvironRec): CMErr;`

Description   `refCon` is the reference constant for the terminal tool.

`theEnvirons` is a data structure containing the connection-environment record. Your application can either construct `theEnvirons` or use the Connection Manager routine `CMGetConnEnvirons`. For more information about `theEnvirons`, see "`CMGetConnEnvirons`" in Chapter 3.

The example that follows shows how `MyEnvironsProc` can point to a Connection Manager routine to retrieve information about the connection environment.

Sample terminal-environment routine

```
FUNCTION MyEnvironsProc(refCon: LONGINT;VAR theEnvirons: ConnEnvironRec): OSErr;
BEGIN
        MyEnvironsProc:= envNotPresent;                  { pessimism }
        theEnvirons.version := curConnEnvRecVers;        { fill in version field }

            IF (gConn <> NIL) THEN                        { Tool sets the version }
            MyEnvironsProc:= CMGetConnEnvirons(gConn,theEnvirons);

END; { MyEnvironsProc }
```

Quick reference

This section provides a reference to Terminal Manager routines and data structures. At the end of this section is a listing of routine selectors for programming in assembly language.

Routines

Terminal Manager routines	See page
`InitTM:TMErr;`	88
`TMActivate(hTerm: TermHandle; activate: BOOLEAN);`	105
`TMAddSearch(hTerm: TermHandle; theString: Str255; where: Rect; searchType: TMSearchTypes; callBack: ProcPtr): INTEGER;`	102
`TMChoose(VAR hTerm: TermHandle; where: Point; idleProc: ProcPtr): INTEGER;`	92
`TMClear(hTerm: TermHandle);`	100
`TMClearSearch(hTerm: TermHandle);`	103
`TMClick(hTerm: TermHandle; theEvent: EventRecord);`	106
`TMCountTermKeys(hTerm): INTEGER;`	112
`TMDefault(VAR theConfig: Ptr; procID: INTEGER; allocate: BOOLEAN);`	91
`TMDispose(hTerm: TermHandle);`	101
`TMDoTermKey(hTerm: TermHandle; theKey: Str255): BOOLEAN;`	111
`TMEnglishToIntl(hTerm: TermHandle; inputPtr: Ptr; VAR outputPtr: Ptr; language: INTEGER): OSErr;`	108
`TMEvent(hTerm: TermHandle; theEvent: EventRecord);`	107
`TMGetConfig(hTerm: TermHandle): Ptr;`	98
`TMGetCursor(hTerm: TermHandle; cursType: TMCursorTypes): Point;`	111
`TMGetIndTermKey(hTerm:TermHandle; id:INTEGER; VAR theKey:Str255);`	112
`TMGetLine(hTerm: TermHandle; lineNo: INTEGER; VAR theTermData:TermDataBlock);`	100
`TMGetProcID(name: Str255): INTEGER;`	88
`TMGetRefCon(hTerm: TermHandle): LONGINT;`	109
`TMGetSelect(hTerm: TermHandle; theData: Handle; VAR theType: ResType): LONGINT;`	104

Terminal Manager routines	*See page*
TMGetTermEnvirons(hTerm: TermHandle; VAR theEnvirons: TermEnvironRec): TMErr;	*112*
TMGetToolName(procID: INTEGER; VAR name: Str255);	*109*
TMGetTMVersion: INTEGER;	*110*
TMGetUserData(hTerm: TermHandle): LONGINT;	*110*
TMGetVersion(hTerm: TermHandle): Handle;	*110*
TMIdle(hTerm: TermHandle);	*99*
TMIntlToEnglish(hTerm: TermHandle; inputPtr: Ptr; VAR outputPtr: Ptr; language: INTEGER): OSErr;	*108*
TMKey(hTerm: TermHandle; theEvent: EventRecord);	*106*
TMMenu(hTerm: TermHandle; menuID: INTEGER; item: INTEGER): BOOLEAN;	*105*
TMNew(termRect: Rect; viewRect: Rect; flags: TMFlags; procID: INTEGER; owner: WindowPtr; sendProc: ProcPtr; cacheProc: ProcPtr; breakProc: ProcPtr; clikLoop: ProcPtr; environsProc: ProcPtr; refCon: LONGINT; userData: LONGINT): TermHandle;	*89*
TMPaint(hTerm: TermHandle; theTermData:TermDataBlock; theRect: Rect);	*99*
TMRemoveSearch(hTerm: TermHandle; refNum: INTEGER);	*103*
TMReset(hTerm: TermHandle);	*101*
TMResize(hTerm: TermHandle; newTermRect: Rect);	*101*
TMResume(hTerm: TermHandle; resume: BOOLEAN);	*105*
TMScroll(hTerm: TermHandle; dH, dV: INTEGER);	*100*
TMSetConfig(hTerm: TermHandle; thePtr: Ptr): INTEGER;	*98*
TMSetRefCon(hTerm: TermHandle; refCon: LONGINT);	*109*
TMSetSelection(hTerm: TermHandle; theSelection: TMSelection; selType: TMSelTypes);	*104*
TMSetupCleanup(procID: INTEGER; theConfig: Ptr; count: INTEGER; theDialog: DialogPtr; VAR magicCookie: LONGINT);	*96*
TMSetupFilter(procID: INTEGER; theConfig: Ptr; count: INTEGER; theDialog: DialogPtr; VAR theEvent: EventRecord; VAR theItem: INTEGER; VAR magicCookie: LONGINT): BOOLEAN;	*95*
TMSetupItem(procID: INTEGER; theConfig: Ptr; count: INTEGER; theDialog: DialogPtr; VAR theItem: INTEGER; VAR magicCookie: LONGINT);	*96*

Terminal Manager routines	*See page*
`TMSetupPostflight(procID: INTEGER);`	*97*
`TMSetupPreflight(procID: INTEGER; VAR magicCookie: LONGINT): Handle;`	*94*
`TMSetupSetup(procID: INTEGER; theConfig: Ptr; count: INTEGER; theDialog: DialogPtr; VAR magicCookie: LONGINT);`	*95*
`TMSetUserData(hTerm: TermHandle; userData: LONGINT);`	*110*
`TMStream(hTerm: TermHandle; theBuffer: Ptr; theLength: LONGINT; flags: CMFlags): LONGINT;`	*99*
`TMUpdate(hTerm: TermHandle; visRgn: RgnHandle);`	*106*
`TMValidate(hTerm: TermHandle): BOOLEAN;`	*91*

Routines in your application	*See page*
`MySendProc (thePtr: Ptr; theSize: LONGINT; refCon: LONGINT; flags: CMFlags): LONGINT;`	*114*
`MyBreakProc(duration: LONGINT; refCon: LONGINT);`	*115*
`MyCacheProc(refCon: LONGINT; theTermData:TermDataBlock): LONGINT;`	*116*
`MyCallBack(hTerm: TermHandle; refNum: INTEGER; foundRect: Rect);`	*117*
`MyClikLoop(refCon: LONGINT): BOOLEAN;`	*118*
`MyEnvironsProc(refCon: LONGINT; VAR theEnvirons: ConnEnvironRec): CMErr;`	*118*

Terminal record

```
TYPE
        TermHandle          =          ^TermPointer;
        TermPointer         =          ^TermRecord;
        TermRecord          =          RECORD
            procID          =          INTEGER

            flags           :          TMFlags;
            errCode         :          TMErr;

            refCon          :          LONGINT;
            userData        :          LONGINT;

            defProc         :          ProcPtr;

            config          :          Ptr;
            oldConfig       :          Ptr;
```

```
            environsProc    :       ProcPtr;
            reserved1       :       LONGINT;
            reserved2       :       LONGINT;

            tmPrivate       :       Ptr;

            sendProc        :       ProcPtr;
            breakProc       :       ProcPtr;
            cacheProc       :       ProcPtr;
            clikLoop        :       ProcPtr;


            owner           :       WindowPtr;
            termRect        :       Rect;
            viewRect        :       Rect;
            visRect         :       Rect;

            lastIdle        :       LONGINT;

            selection       :       TMSelection;
            selType         :       TMSelTypes;

            mluField        :       LONGINT;
        END;
```

Constants and data types

```
TYPE
        TMSelection             =       RECORD
            CASE INTEGER OF
            1:      (
                    selRect     :       Rect;
                    );
            2:      (
                    selRgnHandle :      RgnHandle;
                    filler       :      LONGINT;
                    );
            END;


TYPE
        TermDataBlockH      =       ^TermDataPtr;
        TermDataBlockPtr    =       ^TermDataBlock;
        TermDataBlock       =       RECORD
            flags           :       TMTermTypes;
            theData         :       Handle;
            auxData         :       Handle;
            reserved        :       LONGINT;
        END;
```

```
TYPE
        TermEnvironPtr          =       ^TermEnvironRec;
        TermEnvironRec          =       RECORD
                version         :       INTEGER;
                termType        :       TMTermTypes;
                textRows        :       INTEGER;
                textCols        :       INTEGER;
                cellSize        :       Point;
                graphicSize     :       Rect;
                slop            :       Point;
                auxSpace        :       Rect;
        END;


TYPE
        TMErr                   =       OSErr;


CONST
        tmGenericError          =       -1;
        tmNoErr                 =       0;
        tmNotSupported          =       7;
        tmNoTools               =       8;


CONST
        curTermEnvRecVers       =       0;
        curTMVersion            =       1;

{ bit masks for flags field of terminal record }
        tmInvisible             =       $00000001;
        tmSaveBeforeClear       =       $00000002;
        tmNoMenus               =       $00000004;
        tmAutoScroll            =       $00000008;



{ selection types }
        selTextNormal           =       $0001;
        selTextBoxed            =       $0002;
        selGraphicsMarquee      =       $0004;
        selGraphicsLasso        =       $0008;



{ search modifiers }
        searchNoDiacrit         =       $0100;
        searchNoCase            =       $0200;
```

```
TYPE
        TMSearchTypes          =          INTEGER;


{ terminal types in TermEnvironRec data structure }
CONST
        tmTextTerminal         =          $0001;
        tmGraphicsTerminal     =          $0002;


{ TMChoose return values }
        chooseDisaster         =          -2;
        chooseFailed           =          -1;
        chooseOKMinor          =          1;
        chooseOKMajor          =          2;
        chooseCancel           =          3;
```

Terminal Manager routine selectors

◆ *Assembly note:* Your application can access Communications Toolbox routines through a
Macintosh Operating System trap. To call a routine, your application pushes the appropriate
parameters onto the stack and invokes the trap macro that has the same name as the routine,
preceded by an underscore. When expanded, these macros place the routine selector onto the
stack, set A0 to point to the selector, and invoke the trap _CommToolboxDispatch ($A08B).
Upon returning from the trap, the trap macro pops the routine selector off the stack and places
the return value into D0. It is your application's responsibility to clean up the stack by removing
the parameters that were pushed onto the stack prior to invoking the trap macro.

InitTM	.EQU	769	TMEnglishToIntl	.EQU	798
TMActivate	.EQU	775	TMEvent	.EQU	813
TMAddSearch	.EQU	807	TMGetConfig	.EQU	795
TMChoose	.EQU	812	TMGetCursor	.EQU	810
TMClear	.EQU	781	TMGetIndTermKey	.EQU	816
TMClearSearch	.EQU	809	TMGetLine	.EQU	784
TMClick	.EQU	777	TMGetProcID	.EQU	799
TMCountTermKeys	.EQU	815	TMGetRefCon	.EQU	802
TMDefault	.EQU	789	TMGetSelect	.EQU	783
TMDispose	.EQU	771	TMGetTermEnvirons	.EQU	811
TMDoTermKey	.EQU	814	TMGetTMVersion	.EQU	806

TMGetToolName	.EQU	800		TMSetConfig	.EQU	796
TMGetUserData	.EQU	804		TMSetRefCon	.EQU	801
TMGetVersion	.EQU	805		TMSetSelection	.EQU	785
TMIdle	.EQU	787		TMSetupCleanup	.EQU	794
TMIntlToEnglish	.EQU	797		TMSetupFilter	.EQU	792
TMKey	.EQU	772		TMSetupItem	.EQU	793
TMMenu	.EQU	779		TMSetupPostflight	.EQU	817
TMNew	.EQU	770		TMSetupPreflight	.EQU	790
TMPaint	.EQU	774		TMSetupSetup	.EQU	791
TMRemoveSearch	.EQU	808		TMSetUserData	.EQU	803
TMReset	.EQU	780		TMStream	.EQU	778
TMResize	.EQU	782		TMUpdate	.EQU	773
TMResume	.EQU	776		TMValidate	.EQU	788
TMScroll	.EQU	786				

Chapter 5 File Transfer Manager

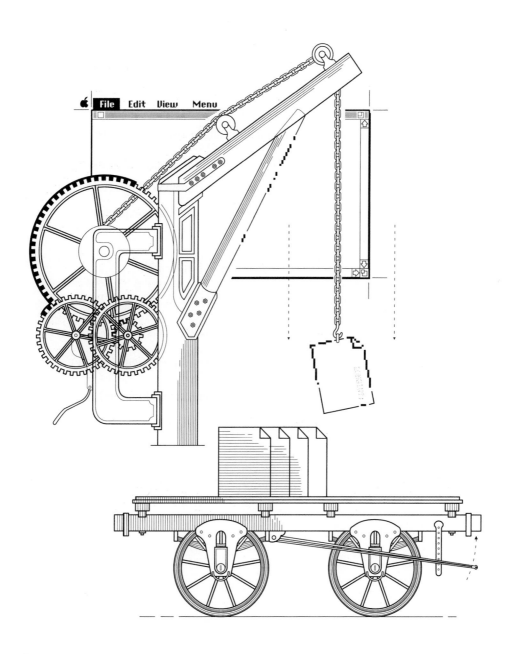

THIS CHAPTER describes the File Transfer Manager, the Communications Toolbox manager that allows applications to implement file transfer services without having to take into account underlying file transfer protocols. This chapter describes fundamental concepts about the File Transfer Manager. Then it describes the **file transfer record,** which is the most important record of the File Transfer Manager. Next, this chapter presents a detailed description of each routine provided by the File Transfer Manager. At the end of the chapter, you'll find a "Quick Reference" to routines, data structures, and routine selectors for programming in assembly language.

In this chapter, the term *your application* refers to the application you are writing for the Macintosh, which will implement communications services for users. Be careful not to confuse the services your application provides with the services that tools provide.

To use the File Transfer Manager, you need to be familiar with

- the Resource Manager (described in *Inside Macintosh,* Volumes I, IV, V)

- the File Manager (described in *Inside Macintosh,* Volumes II, IV, V)

- the Standard File Package (described in *Inside Macintosh,* Volumes I, IV)

- the Connection Manager (described in Chapter 3 of this document)

About the File Transfer Manager

By using File Transfer Manager routines, your application can send files to or receive files from another entity without having to take into account underlying file transfer protocols. **File transfer tools,** which are discussed in Chapter 11, are responsible for implementing file transfer services according to specific protocols.

The File Transfer Manager provides generic file transfer services for a transfer between your application and another computer process. The other process can be running on the same computer as your application, or on any other type of computer.

Here's what happens inside the File Transfer Manager. An application makes a request of the File Transfer Manager when it needs it to send a file or perform some other file transfer function. The File Transfer Manager then sends this request to one of the tools that it manages. The tool provides the service according to the specifics of its file transfer protocol. Once the tool has finished, it passes back to the application any relevant parameters and return codes.

Figure 5-1 shows the data flow into and out of the File Transfer Manager.

■ **Figure 5-1** Data flow into and out of the File Transfer Manager

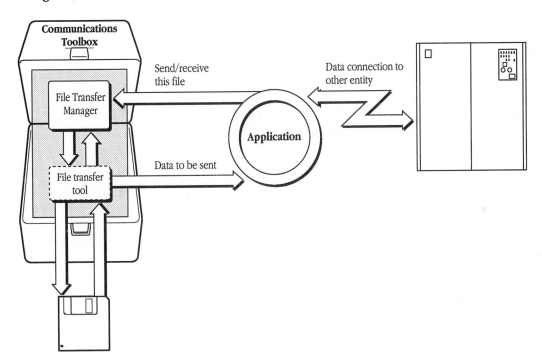

The most important data structure maintained by the File Transfer Manager is the file transfer record, which contains all the specifics about a file transfer. For example, the file transfer record might show that the File Transfer Manager should use the XMODEM tool to perform file transfers, and that the tool should not display any custom menus while transferring files.

One important aspect of the file transfer record is that it allows you to use protocol-independent routines. Protocol-independent routines allow applications to use File Transfer Manager services without regard for the underlying file transfer protocols. In other words, when an application wants to transfer a file from a remote entity, it tells the File Transfer Manager to get the file, and the File Transfer Manager figures out exactly how to implement the transfer for a specific protocol.

Another important feature of the file transfer record is that it lets you use multiple instances of the same tool. The same tool can be used by different processes at the same time, as in a MultiFinder environment, or by different threads in a given application.

The file transfer record is described in greater detail later in this chapter.

Besides providing basic file transfer routines, the File Transfer Manager includes routines that help your application configure a file transfer tool, either by presenting the user with a dialog box or by interfacing directly with a scripting language. The File Transfer Manager also contains routines that can help you localize your applications in other languages.

You can write applications that use the File Transfer Manager with other Communications Toolbox managers to create a communications application with basic connection, terminal emulation, and file transfer capabilities. Or, you can use the File Transfer Manager with some other connection service and terminal emulation service. You can also write your own file transfer tool for the File Transfer Manager to use. (This procedure is discussed in Chapters 8 and 11.) Regardless of which you choose, your application needs to be able to handle different file transfer tools so that users can change tools and still be able to use your program.

The file transfer record

The file transfer record contains information needed by your application and the file transfer tool to send files, such as whether to send data or receive data, and where to find the routines that perform the actual sending and receiving of files. The file transfer record also contains pointers to File Transfer Manager internal data structures. Most of the fields in the file transfer record are filled in when an application calls FTNew, described later in this chapter.

Because the context for a given file transfer is maintained in a file transfer record, an application can perform several file transfers simultaneously (using one or more file transfer tools), by creating a separate file transfer record for each transfer. For details, see "FTNew Creating a File Transfer Record," later in this chapter.

△ **Important**   Your application, in order to be compatible with future releases of the File Transfer Manager, should not directly manipulate the fields of the file transfer record (with the exception of config and oldConfig). The File Transfer Manager provides routines that applications and tools can use to change the fields in the file transfer record. These routines are discussed later in this chapter. △

File transfer record data structure

```
TYPE
        FTHandle            =       ^FTPtr;
        FTPtr               =       ^FTRecord;
        FTRecord            =       PACKED RECORD

            procID          :       INTEGER;


            flags           :       FTFlags;
            errCode         :       FTErr;

            refCon          :       LONGINT;
            userData        :       LONGINT;

            defProc         :       ProcPtr;

            config          :       Ptr;
            oldConfig       :       Ptr;

            environsProc    :       ProcPtr;
            reserved1       :       LONGINT;
            reserved2       :       LONGINT;

            ftPrivate       :       Ptr;

            sendProc        :       ProcPtr;
            recvProc        :       ProcPtr;
            writeProc       :       ProcPtr;
            readProc        :       ProcPtr;

            owner           :       WindowPtr;

            direction       :       FTDirection;
            theReply        :       SFReply;

            writePtr        :       LONGINT;
            readPtr         :       LONGINT;
            theBuf          :       ^char;
            bufSize         :       LONGINT;
            autoRec         :       Str255;
            attributes      :       FTAttributes;
        END;
```

procID

`procID` is the file transfer tool ID. This value is dynamically assigned by the File Transfer Manager when your application calls `FTGetProcID`.

flags

`flags` is a bit field that your application can use to determine when a file transfer has finished, and if the file transfer was successful. Valid values are as follows:

```
CONST
        ftIsFTMode       =       $00000001;
        ftNoMenus        =       $00000002;
        ftQuiet          =       $00000004;
        ftSucc           =       $00000080;

TYPE
        FTFlags          =       LONGINT;
```

`ftIsFTMode` indicates whether a file transfer is in progress. A tool turns this bit on just prior to performing the actual file transfer, and turns it off when the file transfer stops.

The file transfer tool will not display any custom menus if your application sets the `ftNoMenus` bit. The file transfer tool will not display any status dialog boxes or error alerts if your application sets the `ftQuiet` bit. If your application turns `ftQuiet` on, it is responsible for displaying status dialog boxes and error alerts that the tool would have displayed. Applications typically use these two bits to hide the file transfer tool from the user.

`ftSucc` is a bit set by the file transfer tool when a file transfer is completed successfully.

Your application can first check to see if `ftIsFTMode` toggles from on to off to find out when the file transfer has been completed. Then, it can check `ftSucc` to see if the file transfer was completed successfully.

The other bits of `flags` are reserved by Apple Computer, Inc.

errCode

`errCode` contains the last error reported to the File Transfer Manager. If `errCode` is negative, an operating system error occurred. If `errCode` is positive, a File Transfer Manager error occurred. Valid values are as follows:

```
CONST
        ftGenericError        =        -1;
        ftNoErr               =         0;
        ftRejected            =         1;
        ftFailed              =         2;
        ftTimeOut             =         3;
        ftTooManyRetry        =         4;
        ftNotEnoughDspace     =         5;
        ftRemoteCancel        =         6;
        ftWrongFormat         =         7;
        ftNoTools             =         8;
        ftUserCancel          =         9;
        ftNotSupported        =        10;
```

```
TYPE
        FTErr                   =           OSErr;
```

refCon

refCon is a four-byte field that your application can use.

userData

userData is a four-byte field that your application can use.

defProc

defProc is a pointer to the file transfer tool's main definition procedure, which is contained in a code resource of type 'fdef'.

config

config is a pointer to a data block that is private to the file transfer tool. It can contain information like retry and timeout values, but the contents vary from tool to tool.

Your application can store the contents of config to save the state of a file transfer in a document. The structure, size, and contents of the configuration record are set by the tool. Your application can determine the size of the configuration record by calling GetPtrSize, overwrite its contents using BlockMove, and validate the contents with FTValidate.

Your application can use FTGetConfig and FTSetConfig to manipulate fields in this record. For details, read "Interfacing with a Scripting Language," later in this chapter. Your application can save the state of the file transfer record by saving the string FTGetConfig returns. Also, your application can restore the configuration of the file transfer record by passing a saved string to FTSetConfig. You can find a description of config from a file transfer tool perspective in Chapter 8.

oldConfig

oldConfig is a pointer to a data block that is private to the file transfer tool and contains the most recently saved version of config. Your application is responsible for setting oldConfig when the user saves a session document.

environsProc

environsProc is a pointer to a routine in your application that the file transfer tool calls to obtain a record describing the connection environment. For more information about environsProc, see "MyEnvironsProc Getting Connection Environment Information," later in this chapter.

reserved1 and reserved2

reserved1 and reserved2 are fields reserved for the File Transfer Manager. Your application must not use this field.

ftPrivate

ftPrivate is a pointer to a data block that is private to the file transfer tool. Your application must not use this field.

sendProc

sendProc is a pointer to a routine that your application uses to send data. This routine is discussed under "MySendProc Sending Data, " later in this chapter.

recvProc

recvProc is a pointer to a routine that your application uses to request data. This routine is discussed under "MyRecvProc Receiving Data," later in this chapter.

writeProc

writeProc is a pointer to a routine in your application that writes data to a file. If this field is NIL, the file transfer tool performs standard file operations (that is, writing to a disk). The file transfer tool checks this field to see if your application has a writeProc routine. If it does, the tool lets writeProc handle writing data.

This routine can be used to perform postprocessing upon a file being received, and is discussed under "MyWriteProc Writing Data," later in this chapter.

readProc

readProc is a pointer to a routine in your application that reads data from a file. If this field is NIL, the file transfer tool performs standard file operations (that is, reading data from a disk). The file transfer tool checks this field to see if your application has a readProc routine. If it does, the tool lets readProc handle reading data.

This routine can be used to perform preprocessing upon a file being sent, and is discussed under "MyReadProc Reading Data," later in this chapter.

owner

owner is a pointer to a window (or grafPort) relative to which the file transfer status dialog box is positioned. If this field is NIL, the file transfer tool will not display a file transfer status dialog box.

direction

direction is a field that indicates whether a file is being sent to or received from another entity. Your application passes this field as a parameter to FTStart (described later in this chapter). Valid values in this field are as follows:

```
CONST
        ftReceiving         =       0;
        ftTransmitting      =       1;
        ftFullDuplex        =       2;

TYPE
        FTDirection         =       INTEGER;
```

theReply

theReply is an SFReply data structure. The SFReply data structure should contain the reference number of the working directory of the default volume for files being sent or received. If a file is being sent, the data structure should also contain the name of the file to be sent. If a file is being received and your application has information about the filename (for example, from a scripting language), the data structure should contain the filename to be used. Otherwise, pass an empty string for theReply.filename.

writePtr, readPtr, theBuf, and **bufSize**

writePtr, readPtr, theBuf, and bufSize are properties of a particular file transfer tool.

autoRec

autoRec is a string that represents the start sequence a remote entity sends, causing the Macintosh to enter a file-reception mode. If this string is of length 0, remote-entity-initiated file transfers are not supported by the file transfer tool. It is the application's responsibility to make use of this field by searching the data stream for this sequence of characters. The Connection Manager, described in Chapter 3, provides routines that your application can use to search an incoming data stream for a specified sequence of characters.

attributes

attributes is a field that describes the file transfer protocol supported by the file transfer tool. The bits in attributes are as follows:

```
CONST
        ftSameCircuit        =        $0001;
        ftSendDisable        =        $0002;
        ftReceiveDisable     =        $0004;
        ftTextOnly           =        $0008;


TYPE
        FTAttributes         =        INTEGER
```

ftSameCircuit indicates whether the file transfer tool creates its own data connection or expects the application to provide the connection. If this bit is set, the file transfer tool uses the data connection provided by the application. This bit is set by the file transfer tool.

ftSendDisable indicates that the file transfer tool does not allow users to send files. Some tools that support sending files turn this bit on when they are in a mode that does not allow users to initiate sending files. When this bit is on, your application should dim any menu items that allow users to send files.

ftReceiveDisable indicates that the file transfer tool does not allow users to receive files. Some tools that support receiving files turn this bit on when they are in a mode that does not allow users to initiate receiving files. When this bit is on, your application should dim any menu items that allow users to receive files.

ftTextOnly indicates that the file transfer tool sends and receives only text files (files of type TEXT); the tool does not handle resource forks. The file transfer tool sets this bit.

The other bits of this field are reserved by Apple Computer, Inc.

File Transfer Manager routines

The following sections describe the routines that tools and applications can use to access File Transfer Manager services. Your application cannot call these routines from interrupt level.

Below is a listing of the routines described in this section in the order in which they are presented.

InitFT / 138

FTGetProcID / 139

FTNew / 139

FTDefault / 141

FTValidate / 141

FTChoose / 142

FTSetupPreFlight / 144

FTSetupSetup / 145

FTSetupFilter / 145

FTSetupItem / 146

FTSetupCleanup / 146

FTSetupPostFlight / 147

FTGetConfig / 148

FTSetConfig / 148

FTStart / 149

FTExec / 150

FTAbort / 150

FTDispose / 150

FTActivate / 151

FTResume / 151

FTMenu / 152

FTEvent / 152

FTIntlToEnglish / 153

FTEnglishToIntl / 153

FTGetToolName / 154

FTSetRefCon / 154

FTGetRefCon / 154

FTSetUserData / 155

FTGetUserData / 155

FTGetVersion / 155

FTGetFTVersion / 155

Preparing for a file transfer

Before your application can start a file transfer, it must initialize the File Transfer Manager (by calling `initFT`), find out the `procID` of the tool it requires (by calling `FTGetProcID`), create a file transfer record (by calling `FTNew`), and then configure the file transfer tool (by restoring `config` from a saved document; or by calling `FTChoose`, the file transfer tool custom tool-settings routines, or `FTSetConfig`).

Initializing the File Transfer Manager

`InitFT` initializes the File Transfer Manager. Your application must call this routine after calling the standard Macintosh Toolbox initialization routines.

▲ **Warning** Your application must initialize the Communications Resource Manager (by calling `InitCRM`) and then the **Communications Toolbox Utilities** (by calling `InitCTBUtilities`), regardless of whether it uses any of their calls, before it initializes the File Transfer Manager. ▲

Function   `InitFT: FTErr;`

Description   `InitFT` returns an operating system error code if appropriate. Your application must check for the presence of the Communications Toolbox before calling this function. Sample code under "Determining Whether the Managers are Installed" in Appendix C shows you how your application can make this check.

Result Codes   `ftGenericError, ftNoErr, ftNoTools`

Getting current `procID` information

Your application should call `FTGetProcID` just before creating a new file transfer record, to find out the `procID` of a tool.

Function

`FTGetProcID(name: Str255): INTEGER;`

Description

`name` specifies a file transfer tool. If a file transfer tool is available with the specified name, its `procID` is returned. If `name` refers to a nonexistent file transfer tool, `FTGetProcID` returns –1.

Creating a file transfer record

Before your application can transfer files, it must create a file transfer record. `FTNew` creates a new file transfer record, fills in the fields that it can, based upon the parameters that were passed to it, and returns a handle to the new record in `FTHandle`. `FTNew` automatically makes two calls to `FTDefault` (described later in this chapter) to fill in `config` and `oldConfig`. The File Transfer Manager then loads the file transfer tool's main definition procedure, moves it high in the current heap, and locks it. If an error occurs that prevents a new file transfer record from being created (for example, running out of memory), `FTNew` passes back `NIL` in `FTHandle`.

Function

`FTNew(procID: INTEGER; flags: FTFlags; sendProc: ProcPtr; recvProc: ProcPtr; readProc: ProcPtr; writeProc: ProcPtr; environsProc: ProcPtr;  owner: WindowPtr; refCon: LONGINT; userData: LONGINT): FTHandle;`

Description

`procID` specifies the file transfer tool the File Transfer Manager will use to transfer data.

`flags` is a bit field with the following masks:

```
CONST
     ftIsFTMode      =        $0001;
     ftNoMenus       =        $0002;
     ftQuiet         =        $0004;
     ftSucc          =        $0080;

TYPE
     FTFlags         =        LONGINT;
```

`flags` represents a request from your application for a level of service. Your application can set only two of these bits, `ftNoMenus` and `ftQuiet`. If your application sets `ftNoMenus`, the file transfer tool will not display any custom menus. If your application sets `ftQuiet`, the file transfer tool will not display any windows. Applications typically use these bits to hide the file transfer tool from the user.

Apple Computer, Inc. has reserved the bits of `flags` that are not shown in this document. Do not use them, or your code may not work in the future.

`ftSucc` is a bit that is set by the file transfer tool when a file transfer is completed successfully. Your application should not set this bit.

Your application can check to see if `ftIsFTMode` toggles from on to off to find out when the file transfer has been completed. Then it can check `ftSucc` to see if the file transfer was completed successfully.

`sendProc` is a pointer to a routine that the application uses to send data.

`recvProc` is a pointer to a routine that the application uses to request data.

`readProc` is a pointer to a routine in your application that reads data from a file. The file transfer tool checks this field to see if your application has a `readProc` routine. If it does, the tool lets `readProc` handle reading data. If `NIL`, the file transfer tool performs standard file operations (that is, reading data from a disk).

This function can be used to perform preprocessing upon a file being sent, and is discussed later in this chapter, in "Routines Your Application Provides."

`writeProc` is a pointer to a routine in your application that writes data to a file. The file transfer tool checks this field to see if your application has a `writeProc` routine. If it does, the tool lets the `writeProc` handle writing data. If `NIL`, the file transfer tool performs standard file operations (that is, writing to a disk).

This function can be used to perform post-processing upon a file being received, and is discussed later in this chapter, in "Routines Your Application Provides."

`environsProc` is a pointer to a routine that the file transfer tool can call when it wants to get information about the connection. See Chapter 3 for more information about the `CMGetConnEnvirons` routine.

`owner` is a pointer to a window, relative to which the file transfer status dialog box is positioned. If this field is `NIL`, the File Transfer Manager will not display a file transfer status dialog box.

`refCon` and `userData` are fields that your application can use.

Initializing the file transfer record

FTDefault fills the specified configuration record with the default configuration specified by the file transfer tool. FTNew calls this procedure automatically when it fills in the config and oldConfig fields in a new file transfer record.

Procedure

```
FTDefault(VAR theConfig: Ptr; procID: INTEGER; allocate: BOOLEAN);
```

Description

If allocate is TRUE, the tool allocates space for theConfig in the current heap zone.

Validating the file transfer record

FTValidate performs an internal consistency check on the configuration and private data records of the file transfer record. FTNew and FTSetConfig call this routine after they have created a new file transfer record, to make sure that the the record contains values identical to those specified by the file transfer tool.

Function

```
FTValidate(hFT: FTHandle): BOOLEAN;
```

Description

If the validation fails, the File Transfer Manager returns TRUE and the file transfer tool fills the configuration record with default values by calling FTDefault.

Your application can call this routine after restoring a configuration, to verify that the file transfer record contains the correct information, in a manner similar to that shown next.

```
BlockMove(saveConfig,hFT^^.config,GetPtrSize(hFT^^.config));
IF FTValidate(hFT) THEN BEGIN
     { validate failed }
     END
     ELSE BEGIN
             { validate succeeded }
             END
```

Configuring a file transfer tool

An application can configure a file transfer tool in one of three ways. The easiest and most straightforward way is by calling the FTChoose routine. This routine presents the user with a dialog box similar to the one shown in *Figure 5-2.*

■ **Figure 5-2** A sample tool-settings dialog box

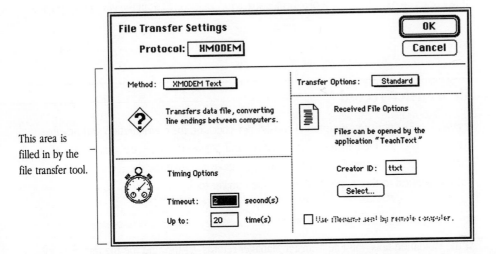

This area is filled in by the file transfer tool.

The second way an application can configure a file transfer tool is by presenting the user with a custom tool-settings dialog box. This method is much more difficult and involves calling six routines. The routines are described in the next section, "Custom Configuration of a File Transfer Tool," and "The Custom Tool-Settings Dialog Box" in Appendix C provides example code.

The third way your application can configure a file transfer tool is by using the scripting language interface, described under "Interfacing with a Scripting Language," later in this chapter. This method allows your application to bypass user interface elements.

Function

FTChoose(VAR hFt:FTHandle; where: Point; idleProc: ProcPtr): INTEGER;

Description

where is the point, specified in global coordinates, where the upper-left corner of the dialog box should appear. It is recommended that your application place the dialog box as close as possible to the upper-left corner of the screen, because the size of the dialog box varies from tool to tool.

idleProc is a procedure with no parameters that the File Transfer Manager will automatically call every time FTChoose loops through the setup dialog filter procedure. Pass NIL if your application has no idleProc.

`FTChoose` returns one of the following values:

```
CONST
    chooseDisaster        =      -2;
    chooseFailed          =      -1;
    chooseOKMinor         =       1;
    chooseOKMajor         =       2;
    chooseCancel          =       3;
```

`chooseDisaster` means that the `FTChoose` operation failed, destroyed the file transfer record, and returned `NIL` in the file transfer handle.

`chooseFailed` means that the `FTChoose` operation failed and the file transfer record was not changed.

`chooseOKMinor` means that the user clicked OK in the dialog box, but did not change the file transfer tool being used.

`chooseOKMajor` means that the user clicked OK in the dialog box and also changed the file transfer tool being used. The old file transfer handle is destroyed by the File Transfer Manager, by calling `FTDispose`. The file transfer is closed down, all pending read and write operations are terminated, and a new file transfer handle is returned in `hFT`.

`chooseCancel` means that the user clicked Cancel in the dialog box.

Custom configuration of a file transfer tool

Your application creates a custom tool-settings dialog box and presents it to the user by using six File Transfer Manager routines: `FTSetupPreflight`, `FTSetupSetup`, `FTSetupItem`, `FTSetupFilter`, `FTSetupCleanup`, and `FTSetupPostflight`. Using these routines is more involved than calling `FTChoose`, but they provide your application with much more flexibility. Refer to the code sample in "The Custom Tool-Settings Dialog Box" in Appendix C to see how an application calls these routines.

To build a list of file transfer tools, use the routine `CRMGetIndToolName`, which is described in Chapter 6.

`FTSetupPreflight`

Setting up the tool-settings dialog box

`FTSetupPreflight` returns a handle to a dialog item list that your application appends to the tool-settings dialog box. The handle comes from the file transfer tool. (The calling application uses `AppendDITL`, discussed in Chapter 7.) This handle is not a resource handle. Your application is responsible for disposing of the handle when done with it.

The file transfer tool can use `FTSetupPreflight` to allocate a block of private storage, and to store the pointer to that block in `magicCookie`. `magicCookie` should be passed to the other routines that are used to set up the tool-settings dialog box.

Function   `FTSetupPreflight(procID: INTEGER; VAR magicCookie: LONGINT): Handle;`

Description   `procID` is the ID for the file transfer tool that is being configured. Your application should get this value by using the `FTGetProcID` routine, discussed earlier in this chapter.

◆ *Note:* The `refcon` of the custom tool-settings dialog box should point to a data structure (an example of which is shown next) in which the first two bytes are the tool `procID` and the next four bytes are `magicCookie`. `UserItem` routines, for example, may require `procID` to obtain tool resources.

```
TYPE
    chooseDLOGdata=RECORD
            procID:INTEGER
            magicCookie:LONGINT
END;
```

Setting up tool-settings dialog box items

FTSetupSetup tells the file transfer tool to set up controls (such as radio buttons or check boxes) in the dialog item list returned by FTSetupPreflight.

Procedure   FTSetupSetup(procID: INTEGER; theConfig: Ptr; count: INTEGER; theDialog: DialogPtr; VAR magicCookie: LONGINT);

Description   procID is the ID for the file transfer tool being configured. Your application should use the same value for procID as it passed to FTSetupPreflight.

theConfig is a pointer to a configuration record for the tool being configured.

count is the number of the first item in the dialog item list appended to the dialog box.

theDialog is the dialog box in which configuration is taking place.

magicCookie is a pointer to private storage for the file transfer tool.

Filtering tool-settings dialog box events

Your application calls FTSetupFilter as a filter procedure before it calls the standard modal dialog box filter procedure for the tool-settings dialog box. This routine allows file transfer tools to filter events in the tool-settings dialog box.

Function   FTSetupFilter(procID: INTEGER; theConfig: Ptr; count:INTEGER; theDialog: DialogPtr; VAR theEvent: EventRecord; VAR theItem: INTEGER; VAR magicCookie: LONGINT): BOOLEAN;

Description   procID is the ID for the file transfer tool that is being configured. Your application should use the same value for procID as it passed to FTSetupPreflight.

theConfig is the pointer to the configuration record for the tool being configured.

count is the number of the first item in the dialog item list appended to the dialog box.

theDialog is the dialog box performing the configuration.

theEvent is the event record for which filtering is to take place.

theItem can return the item clicked in the dialog box.

magicCookie is a pointer to private storage for the file transfer tool.

If the event passed in was handled, FTSetupFilter returns TRUE. FALSE indicates that your application should perform standard dialog box filtering.

Processing tool-settings dialog box events

FTSetupItem processes events for controls in the custom tool-settings dialog box.

Procedure
```
FTSetupItem(procID: INTEGER; theConfig: Ptr; count: INTEGER;
theDialog: DialogPtr; VAR theItem: INTEGER; VAR magicCookie:
LONGINT);
```

Description
procID is the ID for the file transfer tool being configured. Your application should use the same value for procID as it passed to FTSetupPreflight.

theConfig is a pointer to the configuration record for the tool being configured.

count is the number of the first item in the dialog item list appended to the dialog box.

theDialog is the dialog box performing the configuration.

theItem is the item clicked in the dialog box. This value can be modified and sent back.

magicCookie is a pointer to private storage for the file transfer tool.

FTSetupCleanup

Performing clean-up operations

FTSetupCleanup disposes of any storage allocated in FTSetupPreflight and performs other clean-up operations.

Procedure
```
FTSetupCleanup(procID: INTEGER; theConfig: Ptr; count: INTEGER;
theDialog: DialogPtr; VAR magicCookie: LONGINT);
```

Description
procID is the ID for the file transfer tool that is being configured. Your application should use the same value for procID as it passed to FTSetupPreflight.

theConfig is the pointer to the configuration record for the tool being configured.

count is the number of the first item in the dialog item list appended to the dialog box.

theDialog is the dialog box performing the configuration.

magicCookie is a pointer to private storage for the file transfer tool.

Closing the tool file

FTSetupPostflight closes the tool file if it is not being used by any session.

Procedure FTSetupPostflight (procID:INTEGER);

Description procID is the ID for the file transfer tool that is being configured. Your application should use the same value for procID as it passed to FTSetupPreflight.

Interfacing with a scripting language

Your application does not have to rely on users making selections from dialog boxes in order to configure a file transfer tool. `FTGetConfig` and `FTSetConfig` provide the services that your application needs to interface with a scripting language.

FTGetConfig

Getting the configuration string

FTGetConfig gets a configuration string from the file transfer tool.

Function   `FTGetConfig(hFT: FTHandle): Ptr;`

Description   `FTGetConfig` returns a null-terminated, C-style string from the file transfer tool containing tokens that fully describe the configuration of the file transfer record. For an example, see the description of the next routine. If an error occurs, `FTGetConfig` returns `NIL`.

        It is the responsibility of your application to dispose of `Ptr`.

FTSetConfig

Setting the configuration with a string

FTSetConfig passes a configuration string to the file transfer tool.

Function   `FTSetConfig(hFT: FTHandle; thePtr: Ptr): INTEGER;`

Description   `FTSetConfig` passes a null-terminated, C-style string (see the example string later in this section) to the file transfer tool for parsing. The string is pointed to by `thePtr` and must contain tokens that describe the configuration of the file transfer record. The string can be any length.

        `FTSetConfig` ignores items it does not recognize or find relevant; such an occurrence causes the file transfer tool to stop parsing the string and to return the character position where the error occurred. If the file transfer tool successfully parses the string, it returns `ftNoErr`. If the file transfer tool does not successfully parse the string, it returns one of the following values: a number less than –1 to indicate an `OSErr`, –1 to indicate an unknown error, or a positive number to indicate the character position where parsing was stopped.

        Individual file transfer tools are responsible for the parsing operation.

Sample   *A null-terminated, C-style configuration string*

       `InterCharDelay 0 InterLineDelay 0 WordWrap False Ending CR\0`

Transferring files

When your application has performed the necessary steps described in the previous sections, it is ready to start transferring files. Your application must perform two steps: first, it must call `FTStart` to open the file and initialize tool-private variables; second, it must call `FTExec` to process data every time it goes through its main event loop.

FTStart

Starting a file transfer

`FTStart` opens the file that is going to be involved in the file transfer, and initializes tool-private variables.

The value in the `owner` field in the file transfer record controls the appearance of a status dialog box.

The code that performs the actual sending, receiving, reading, and writing of data is the responsibility of your application. Your application specifies these routines when it creates the file transfer record. For a description of the parameters that will be passed to these routines, see "Routines Your Application Provides," later in this chapter.

Function
```
FTStart(hFT: FTHandle; direction:FTDirection; fileInfo:SFReply):
FTErr;
```

Description
`direction` describes the direction of the file transfer and can be either `ftReceiving`, `ftTransmitting`, or `ftFullDuplex`.

Once the file transfer has started, your application needs to call `FTExec` every time it goes through its main event loop. Calling `FTExec` gives the tool time to send and receive a packet of data, among other things.

Result Codes
`ftGenericError, ftNoErr, ftRejected, ftFailed, ftTimeout, ftTooManyRetry, ftNotEnoughDspace, ftRemoteCancel, ftWrongFormat, ftUserCancel, ftNotSupported.`

Processing file transfer data

FTExec is the soul of the file transfer process because it allows the file transfer tool to implement the file transfer protocol. FTExec handles the disk input and output, either through your application or by performing local disk input and output, if specified by your application. Every time your application calls FTExec, a little piece of data is processed until there is no more data.

When sending files, the file transfer tool reads data from your application with a readProc, and sends it to the connection with a sendProc. When receiving files, the file transfer tool gets data from your application with a recvProc, and checks if the data arrived correctly. The file transfer tool then writes the data with a writeProc.

The readProc, sendProc, recvProc, and writeProc routines are discussed in "Routines Your Application Provides" later in this chapter.

At the end of the file transfer, the file transfer tool is responsible for closing the file, releasing any memory allocated, and resetting the ftIsFTMode bit in the file transfer record.

Procedure   FTExec(hFT: FTHandle);

Stopping a file transfer

FTAbort aborts a file transfer in progress. The file transfer tool sends the appropriate canceling characters to the remote computer, and stops the file transfer.

Function   FTAbort(hFT: FTHandle): FTErr;

Result Codes   ftGeneric, ftNoErr, ftRejected, ftFailed, ftNotSupported.

Disposing of a file transfer record

FTDispose disposes of the file transfer record and all associated data structures. The file transfer tool stops any file transfer in progress (as specified by the file transfer record).

Procedure   FTDispose(hFT: FTHandle);

Handling events

The File Transfer Manager event-processing routines provide useful extensions to the Macintosh Toolbox Event Manager. This section explains the three procedures that the Communications Toolbox provides: FTActivate, FTResume, and FTEvent. See "Other Events" in Chapter 2 for sample code showing how an application can determine if an event needs to be handled by one of these routines.

FTActivate

Activate events

FTActivate processes an activate or deactivate event (for instance, installing or removing a custom tool menu) for a window associated with the file transfer.

Procedure

FTActivate(hFT: FTHandle; activate: BOOLEAN);

Description

If activate is TRUE, the file transfer tool processes an activate event. Otherwise, it processes a deactivate event.

FTResume

Resume events

FTResume is called when your application receives a suspend or a resume event. The file transfer tool may decide to change timeout values or other parameters, depending on whether the application is running in the foreground.

Procedure

FTResume(hFT: FTHandle; resume: BOOLEAN);

Description

If resume is TRUE, the file transfer tool processes a resume event. Otherwise, it processes a suspend event.

Menu events

Your application must call FTMenu when the user chooses an item from a menu installed by the file transfer tool.

Function   FTMenu(hFT: FTHandle; menuID: INTEGER; item: INTEGER): BOOLEAN;

Description   FTMenu returns FALSE if the file transfer tool did not handle the menu event. FTMenu returns TRUE if the file transfer tool did handle the menu event.

FTEvent

Other events

When your application receives an event, it should check if the refcon of the window is a tool's hFT. Such an event occurs, for example, when the user clicks a button in a dialog box displayed by the file transfer tool. If it does belong to a file transfer tool's window, your application can call FTEvent.

Procedure   FTEvent(hFT: FTHandle; theEvent: EventRecord);

Description   A window (or dialog box) created by a file transfer tool has a file transfer record handle stored in the refCon field for windowRecord.

Localizing configuration strings

The Communications Toolbox provides two routines that make it easier to localize configuration strings.

`FTIntlToEnglish`

Translating into English

`FTIntlToEnglish` converts a configuration string, which is pointed to by `inputPtr`, to an American English configuration string pointed to by `outputPtr`.

Function
```
FTIntlToEnglish(hFT: FTHandle; inputPtr: Ptr; VAR outputPtr: Ptr;
language: INTEGER): OSErr;
```

Description
This function returns an operating system error code if any internal errors occur.

The file transfer tool allocates space for `outputPtr`. Your application is responsible for disposing of the pointer with `DisposPtr` when done with it.

`language` specifies the language from which the string is to be converted. Valid values for this field are shown in the description of the Script Manager in *Inside Macintosh*, Volume V. If the language specified is not supported, this routine returns `noErr`, but `outputPtr` is NIL.

`FTEnglishToIntl`

Translating from English

`FTEnglishToIntl` converts an American English configuration string, which is pointed to by `inputPtr`, to a configuration string pointed to by `outputPtr`.

Function
```
FTEnglishToIntl(hFT: FTHandle; inputPtr: Ptr; VAR outputPtr: Ptr;
language: INTEGER): OSErr;
```

Description
This function returns an operating system error code if any internal errors occur.

The file transfer tool allocates space for `outputPtr`; your application is responsible for disposing of the pointer with `DisposPtr` when done with it.

`language` specifies the language to which the string is to be converted. Valid values for this field are shown in the description of the Script Manager in *Inside Macintosh*, Volume V. If the language specified is not supported, `noErr` is still returned, but `outputPtr` is NIL.

Miscellaneous routines

The routines described in this section perform a variety of tasks.

`FTGetToolName`

Getting the name of a tool

FTGetToolName returns in name the name of the tool specified by procID.

Procedure   `FTGetToolName(procID: INTEGER; VAR name: Str255);`

Description   If procID references a file transfer tool that does not exist, the File Transfer Manager sets name to an empty string.

`FTSetRefCon`

Setting the file transfer record's reference constant

FTSetRefCon sets the file transfer record refCon to the given value. It is very important that your application use this routine to change the value of the reference constant, instead of changing it directly.

Procedure   `FTSetRefCon(hFT: FTHandle; refCon: LONGINT);`

`FTGetRefCon`

Getting the file transfer record reference constant

FTGetRefCon returns the file transfer record reference constant.

Function   `FTGetRefCon(hFT: FTHandle): LONGINT;`

FTSetUserData

Setting the `userData` field

`FTSetUserData` sets the file transfer record's `userData` field to the given value. It is very important that your application use this routine to change the value of the `userData` field, instead of changing it directly.

Procedure `FTSetUserData(hFT: FTHandle; userData: LONGINT);`

FTGetUserData

Getting the `userData` field

`FTGetUserData` returns the file transfer record's `userData` field.

Function `FTGetUserData(hFT: FTHandle) : LONGINT;`

FTGetVersion

Getting `'vers'` resource information

`FTGetVersion` returns a handle to a relocatable block that contains the information in the file transfer tool's `'vers'` resource with ID=1. Your application is responsible for disposing of the handle when done with it.

◆ *Note:* The handle returned is *not* a resource handle.

Function `FTGetVersion(hFT: FTHandle): Handle;`

FTGetFTVersion

Getting the File Transfer Manager version number

`FTGetFTVersion` returns the version number of the File Transfer Manager.

Function `FTGetFTVersion: INTEGER;`

Description The version number of the File Transfer Manager described in this document is:

```
CONST
      curFTVersion  =      1;
```

Routines your application provides

Your application is responsible for providing routines it will use to send, receive, read, and write data during a file transfer. Your application might also need to include a routine that can provide information to the file transfer tool about the connection environment. When your application creates a new file transfer record, it specifies pointers to these routines.

Sending and receiving files are both two-step processes. When sending a file, the file transfer tool calls `MyReadProc` to read the data into a buffer, and then `MySendProc` to send the processed data. When receiving a file, the file transfer tool calls `MyRecvProc` to get the data, and then `MyWriteProc` to write the processed data to the appropriate medium.

Your application must include the send and receive routines described in this section. The other routines are optional.

MyReadProc

Reading data

MyReadProc is a routine in your application that the file transfer tool calls to read data from a file. After `MyReadProc` reads the data, the file transfer tool typically sends the data by calling the `MySendProc` routine, which is described next. `MyReadProc` is also responsible for opening and closing the file from which the outgoing data is read.

Function   MyReadProc(VAR count : LONGINT; bufPtr : Ptr; refCon : LONGINT; fileMsg : INTEGER) : OSErr;

Description   MyReadProc must return an error code when appropriate.

count is a bit field with the following bit masks defined:

```
CONST
        ftOpenDataFork        =        $00000001;
        ftOpenRsrcFork        =        $00000002;
```

refCon is the reference constant of the file transfer record.

fileMsg specifies which service the file transfer tool requires `MyReadProc` to provide.

```
CONST
            ftReadOpenFile        =        0;
            ftReadDataFork        =        1;
            ftReadRsrcFork        =        2;
            ftReadAbort           =        3;
            ftReadComplete        =        4;
```

ftReadOpenFile

ftReadOpenFile indicates that the file transfer tool requires `MyReadProc` to open a file. The bits set in `count` specify whether `MyReadProc` should open the resource fork, data fork, or both. `bufPtr` points to a parameter block that specifies the file `MyReadProc` should open. The parameter block the file transfer tool passes to `MyReadProc` is the same as that returned from calling `PBGetFInfo`.

`ftReadDataFork` and `ftReadRsrcFork`

These messages indicate that the file transfer tool requires `MyReadProc` to read data from an open file, which it had previously opened in response to `ftReadOpenFile`. `count` specifies the number of bytes `MyReadProc` should read. When finished reading, `MyReadProc` puts the actual number of bytes read into `count`. `bufPtr` points to the buffer into which `MyReadProc` should read data.

`ftReadAbort` and `ftReadComplete`

These messages indicate that `MyReadProc` should close the file it had opened in response to `ftReadOpenFile`.

`MySendProc`

Sending data

`MySendProc` is a routine in your application that the file transfer tool calls to send data that is in a buffer.

Function
`MySendProc(thePtr: Ptr; theSize: LONGINT; refCon: LONGINT; channel: CMChannel; flags: CMFlags):LONGINT;`

Description
`MySendProc` must return the actual number of bytes it sent.

`thePtr` is a pointer to a block of data in memory that is to be sent.

`theSize` is the length of that block.

`refCon` is the reference constant of the file transfer record.

`channel` specifies the channel that the file transfer tool can use. Your application should specify one of the following values for channel: `CMData`, `CMCntl`, or `CMAttn`.

`flags` is described in Chapter 3 under the description of `CMWrite`.

Sample send routine

```
FUNCTION MySendProc(thePtr: Ptr;theSize: LONGINT;refcon: LONGINT;
                channel: CMChannel;flags: INTEGER) : LONGINT;
VAR
      theErr : CMErr;                        { Errors on a write }

BEGIN
      MySendProc:= 0;                              { Assume the worst }

      IF gConn <> NIL THEN BEGIN        { Send the data }
            theErr := CMWrite(gConn,thePtr,theSize,channel,FALSE, NIL, 0, flags);
            IF (theErr = noErr) THEN
                  MySendProc:= theSize  { if ok, we sent all }
            ELSE
                  ;                      { Handle errors }
      END; { Good Connection        }

END; { MySendProc }
```

Receiving data

MyRecvProc is a routine in your application that the file transfer tool uses to receive data into a buffer from the connection.

Function

```
MyRecvProc (thePtr: Ptr; theSize: LONGINT; refCon: LONGINT; channel:
CMChannel; VAR flags: CMFlags):LONGINT;
```

Description

MyRecvProc must return the actual number of bytes it received.

thePtr is a pointer to a block of data in memory where the incoming data is to be placed.

theSize is the length of that data.

refCon is the reference constant of the file transfer record.

channel specifies the data channel that the file transfer tool can use. Your application should specify one of the following values for channel: CMData, CMCntl, or CMAttn.

flags is described in Chapter 3 under the description of CMRead.

Sample receive routine

```
FUNCTION MyRecvProc (thePtr: Ptr;theSize: LONGINT;refcon: LONGINT;
                channel: CMChannel;VAR flags: INTEGER) : LONGINT;
VAR
        theErr : CMErr;                 { Any errors }

BEGIN
        MyRecvProc := 0;                        { Assume the worst }

        IF gConn <> NIL THEN BEGIN
                                        { Read all the data }
                theErr := CMRead(gConn,thePtr,theSize,channel,FALSE,NIL,0,flags);
                IF (theErr <> noErr) THEN
                        MyRecvProc := theSize           { if ok, we got all }
                ELSE
                        ;                       { Handle errors }
        END; { Good Connection }

END; { MyRecvProc }
```

Writing data

MyWriteProc is a routine in your application that the file transfer tool calls to write data to a file. MyWriteProc is also responsible for opening and closing the file to which the outgoing data is written.

Function

```
MyWriteProc(VAR count: LONGINT; bufPtr: Ptr; refCon: LONGINT;
fileMsg: INTEGER): OSErr;
```

Description

MyWriteProc must return an error code when appropriate.

count is a bit field with the following bit masks defined:

```
CONST
      ftOpenDataFork          =       1;
      ftOpenRsrcFork          =       2;
```

refCon is the reference constant of the file transfer record.

fileMsg specifies which service the file transfer tool requires MyWriteProc to provide.

```
CONST
      ftWriteOpenFile         =       0;
      ftWriteDataFork         =       1;
      ftWriteRsrcFork         =       2;
      ftWriteAbort            =       3;
      ftWriteComplete         =       4;
      ftWriteFileInfo         =       5;
```

ftWriteOpenFile

ftWriteOpenFile indicates that the file transfer tool requires MyWriteProc to open a file. The bits set in count specify whether MyWriteProc should open the resource fork, data fork, or both. bufPtr points to a parameter block that specifies the file MyWriteProc should open. The parameter block the file transfer tool passes to MyWriteProc is the same as that returned from calling PBGetFInfo.

Note that MyWriteProc creates the file specified by the parameter block. If the file transfer protocol in use does not specify the filename for the incoming file, MyWriteProc must generate one. Your application must handle filename conflicts and AppleShare® file server permission problems if they arise.

ftWriteDataFork and ftWriteRsrcFork

These messages indicate that the file transfer tool requires MyWriteProc to open a file. count specifies the number of bytes to write. When finished writing data, MyWriteProc should set count to the actual number of bytes written. bufPtr points to the buffer into which MyWriteProc should write data.

ftWriteAbort

`ftWriteAbort` indicates that `MyWriteProc` should close the open file and delete it.

ftWriteComplete

`ftWriteComplete` indicates that `MyWriteProc` should close the open file.

ftWriteFileInfo

`ftWriteFileInfo` indicates that the file transfer tool requires `MyWriteProc` to change file information. `bufPtr` points to a parameter block that `MyWriteProc` can pass to the File Manager routine `PBSetFInfo`.

MyEnvironsProc

Getting the connection environment

Sometimes the file transfer tool needs to know about the type of connection on which to transfer files. For example, some file transfer protocols require an 8-bit data channel. To get this information, the file transfer tool calls a routine in your application, `MyEnvironsProc`.

Function
MyEnvironsProc(refCon: LONGINT; VAR theEnvirons: ConnEnvironRec): CMErr;

Description
`refCon` is the reference constant of the file transfer record.

`theEnvirons` is a data structure containing the connection-environment record. Your application can either construct `theEnvirons` or use the Connection Manager routine `CMGetConnEnvirons`. For more information about `theEnvirons`, see "`CMGetConnEnvirons` Getting the Connection Environment" in Chapter 3.

The example that follows shows how `MyEnvironsProc` can point to a Connection Manager routine to retrieve information about the connection environment.

Result Codes
cmGenericError, cmNoErr, cmNotSupported, envVersTooBig.

Sample connection-environment routine

```
FUNCTION MyEnvironsProc(refCon: LONGINT;VAR theEnvirons: ConnEnvironRec): OSErr;
BEGIN
        MyEnvironsProc:= envNotPresent;       { pessimism }

        { Get the connection info }
        IF gConn <> NIL THEN            { Tool sets the version }
                MyEnvironsProc:= CMGetConnEnvirons(gConn,theEnvirons);

END; { MyEnvironsProc}
```

Quick reference

This section provides a reference to File Transfer Manager routines and data structures. At the end of this section is a listing of routine selectors for programming in assembly language.

Routines

File Transfer Manager routines	*See page*
`FTAbort(hFT: FTHandle): FTErr;`	*150*
`FTActivate(hFT: FTHandle; activate: BOOLEAN);`	*151*
`FTChoose(VAR hFT: FTHandle; where: Point; idleProc: ProcPtr): INTEGER;`	*142*
`FTDefault(VAR theConfig: Ptr; procID: INTEGER; allocate: BOOLEAN);`	*141*
`FTDispose(hFT: FTHandle);`	*150*
`FTEnglishToIntl(hFT: FTHandle; inputPtr: Ptr; VAR outputPtr: Ptr; language: INTEGER): OSErr;`	*153*
`FTEvent(hFT: FTHandle; theEvent: EventRecord);`	*152*
`FTExec(hFT: FTHandle);`	*150*
`FTGetConfig(hFT: FTHandle): Ptr;`	*148*
`FTGetFTVersion: INTEGER;`	*155*
`FTGetToolName(procID: INTEGER; VAR name: Str255);`	*154*
`FTGetProcID(name: Str255): INTEGER;`	*139*
`FTGetRefCon(hFT: FTHandle): LONGINT;`	*154*
`FTGetUserData(hFT: FTHandle) : LONGINT;`	*155*
`FTGetVersion(hFT: FTHandle): Handle;`	*155*
`FTIntlToEnglish(hFT: FTHandle; inputPtr: Ptr; VAR outputPtr: Ptr; language: INTEGER): OSErr;`	*153*
`FTMenu(hFT: FTHandle; menuID: INTEGER; item: INTEGER): BOOLEAN;`	*152*
`FTNew(procID: INTEGER; flags: FTFlags; sendProc: ProcPtr; recvProc: ProcPtr; readProc: ProcPtr; writeProc: ProcPtr; environsProc: ProcPtr; owner: WindowPtr; refCon: LONGINT; userData: LONGINT): FTHandle;`	*139*
`FTResume(hFT: FTHandle; resume: BOOLEAN);`	*151*
`FTSetConfig(hFT: FTHandle; thePtr: Ptr): INTEGER;`	*148*
`FTSetRefCon(hFT: FTHandle; refCon: LONGINT);`	*154*

File Transfer Manager routines   **See page**

FTSetupCleanup(procID: INTEGER; theConfig: Ptr;   146
count: INTEGER; theDialog: DialogPtr; VAR
magicCookie: LONGINT);

FTSetupFilter(procID: INTEGER; theConfig: Ptr; count: 145
INTEGER; theDialog: DialogPtr; VAR theEvent:
EventRecord; VAR theItem: INTEGER; VAR magicCookie:
LONGINT): BOOLEAN;

FTSetupItem(procID: INTEGER; theConfig: Ptr; count: 146
INTEGER; theDialog: DialogPtr; VAR theItem: INTEGER;
VAR magicCookie: LONGINT);

FTSetupPostflight(procID: INTEGER);   147

FTSetupPreflight(procID: INTEGER; VAR magicCookie: 144
LONGINT): Handle;

FTSetupSetup(procID: INTEGER; theConfig: Ptr; count: 145
INTEGER; theDialog: DialogPtr; VAR magicCookie:
LONGINT);

FTSetUserData(hFT: FTHandle; userData: LONGINT);   155

FTStart(hFT: FTHandle; direction: FTDirection;   149
fileInfo: SFReply): FTErr;

FTValidate(hFT: FTHandle): BOOLEAN;   141

InitFT: FTErr;   138

Routines in your application   **See page**

MyEnvironsProc(refCon: LONGINT; VAR theEnvirons: 160
ConnEnvironRec): CMErr;

MyReadProc(VAR count : LONGINT; bufPtr : Ptr; refCon :   156
LONGINT; fileMsg : INTEGER) : OSErr;

MyRecvProc(thePtr: Ptr; theSize: LONGINT; refCon: 158
LONGINT; channel: CMChannel; VAR flags:
CMFlags):LONGINT;

MySendProc(thePtr: Ptr; theSize: LONGINT; refCon: 157
LONGINT; channel: CMChannel; flags: CMFlags):LONGINT;

MyWriteProc(VAR count: LONGINT; bufPtr: Ptr; refCon: 159
LONGINT; fileMsg: INTEGER): OSErr;

File transfer record

```
TYPE
        FTHandle            =       ^FTPtr;
        FTPtr               =       ^FTRecord;
        FTRecord            =       PACKED RECORD

            procID          :       INTEGER;


            flags           :       FTFlags;
            errCode         :       FTErr;

            refCon          :       LONGINT;
            userData        :       LONGINT;

            defProc         :       ProcPtr;

            config          :       Ptr;
            oldConfig       :       Ptr;

            environsProc    :       ProcPtr;
            reserved1       :       LONGINT;
            reserved2       :       LONGINT;

            ftPrivate       :       Ptr;

            sendProc        :       ProcPtr;
            recvProc        :       ProcPtr;
            writeProc       :       ProcPtr;
            readProc        :       ProcPtr;

            owner           :       WindowPtr;

            direction       :       FTDirection;
            theReply        :       SFReply;

            writePtr        :       LONGINT;
            readPtr         :       LONGINT;
            theBuf          :       ^char;
            bufSize         :       LONGINT;
            autoRec         :       Str255;
            attributes      :       FTAttributes;
        END;
```

Constants and data types

```
CONST
        curFTVersion            =       1;

TYPE
        FTDirection             =       INTEGER;

CONST
        ftReceiving             =       0;
        ftTransmitting          =       1;
        ftFullDuplex            =       2;


{ file transfer attributes }
TYPE
        FTAttributes            =       INTEGER
CONST
        ftSameCircuit           =       $0001;
        ftSendDisable           =       $0002;
        ftReceiveDisable        =       $0004;
        ftTextOnly              =       $0008;


{ file transfer flags }
TYPE
        FTFlags                 =       LONGINT;

CONST
        ftIsFTMode              =       $0001;
        ftNoMenus               =       $0002;
        ftQuiet                 =       $0004;
        ftSucc                  =       $0080;

{ Choose return values }
CONST
        chooseDisaster          =       -2;
        chooseFailed            =       -1;
        chooseOKMinor           =       1;
        chooseOKMajor           =       2;
        chooseCancel            =       3;
```

Errors

```
TYPE
     FTErr                   =       OSErr;

CONST
     ftGenericError          =       -1;
     ftNoErr                 =        0;
     ftRejected              =        1;
     ftFailed                =        2;
     ftTimeOut               =        3;
     ftTooManyRetry          =        4;
     ftNotEnoughDspace       =        5;
     ftRemoteCancel          =        6;
     ftWrongFormat           =        7;
     ftNoTools               =        8;
     ftUserCancel            =        9;
     ftNotSupported          =       10;
```

File Transfer Manager routine selectors

◆ *Assembly note:* Your application can access Communications Toolbox routines through a Macintosh Operating System trap. To call a routine, your application pushes the appropriate parameters onto the stack and invokes the trap macro that has the same name as the routine, preceded by an underscore. When expanded, these macros place the routine selector onto the stack, set A0 to point to the selector, and invoke the trap `_CommToolboxDispatch ($A08B)`. Upon returning from the trap, the trap macro pops the routine selector off the stack and places the return value into D0. It is your application's responsibility to clean up the stack by removing the parameters that were pushed onto the stack prior to invoking the trap macro.

FTAbort	.EQU	525	FTGetProcID	.EQU	519
FTActivate	.EQU	544	FTGetRefCon	.EQU	515
FTChoose	.EQU	540	FTGetToolName	.EQU	518
FTDefault	.EQU	528	FTGetUserData	.EQU	517
FTDispose	.EQU	521	FTGetVersion	.EQU	538
FTEnglishToIntl	.EQU	537	FTIntlToEnglish	.EQU	536
FTEvent	.EQU	541	FTMenu	.EQU	543
FTExec	.EQU	522	FTNew	.EQU	520
FTGetConfig	.EQU	534	FTResume	.EQU	526
FTGetFTVersion	.EQU	539	FTSetConfig	.EQU	535

FTSetRefCon	.EQU	514	FTSetupSetup	.EQU	530
FTSetupCleanup	.EQU	533	FTSetUserData	.EQU	516
FTSetupFilter	.EQU	531	FTStart	.EQU	523
FTSetupItem	.EQU	532	FTValidate	.EQU	527
FTSetupPostflight	.EQU	542	InitFT	.EQU	513
FTSetupPreflight	.EQU	529			

Chapter 6 **Communications Resource Manager**

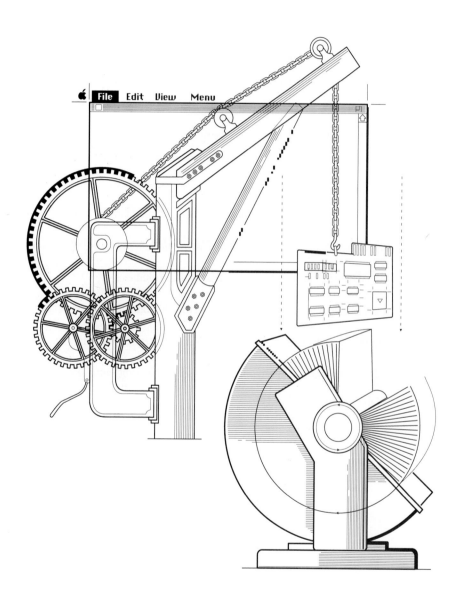

THIS CHAPTER describes the Communications Resource Manager, the Communications Toolbox manager that makes it easier for your code to manage communications resources and devices. This chapter describes the data structures and routines your code can use to implement device management. Next, it presents the routines your code can use to perform resource management. At the end of the chapter, you'll find a "Quick Reference" to routines, data structures, and routine selectors for programming in assembly language.

In this chapter, the term *your code* refers to the application, tool, or driver you are writing for the Macintosh, which will implement communications services for users.

To use the Communications Resource Manager, you need to be familiar with

- the Resource Manager (described in *Inside Macintosh*, Volumes I, IV, V)

- the Device Manager (described in *Inside Macintosh*, Volumes I, IV, V)

- the Memory Manager (described in *Inside Macintosh*, Volumes I, IV, V)

- the Operating System Utilities (described in *Inside Macintosh*, Volume II)

- the MultiFinder programming environment (described in *Programmer's Guide to MultiFinder*)

About the Communications Resource Manager

Your code uses the services provided by the Communications Resource Manager for two purposes: to manage devices (such as internal modems and serial cards) and to manage resources. Device management is essential when your code needs to know about new cards that have been installed in a Macintosh. Resource management is required when your code is sharing resources with other applications (as it does when a Macintosh runs under MultiFinder). The resource management services provided by the Communications Resource Manager are an extension to the services provided by the Resource Manager in the Macintosh Toolbox.

The way your code uses the Communications Resource Manager is very similar to the way it uses other Communications Toolbox managers. Your code calls a Communications Resource Manager routine, which, upon completion, returns to your code any relevant parameters and return codes. *Figure 6-1* shows the data flow into and out of the Communications Resource Manager.

■ **Figure 6-1** Data flow into and out of the Communications Resource Manager

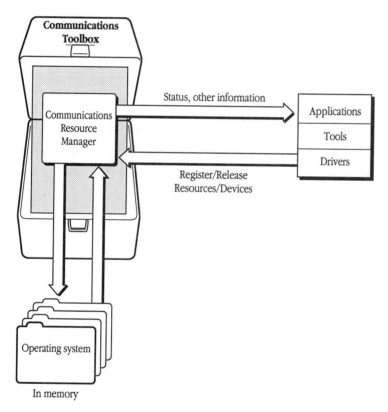

Device management

The way Macintosh applications interact with special interface cards varies from card to card, making the task of programming the Macintosh to use these cards quite complex. The Communications Toolbox solves this problem by providing applications with standardized routines and data structures that they can use to keep track of communications devices users have installed.

The data structure that is most important in supporting communications device management is the **communications resource record,** which is stored as an operating system queue. The communications resource record comprises fields containing information such as the type of device the record represents, and whether the device is available for use. The communications resource record is described later in this chapter.

The Communications Resource Manager and your code keep track of communications devices by placing a communications resource record into the queue for each communications device. Initially, when your code calls `InitCRM` (discussed later in this chapter), this queue contains two records, one for each of the serial drivers. Your code can then add and delete communications resource records.

By making use of Communications Toolbox routines, your code can register new devices, allocate devices, and look for specific kinds of devices. And device drivers, if properly coded, can resolve conflicts when two or more applications need to use a communications resource at the same time. This situation often arises in a MultiFinder environment.

Resource management

When your code shares resources with other applications, problems can arise if one of the applications accidentally disposes of a resource needed by another application. The Communications Toolbox provides routines that your code can use to share resources without confronting this kind of problem. These routines keep track of how many times a resource is simultaneously in use in an internal Communications Resource Manager data structure for every communications resource. Every time code requests a resource, the Communications Resource Manager *increases* the "use count" for that resource by 1. Every time code releases a communications resource, the Communications Resource Manager *decreases* the value by 1. This enables the Communications Resource Manager to keep track of which resources are being used; when a resource's use count reaches 0, it is released.

The communications resource record

The most important data structure to the Communications Resource Manager is the communications resource record. It contains information like the name and type of each device connected to the Macintosh, and whether a device is in use.

At startup time, the Communications Resource Manager builds a queue of communications resource records. If the Communications Resource Manager is installed, the queue will consist of a minimum of two devices of type `crmSerialDevice`.

When your code installs a new record into the queue, it must fill in the following fields in the communications resource record: `crmDeviceType`, `crmAttributes`, `crmStatus`, and `crmRefCon`. The Communications Resource Manager fills in the other fields.

Communications resource record data structure

```
TYPE
        CRMRecPtr           =       ^CRMRec;
        CRMRec              =       RECORD
            qLink           :       QElemPtr;
            qType           :       INTEGER;
            crmVersion      :       INTEGER;

            crmPrivate      :       LONGINT;
            crmReserved     :       INTEGER;

            crmDeviceType   :       LONGINT;
            crmDeviceID     :       LONGINT;
            crmAttributes   :       LONGINT;
            crmStatus       :       LONGINT;

            crmRefCon       :       LONGINT;
        END;
```

qLink

`qLink` points to the next `CRMRec` in the Communications Resource Manager's queue of communications resource records.

qType

`qType` is a constant that your code must fill with the constant `crmType`.

crmVersion

`crmVersion` is the version number of the `CRMRec` data structure. At this time there is only one version, so the Communications Resource Manager fills this with the constant `crmRecVersion`.

crmPrivate and crmReserved

crmPrivate and crmReserved are private to the Communications Resource Manager; your code must not use them.

crmDeviceType

crmDeviceType is the type of device. For example, a serial port has a crmDeviceType of crmSerialDevice.

crmDeviceID

crmDeviceID is an identifier that your code can use to distinguish between multiple devices of the same device type. The Communications Resource Manager fills in this field when your code calls the CRMInstall routine.

crmAttributes

crmAttributes specifies the attributes of a specific device type. This field can hold either a pointer to the data or the actual data that describes the device. A sample crmAttributes data structure appears later in this chapter in the section "Registering a Device."

crmStatus

crmStatus specifies the status of a device. Your code can use this field for device arbitration purposes.

crmRefCon

crmRefCon is not used in this release of the Communications Resource Manager.

Communications Resource Manager routines

The following sections describe the routines that applications use to access Communications Resource Manager services. Your application cannot call these routines from interrupt level.

Below is a listing of the routines described in this section in the order in which they are presented. You can use the list as a reference tool to find the description of a routine. Or, you can use the index at the end of this document, which lists these routines alphabetically.

InitCRM / 174
CRMInstall / 174
CRMSearch / 175
CRMRemove / 175
CRMGetCRMVersion / 176
CRMGetHeader / 176
CRMGetResource / 177
CRMGet1Resource / 177
CRMGetIndResource / 177

CRMGet1IndResource / 177
CRMGetNamedResource / 178
CRMGet1NamedResource / 178
CRMGetIndex / 178
CRMReleaseResource / 178
CRMGetIndToolName / 179
CRMRealToLocalID / 180
CRMLocalToRealID / 181

Initializing the Communications Resource Manager

InitCRM initializes the Communications Resource Manager.

▲ **Warning** Your code must call this routine after calling the standard Macintosh Toolbox initialization routines and before calling any of the other Communications Toolbox manager initialization routines. ▲

Function InitCRM:CRMErr;

Description InitCRM returns an operating system error code if appropriate.

Your code must check for the presence of the Communications Toolbox before calling this function. Sample code under "Determining Whether the Managers Are Installed" in Appendix C shows you how your application can make this check.

Result Codes crmGenericError, crmNoErr.

CRMInstall

Installing devices

CRMInstall installs a device into the Communications Resource Manager's queue. Devices in the Communications Resource Manager queue typically have their CRMRec records allocated in the system heap. If your code installs a CRMRec at startup time, be sure that your code increases the size of the system heap appropriately.

For more information on how to register a device with the Communications Resource Manager, read "Registering a Device," later in this chapter.

Procedure CRMInstall(crmReqPtr: QElemPtr);

Description CRMInstall installs the communications resource record crmReqPtr into the Communications Resource Manager queue.

▲ **Warning** A CRMRec allocated in the application heap needs to be removed before the application heap is reinitialized; otherwise, the Communications Resource Manager queue may be damaged. ▲

Searching for devices

Your code can use CRMSearch to order the Communications Resource Manager queue, or to add new elements to the end of the queue.

Function   CRMSearch(crmReqPtr: QElemPtr): QElemPtr;

Description   crmReqPtr specifies communications resource record search criteria.

CRMSearch searches for a device in the Communications Resource Manager queue that has two characteristics: the same deviceType, and a deviceID greater than the deviceID in the record specified by crmReqPtr. CRMSearch returns a pointer to the first record that it finds that meets these two conditions. Or, if no records meet the search criteria, it returns NIL.

When searching for the first element in the queue, your code must pass 0 in deviceID.

Removing devices

CRMRemove removes a device from the Communications Resource Manager queue.

Function   CRMRemove(crmReqPtr: QElemPtr): OSErr;

Description   crmReqPtr specifies the device to be removed.

Getting the version number

CRMGetCRMVersion returns the version number of the Communications Resource Manager.

Function   CRMGetCRMVersion:INTEGER;

Description   The Communications Resource Manager version described in this document is:

```
CONST
     curCRMVersion          =          1;
```

Getting to the head of the queue

CRMGetHeader returns a pointer to the head of the Communications Resource Manager queue.

Function   CRMGetHeader: QHdrPtr;

Resource management routines

The nine routines described in this section make it easier for your code to manage communications resources. Your code should use these routines so that the Communications Resource Manager can keep track of how many times a resource is simultaneously in use.

The names of these routines are similar to the names of Resource Manager routines available in the Macintosh Toolbox. Communications Resource Manager routines also operate very much like Resource Manager routines; in fact, most of them make use of their counterparts in the Macintosh Toolbox.

CRMGetResource and CRMGet1Resource

Loading resources

CRMGetResource and CRMGet1Resource call the Resource Manager routines GetResource and Get1Resource, respectively, and return a handle to the specified communications resource. The Communications Resource Manager then adds the handle to the list of resources that it is managing, and increases by one the use count, which indicates how many pieces of code are using a resource.

Function   CRMGetResource(theType: ResType; theID: INTEGER): Handle;

Function   CRMGet1Resource(theType: ResType; theID: INTEGER): Handle;

CRMGetIndResource and CRMGet1IndResource

Loading indexed resources

CRMGetIndResource and CRMGet1IndResource call the Resource Manager routines GetIndResource and Get1IndResource, respectively, and return a handle to the specified communications resource. The Communications Resource Manager then adds the handle to the list of resources that it is managing, and increases by one the use count, which indicates how many pieces of code are using a resource.

Function   CRMGetIndResource(theType: ResType; index: INTEGER): Handle;

Function   CRMGet1IndResource(theType: ResType; index: INTEGER): Handle;

Loading named resources

CRMGetNamedResource and CRMGet1NamedResource call GetNamedResource and Get1NamedResource, respectively, and return a handle to the specified communications resource. The Communications Resource Manager then adds the handle to the list of resources that it is managing, and increases by one the use count, which indicates how many pieces of code are using a resource.

Function   CRMGetNamedResource(theType: ResType; name: Str255): Handle;

Function   CRMGet1NamedResource(theType: ResType; name: Str255): Handle;

CRMGetIndex

Getting a usage index for a resource

CRMGetIndex returns a use count which indicates how many pieces of code are simultaneously using a resource with the specified handle. CRMGetIndex returns 0 if it does not find theHandle in the list of resources the Communications Resource Manager is managing.

Function   CRMGetIndex(theHandle: Handle): LONGINT;

CRMReleaseResource

Releasing resources

CRMReleaseResource decreases by 1 the value that indicates how many pieces of code have requested a resource. If the use count reaches 0, the resource specified by theHandle is released with a call to the Resource Manager routine ReleaseResource.

Procedure   CRMReleaseResource(theHandle: Handle);

▲ **Warning**   Your code must release communications resources by calling CRMReleaseResource. If your code tries to release the resources using the Resource Manager routine ReleaseResource, the results are unpredictable. ▲

Getting the name of a tool

CRMGetIndToolName returns the name of a tool in toolName.

Function

CRMGetIndToolName(bundleType : OSType; index : INTEGER;
VAR toolName : Str255) : OSErr;

Description

The appropriate values for bundleType are as follows:

```
CONST
      ClassCM       =       'cbnd';
      ClassFT       =       'fbnd';
      ClassTM       =       'tbnd';
```

index specifies which occurrence of a particular type of tool to return. For example, if index is 2, the Communications Resource Manager returns the name of the second tool of a particular type in toolName. If the Communications Resource Manager cannot find a tool that matches the specified parameters, an empty string is returned in toolName.

Resource-mapping routines

All resources used by a tool can be referenced by a local ID, which can be mapped (using the tool bundle resource) into the appropriate physical ID. The Communications Toolbox contains two routines that will help you keep things straight: To map from physical ID to local ID, use `CRMRealToLocalID`; to map from local ID to physical ID, use `CRMLocalToRealID`.

`CRMRealToLocalID`

Mapping to Local ID

`CRMRealToLocalID` maps a physical resource ID to a local resource ID.

Function `CRMRealToLocalID(bundleType: ResType; toolID: INTEGER; theKind: ResType; realID: INTEGER): INTEGER;`

Description This routine returns the (physical/local) resource ID if an appropriate entry exists in the tool bundle resource. If no entry is found, –1 is returned.

`bundleType` specifies the type of tool for which the mapping is to take place: `ClassCM` (for connection tools), `ClassTM` (for terminal tools), or `ClassFT` (for file transfer tools).

Here is the format for a connection tool bundle resource (in `Rez` format). The same resource type declaration holds for terminal tools and file transfer tools.

```
type 'cbnd' {                      /* or tbnd, or fbnd */
    integer = $$CountOf(TypeArray) - 1;
    array TypeArray {
        literal longint;     /* Type */
        integer = $$CountOf(IDArray) - 1;
        wide array IDArray {
            integer;         /* Local ID */
            integer;         /* Actual ID */
        };
    };
};
```

Mapping to Real ID

CRMLocalToRealID maps a local resource ID to a physical resource.

Function

CRMLocalToRealID(bundleType: ResType; toolID: INTEGER; theKind: ResType; localID: INTEGER) : INTEGER;

Description

This routine returns the (physical/local) resource ID if an appropriate entry exists in the tool bundle resource. If no entry is found, –1 is returned.

bundleType specifies the type of tool for which the mapping is to take place: ClassCM (for connection tools), ClassTM (for terminal tools), or ClassFT (for file transfer tools).

toolID specifies the bundle resource for the tool.

Registering a device

This section gives some basic information about writing drivers that emulate the behavior of the built-in serial drivers.

Private storage   Your code can reference all private data storage off the `dCtlStorage` field of the `DCtlEntry` for the drivers involved.

Low memory   Do not use any.

Driver naming   Use unique driver names and be prepared to deal with driver name collisions. For example, don't use `.CIn/.COut`.

driver csCode calls   Support all of the `csCode` calls supported by the standard serial drivers. If you need additional `csCode` calls, contact Developer Technical Support to reserve them. `csCode` calls below 256 are reserved for Apple Computer, Inc.

Data structures

Each device in the Communications Resource Manager's queue has a `CRMRec` associated with it. For the `crmDeviceType` field, Apple Computer, Inc. has defined the following value for serial port devices:

```
CONST
      crmSerialDevice        =        1;
```

◆ *Note:* Values for `crmDeviceType` less than 128 are reserved for Apple Computer, Inc. Your code must not use them.

When adding a `CRMRec` to the Communications Resource Manager queue with the `CRMInstall` routine, pass 0 for the `crmDeviceID` field. The device identifier will be assigned by the Communications Resource Manager.

The `crmAttributes` field in the `CRMRec` points to a serial port device-specific data structure. The `crmStatus` field of the `CRMRec` is not used for devices of type `crmSerialDevice` in this version of the Communications Resource Manager.

```
TYPE
        CRMSerialPtr              =         ^CRMSerialRecord;
        CRMSerialRecord           =         RECORD
             version              :         INTEGER;

             inputDriverName      :         StringHandle;
             outputDriverName     :         StringHandle;
             name                 :         StringHandle;
             deviceIcon           :         Handle;

             ratedSpeed           :         LONGINT;
             maxSpeed             :         LONGINT;

             reserved             :         LONGINT;
        END;
```

version

version is the version number of the CRMSerialRecord data structure. For the version of
CRMSerialRecord described in this document, version = curCRMSerRecVer, which equals 0.

inputDriverName

inputDriverName is a pointer to a Pascal-style string, which is the name of the input driver for
the given serial port. This driver should behave like the standard input serial port drivers (.AIn and
.BIn), and support the same csCode calls as do the standard drivers.

outputDriverName

outputDriverName is a pointer to a Pascal-style string, which is the name of the output driver for
the given serial port. This driver should behave like the standard output serial port drivers (.AOut
and .BOut), and support the same csCode calls as do the standard drivers.

name

name is a string handle, which is the name associated with a given port.

deviceIcon

deviceIcon is a handle to a relocatable block that contains an icon and a mask associated with the
given port. Pass NIL if no icon is available.

ratedSpeed

ratedSpeed is the maximum *recommended* speed in bits per second.

maxSpeed

maxSpeed is the maximum speed in bits per second of which the hardware is capable.

Searching for serial port devices

The following routine will search the Communications Resource Manager linked list for devices of a specified type.

```
PROCEDURE FindSerialPorts;
VAR
        theCRM          :       CRMRecPtr;
        theCRMRec       :       CRMRec;
        theErr          :       RMErr;
        theSerial       :       CRMSerialPtr;

        old             :       INTEGER;

BEGIN
        theErr := 0;                            { error status }
        old := 0;                               { index number of ports }
        WHILE (theErr = noErr) DO
        BEGIN
                WITH theCRMRec DO
                BEGIN
                        crmDeviceType := crmSerialDevice;
                        { search for port with index number greater than "old" }
                        crmDeviceID := old;   { to be filled in later }
                END;
                theCRM := @theCRMRec;
                theCRM := CRMRecPtr(CRMSearch(QElemPtr(theCRM)));

                IF theCRM <> NIL THEN           { got one! }
                BEGIN
                        theSerial := CRMSerialPtr(theCRM^.crmAttributes);
                        old := theCRM^.crmDeviceID;

                        WITH theSerial^ DO
                        BEGIN
                        END;
                END
                ELSE
                BEGIN
                        theErr := 1;
                END;
        END; { while }
END;
```

Quick reference

This section provides a reference to Communications Resource Manager routines and data structures. At the end of this section is a listing of routine selectors for programming in assembly language.

Routines

Communications Resource Manager routines	See page
CRMGet1IndResource(theType: ResType; index: INTEGER): Handle;	177
CRMGet1NamedResource(theType: ResType; name: Str255): Handle;	178
CRMGet1Resource(theType: ResType; theID: INTEGER): Handle;	177
CRMGetCRMVersion: INTEGER;	176
CRMGetHeader: QHdrPtr;	176
CRMGetIndex(theHandle: Handle): LONGINT;	178
CRMGetIndResource(theType: ResType; index: INTEGER): Handle;	177
CRMGetIndToolName(bundleType : OSType; index : INTEGER; VAR toolName : Str255) : OSErr;	179
CRMGetNamedResource(theType: ResType; name: Str255): Handle;	178
CRMGetResource(theType: ResType; theID: INTEGER): Handle;	177
CRMInstall(crmReqPtr: QElemPtr);	174
CRMReleaseResource(theHandle: Handle);	178
CRMRemove(crmReqPtr: QElemPtr): OSErr;	175
CRMSearch(crmReqPtr: QElemPtr): QElemPtr;	175
CRMLocalToRealID(bundleType: ResType; toolID: INTEGER; theKind: ResType; localID: INTEGER): INTEGER;	181
CRMRealToLocalID(bundleType: ResType; toolID: INTEGER; theKind: ResType; realID: INTEGER): INTEGER;	180
InitCRM:CRMErr;	174

Constants and data types

```
TYPE
       CRMErr                    =        OSErr;


CONST
       crmGenericError    =        -1;
       crmNoErr           =         0;


CONST

       curCRMVersion      =         1;


{ Communications Resource Manager linked list type }
       crmType            =         9;


{ Version of CRMRec data structure }
       crmRecVersion      =         1;


{ local/real resource ID mapping }
       ClassCM     =      'cbnd';
       ClassTM     =      'tbnd';
       ClassFT     =      'fbnd';


TYPE
       CRMRecPtr                  =        ^CRMRec;
       CRMRec                     =        RECORD
             qLink            :        QElemPtr;
             qType            :        INTEGER;
             crmVersion       :        INTEGER;

             crmPrivate       :        LONGINT;
             crmReserved      :        INTEGER;

             crmDeviceType    :        LONGINT;
             crmDeviceID      :        LONGINT;
             crmAttributes    :        LONGINT;
             crmStatus        :        LONGINT;

             crmRefCon        :        LONGINT;
       END;
```

```
TYPE
        CRMSerialPtr                =       ^CRMSerialRecord;
        CRMSerialRecord             =       RECORD
                version             :       INTEGER;

                inputDriverName     :       StringHandle;
                outputDriverName    :       StringHandle;
                name                :       StringHandle;
                deviceIcon          :       Handle;

                ratedSpeed          :       LONGINT;
                maxSpeed            :       LONGINT;

                reserved            :       LONGINT;
        END;
```

Communications Resource Manager routine selectors

◆ *Assembly note:* Your application can access Communications Toolbox routines through a Macintosh Operating System trap. To call a routine, your application pushes the appropriate parameters onto the stack and invokes the trap macro that has the same name as the routine, preceded by an underscore. When expanded, these macros place the routine selector onto the stack, set A0 to point to the selector, and invoke the trap `_CommToolboxDispatch` ($A08B). Upon returning from the trap, the trap macro pops the routine selector off the stack and places the return value into D0. It is your application's responsibility to clean up the stack by removing the parameters that were pushed onto the stack prior to invoking the trap macro.

CRMGet1IndResource	.EQU	1290	CRMGetResource	.EQU	1287
CRMGet1NamedResource	.EQU	1292	CRMInstall	.EQU	1283
CRMGet1Resource	.EQU	1288	CRMLocalToRealID	.EQU	1295
CRMGetCRMVersion	.EQU	1286	CRMRealToLocalID	.EQU	1296
CRMGetHeader	.EQU	1282	CRMReleaseResource	.EQU	1293
CRMGetIndex	.EQU	1294	CRMRemove	.EQU	1284
CRMGetIndResource	.EQU	1289	CRMSearch	.EQU	1285
CRMGetIndToolName	.EQU	1297	InitCRM	.EQU	1281
CRMGetNamedResource	.EQU	1291			

Chapter 7 Macintosh Communications Toolbox Utilities

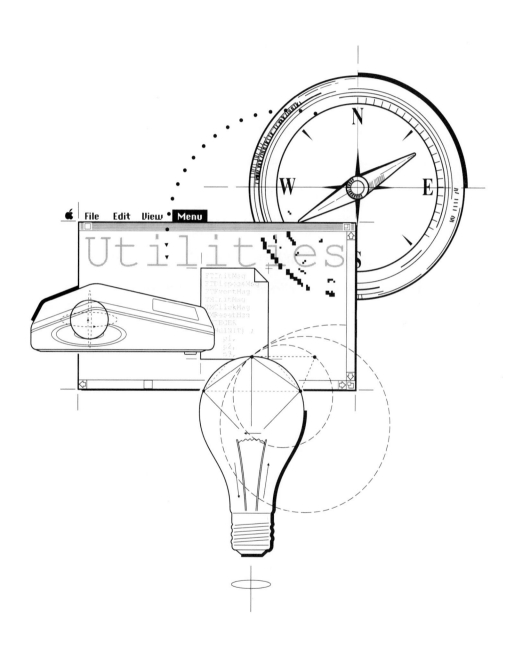

THIS CHAPTER describes the Communications Toolbox utilities, a set of routines that makes it easier for your application to manipulate dialog item lists, control pop-up menus, and search a network for AppleTalk entities. This chapter also details two routines your application can use to initialize the utilities and obtain the version number of the utilities.

At the end of the chapter you'll find a "Quick Reference" to these routines, data structures, and routine selectors for programming in assembly language.

To use the dialog item list manipulation routines, you need to be familiar with

■   the Dialog Manager (described in *Inside Macintosh,* Volumes IV, V)

■   the Control Manager (described in *Inside Macintosh,* Volumes I, IV, V)

■   the Resource Manager (described in *Inside Macintosh,* Volumes I, IV, V)

To use the network look-up utilities, you need to be familiar with

■   AppleTalk (described in *Inside Macintosh,* Volumes II, V)

Communications Toolbox utilities

This section explains the routines and data structures that make up the Communications Toolbox utilities. Your application cannot call these routines from interrupt level.

Below is a listing of the routines described in this section in the order in which they are presented.

InitCTBUtilities / 192   CountDITL / 201

CTBGetCTBVersion / 192   ShortenDITL / 201

'CDEF'/ 193   NuLookup / 203

AppendDITL / 198   NuPLookup / 204

Initializing the Communications Toolbox utilities

InitCTBUtilities initializes the Communications Toolbox utilities.

▲ **Warning**   Your application must call this routine after calling the standard Macintosh Toolbox initialization routines and the Communications Resource Manager initialization routine (InitCRM); your application can then call other Communications Toolbox manager initialization routines. All code that uses any Communications Toolbox routines *must* call this routine once and only once. ▲

Function   InitCTBUtilities: CTBUErr;

Description   InitCTBUtilities returns an operating system error code if appropriate. Your application must check for the presence of the Communications Toolbox before calling this function. Sample code under "Determining Whether the Managers Are Installed" in Appendix C shows you how your application can make this check.

Result Codes   ctbuGenericError, ctbuNoErr.

Getting the Communications Toolbox version number

CTBGetCTBVersion returns the version number of the Communications Toolbox utilities.

Function   CTBGetCTBVersion: INTEGER;

Description   The Communications Toolbox version described in this document is:

```
CONST
     curCTBUVersion        =        1;
```

Pop-up menu control definition procedure

The Communications Toolbox includes a **control definition procedure** ('CDEF') that extends the function of PopUpMenuSelect, which is a part of the Menu Manager in the Macintosh Toolbox. This 'CDEF', with resource ID=63, is available on Macintosh computers running with the Communications Toolbox installed.

The description that follows shows only the parameters your application must pass to NewControl or GetNewControl that differ from those defined in *Inside Macintosh*.

Your application creates a pop-up menu the same way that it would create any other Macintosh control. *Figure 7-1* shows a pop-up menu control in its inactive and active states.

■ **Figure 7-1** Pop-up menu in its inactive and active states

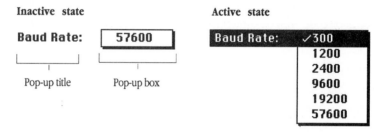

Description　value specifies the manner in which the title of the pop-up menu is to be justified and drawn. value is a bit field with the following masks:

```
CONST
        popupTitleLeftJust      =       $0000;
        popupTitleCenterJust    =       $0001;
        popupTitleRightJust     =       $00FF;

        popupTitleBold          =       $0100;
        popupTitleItalic        =       $0200;
        popupTitleUnderline     =       $0400;
        popupTitleOutline       =       $0800;
        popupTitleShadow        =       $1000;
        popupTitleCondense      =       $2000;
        popupTitleExtend        =       $4000;
        popupTitleNoStyle       =       $8000;
```

To have the pop-up menu draw the title of the control with more than one of the characteristics listed above, pass in `value` the sum of all desired characteristics.

Once a pop-up menu has been created, the pop-up menu `'CDEF'` sets `value` to its minimum valid value. Your application can then use the value of the control to determine the currently selected item.

`min` represents the `menuID` of the menu in the pop-up control when the control is being created. After the control has been created, the pop-up menu `'CDEF'` sets the minimum value of the control to 1.

△ **Important** The popup `'CDEF'` first looks in the menu list using `_GetMHandle`. If it can't find the menu, it creates it using `_GetMenu`. △

`max` contains the width of the pop-up title area when the control is being created. After the control has been created, the pop-up menu `'CDEF'` sets the maximum value of the control to the number of items in the pop-up menu.

`procID` should be an integer equal to `popupMenuCDEFproc` plus the appropriate variation code. `popupMenuCDEFproc` is a constant set by Apple Computer, Inc. and is equal to 1008 (63 times 16). Variation codes are discussed later in "About Variation Codes."

If the pop-up menu is created using the `popupUseAddResMenu` variation code, the pop-up menu `'CDEF'` creates the control and then calls `AddResMenu` to add items to the menu associated with the pop-up menu control. The value in `refCon` is typecast to the type `ResType`, which is used by the routine `AddResMenu`.

For example, if `refCon` is `LONGINT('FONT')`, the pop-up menu control appends a list of the fonts installed in the system to the menu associated with the pop-up menu control.

After the control has been created, your application can use the control's `refCon` field for whatever purpose it requires.

About variation codes

Your application can specify variation codes when it passes a value in `procID`. Variation codes alter the characteristics of the pop-up menu control. To specify the appropriate variation code, your application sums the values that correspond to the desired pop-up menu characteristics with the basic pop-up menu constant `popupMenuCDEFproc`. Valid values are shown next.

Variation code constant	Description
popupFixedWidth	This constant specifies constant control width. If your application specifies this value, the pop-up menu `'CDEF'` will not resize the control horizontally to fit long menu items. The width of the pop-up box where the currently selected item is drawn equals the width of the control, minus the width of the pop-up title your application specifies when it creates the control. If the contents of the pop-up box do not fit into the space provided, the contents is truncated to fit and ellipses (...) are appended to its end. If this variation code is not specified, the contents of the pop-up box are guaranteed to fit, because the pop-up menu `'CDEF'` resizes the control horizontally.
popupUseCQD	This constant specifies the use of Color QuickDraw. If your application specifies this value, the pop-up menu `'CDEF'` uses the colors stored in the menu color table (`'mctb'`) for the color of the pop-up box when Color QuickDraw is available. If Color QuickDraw is unavailable, this variation code is ignored.
	If the grafPort that owns the control is an old-style (classic QuickDraw) grafPort, the pop-up menu control attempts to create a cGrafPort to draw the pop-up menu control in the correct colors and then dispose of it when finished drawing. By using a cGrafPort, the control avoids the distortion that occurs when converting Color QuickDraw colors to classic QuickDraw colors.
popupUseAddResMenu	If your application specifies this value, the pop-up menu `'CDEF'` treats the `refCon` field as a `ResType`, and performs an `AddResMenu` with this resource type on the menu. If the control is being created with the `NewControl` routine, the pop-up menu `'CDEF'` receives `refCon` from your application. If the control is being created with `GetNewControl`, the pop-up menu `'CDEF'` receives `refCon` from the control template (resource type `'CNTL'`).
popupUseWFont	If your application specifies this value, the pop-up menu `'CDEF'` draws the pop-up menu control using the font and size of the grafPort that owns the control. The pop-up menu, when active, also uses the font and size specified by the grafPort, instead of using the standard system font.

The values that correspond to the variation code constants are as follows:

```
CONST
      popupFixedWidth        =        $0001;
      popupUseCQD            =        $0002;
      popupUseAddResMenu     =        $0004;
      popupUseWFont          =        $0008;
```

After the pop-up control has been created

After `NewControl` creates the pop-up menu, `min` contains 1, `max` contains the number of items in the menu that is associated with the control, and `refCon` becomes available for the application to use.

In the process of creating the new control, `NewControl` may modify `boundsRect` to reflect the actual width of the pop-up menu box.

Your application can get the currently selected menu item by calling `GetCtlValue`.

Other pop-up menu control characteristics

There are three pop-up menu control characteristics that you need to be familiar with: how the utility changes the width of the control, how the control changes with regard to system justification, and how your application can access the menu handle.

Whenever the pop-up control is redrawn, the utility calls `CalcMenuSize`. This routine recalculates the size of the menu associated with the control, to allow for the addition of new items in the menu. The pop-up menu `'CDEF'` also updates the width of the pop-up menu control to the sum of the width of the pop-up title, the width of the longest item in the menu (the `menuWidth` field of the menu information record), and some aesthetic white space. As previously described, your application can override this characteristic by using the variation code `popupFixedWidth`.

When the system justification is `teJustRight`, the pop-up control looks like the pop-up menu control shown in *Figure 7-2*.

■ **Figure 7-2** Pop-up menu control when system justification is `teJustRight`

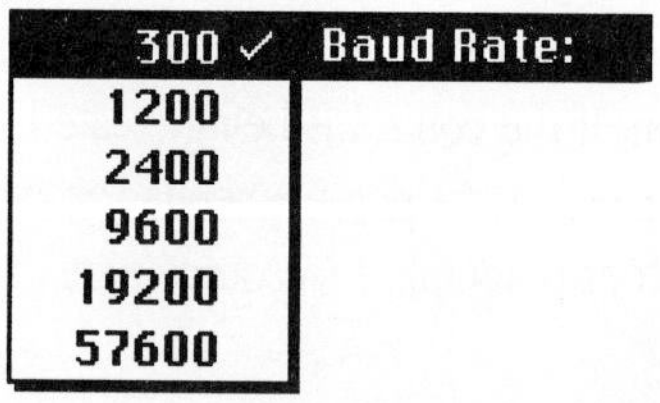

Note that the positions of the pop-up box and the pop-up title are reversed from the standard positions shown in *Figure 7-1*.

Your application obtains the menu handle and the menu ID for the menu associated with the pop-up control by dereferencing the `contrlData` field of the control record. The `contrlData` field is a handle to a block of private information. The first four bytes of this block are the menu handle; the next two bytes are the menu ID for the menu associated with the control. The format of the `popupPrivateData` structure is as follows:

```
TYPE
    popupPrivateData    =       RECORD
        mHandle         :       MenuHandle;
        mID             :       INTEGER;
        mPrivate        :       ARRAY[0..0] OF SignedByte;

    END;
```

Manipulating dialog item lists (DITLs)

As a logical extension to the Dialog Manager routines in the Macintosh Toolbox, the Communications Toolbox provides three procedures to append, shorten, and count the number of items in dialog item lists. You can use these routines regardless of whether your program provides communications services.

AppendDITL

Appending to a dialog item list

AppendDITL lets your application append dialog items to an exisiting dialog box.

Procedure
AppendDITL(theDialog: DialogPtr; theDITL: Handle; method: DITLMethod);

Description
theDialog is a pointer to the dialog box in which you want to append an item list.

theDITL is a handle to the item list that you want to append.

method specifies the manner in which you want the items in the new item list to be appended: overlay, right, or bottom. Here are the acceptable vaules for method, followed by examples of the results of each method:

```
TYPE
    DITLMethod          =       INTEGER

CONST
    overlayDITL         =       0;
    appendDITLRight     =       1;
    appendDITLBottom    =       2;
```

Figure 7-3 shows the initial dialog box, containing items 1 and 2, and the items to be appended, namely items 3 and 4.

■ **Figure 7-3** Initial dialog box and to-be-appended items

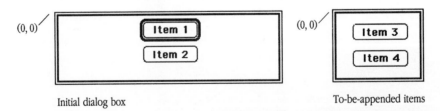

Initial dialog box   To-be-appended items

If your application uses overlayDITL, AppendDITL superimposes the items in the to-be-appended dialog item list onto the dialog item list associated with theDialog, as shown in *Figure 7-4.*

■ **Figure 7-4** Dialog box after appended items are superimposed

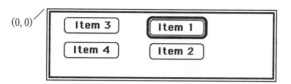

If your application uses `appendDITLRight`, `AppendDITL` offsets the items in the to-be-appended dialog item list by the upper-right coordinate of `theDialog^.portRect`, as shown in *Figure 7-5*. Then `AppendDITL` appends the list to the end of the dialog item list associated with `theDialog`. `AppendDITL` automatically expands the dialog box as needed.

■ **Figure 7-5** Dialog box after items are appended to the right

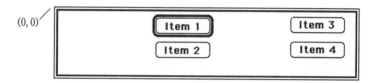

If your application uses `appendDITLBottom`, `AppendDITL` offsets the items in the to-be-appended dialog item list by the lower-left coordinate of `theDialog^.portRect`, as shown in *Figure 7-6*. Then, `AppendDITL` appends the list to the end of the dialog item list associated with `theDialog`, and expands the dialog box as needed.

■ **Figure 7-6** Dialog box after items are appended to the bottom

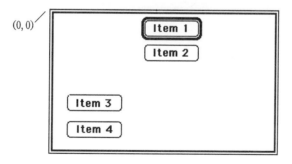

If you know your application will need to restore a window to the size it was before an `AppendDITL` routine, your application should save that size before it calls `AppendDITL`. `ShortenDITL`, the procedure that shortens dialog item lists, will not automatically resize the dialog box. (`ShortenDITL` is described later in this chapter.)

Because `AppendDITL` modifies the contents of `theDITL`, your application must get rid of the dialog item list after calling `AppendDITL`. Here is a typical calling sequence:

```
theDITL := GetResource('DITL', theID);
AppendDITL(theDialog, theDITL, appendDITLBottom);
ReleaseResource(theDITL);
```

Special ways to append items

Your application can append a new dialog item list relative to the location of specific items in the dialog box, rather then appending new dialog items relative to the coordinates of `Dialog^.portRect`. To append a dialog item list in this way, your application uses a negative number in the `method` parameter. This number corresponds to the item that is the point of reference. For instance, if `method` is –2, then the items in the to-be-appended dialog item list have their item boxes offset by the upper-left corner of the item box for item 2 in `theDialog`. *Figure* 7-7 shows how item 3 and item 4 were appended relative to the position of item 2. Item 3, because it was appended relative to the `topLeft` of item 2, appears on top of item 2.

■ **Figure 7-7** Dialog box after items are appended relative to item 2

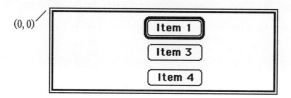

Counting the number of items in a list

CountDITL returns the number of items in the dialog item list associated with theDialog.

Function   CountDITL(theDialog:DialogPtr): INTEGER;

Shortening a dialog item list

ShortenDITL removes items from the end of the given dialog item list, but does not automatically resize the dialog box. If you know that your application will need to resize the dialog box, save the size before calling AppendDITL and use the Window Manager routine SizeWindow.

Procedure   ShortenDITL(theDialog: DialogPtr; numberItems: INTEGER);

Description   theDialog specifies the dialog box to be shortened.

numberItems specifies the number of items to be removed.

Showing AppleTalk entities: `NuLookup` and `NuPLookup`

The network look-up utilities, `NuLookup` and `NuPLookup`, allow your application to present the user with a standard dialog box containing AppleTalk entities. By providing either `NuLookup` or `NuPLookup` with the proper parameters, your application can include in the dialog box one or more types of AppleTalk entities. Both `NuLookup` and `NuPLookup` perform much the same task, but `NuPLookup` gives you a bit more flexibility.

The results of `NuLookup` and `NuPLookup` are displayed in a dialog box similar to the one in *Figure 7-8*, which shows the results of a search for LaserWriter® printers in the **zone** "Blackcap Basin."

■ **Figure 7-8** Network look-up dialog box

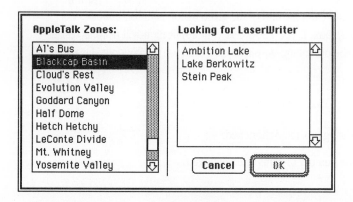

`NuLookup` and `NuPLookup` also provide your application with the option of using filter routines or hook procedures to customize the dialog box or to filter information that would otherwise be included in it. These routines are described later in this chapter, in "Hook and Filter Procedures."

In the network look-up dialog box, pressing the Return key has the same effect as pressing the OK button. Holding down the Command key and pressing the Period key has the same effect as clicking Cancel. The Up Arrow key and the Down Arrow key change the selected name to either the cell above or the cell below. Holding down the Command key while pressing the Up Arrow key or the Down Arrow key moves the selected zone up or down one cell.

Network lookup

NuLookup returns to your application the object/type/zone tuple and AppleTalk node/network/zone numbers tuple for the item that the user selected.

When your application first calls NuLookup, this routine builds a zone list (if possible). Then NuLookup makes a synchronous **Name Binding Protocol (NBP)** lookup for the specified objects. Next, NuLookup builds the preliminary object list and presents the dialog box to the user. At all times while the dialog box is displayed, NuLookup continues an asynchronous NBP lookup with long retry and timeout. It ages objects in the name list so that if an object misses several consecutive asynchronous NBP lookups, it is removed from the list. Items that appear in subsequent NBP lookups are added to the list if they were not already in the look-up list.

Both the zone and name lists are alphabetized by using the international utilities.

Function

```
NuLookup(where: Point; prompt: STR255; numTypes: INTEGER; typeList:
NLType; nameFilter: ProcPtr; zoneFilter: ProcPtr; hookProc: ProcPtr;
VAR theReply: LookupReply): INTEGER;
```

Description

where indicates in global coordinates where NuLookup should place the upper-left corner of the look-up dialog box.

prompt is a string displayed at the top of the look-up dialog box. In *Figure 7-8*, the string "Looking for LaserWriter" was passed to NuLookup.

numTypes is the number of object types that will be included in the lookup. If numTypes is –1, NuLookup searches for all object types.

typeList is a structure of type NLType, which is an array of AppleTalk object types, along with a handle to an icon. If no icon is required, pass NIL for hIcon.

```
TYPE
    NLTypeEntry       =       RECORD
            hIcon      :       Handle;
            typeStr    :       Str32;
    END;

    NLType            =       Array[0..3]of NLTypeEntry;
```

◆ *Assembly note:* Using assembly language, you can specify more than four object types by passing a pointer to an array with the required number of items.

`nameFilter` is a pointer to a procedure that filters object/type/zone tuples from the network look-up dialog box. `zoneFilter` is a pointer to a procedure that filters zones from the network look-up dialog box. `hookProc` is a pointer to a hook procedure that modifies the behavior of items in the dialog box or calls a **background procedure.** These three procedures are described later in this chapter, in "Hook and Filter Procedures." If you do not need these routines in your application, specify `NIL`.

`theReply` is the look-up reply record that contains the object/type/zone tuple for the object, if any, that was selected by the user. The record also contains the AppleTalk address consisting of node/network/zone numbers.

```
TYPE
    LookupReply          =          RECORD
            theEntity    :          EntityName;
            theAddr      :          AddrBlock;
    END;
```

▲ **Warning**   When your application initially passes the `theReply` data structure into the `NuLookup` procedure, `theReply.theEntity` should contain the default zone and name. If the specified object is not in the list of accepted objects in `typeList`, the specified object is ignored, and only the default zone is set. If an appropriate match is found in the initial lookup, the specified zone and the specified name of the given object are selected when the dialog box comes up. ▲

`NuLookup` returns one of three values:

```
CONST
    nlOk        =        0;
    nlCancel    =        1;
    nlEject     =        2;
```

`nlOk` is returned if the user clicks the OK button in the dialog box. `nlCancel` is returned if the user clicks the Cancel button. `nlEject` is returned if the dialog box stops because of the hook procedure.

NuPLookup

A more versatile network lookup

`NuPLookup` performs much the same task as `NuLookup`, except that it gives programmers even greater control over customization of the network look-up dialog box. Additional parameters that can be specified are `userData`, `dialogID`, and `filterProc`.

Function

```
NuPLookup(where: Point; prompt: STR255; numTypes: INTEGER; typeList:
NLType; nameFilter: ProcPtr; zoneFilter: ProcPtr; hookProc: ProcPtr;
userData: LONGINT; dialogID: INTEGER; filterProc: ProcPtr; VAR
theReply: LookupReply): INTEGER;
```

`userData` is a field that the user can specify. It may be referenced from the hook procedure or the filter procedure with the `refCon` field of the dialog box record. `refCon` is a handle to the `userData` value.

The following code fragment demonstrates how to access the `userData` field:

```
TYPE
      LongH          =          ^LongPtr;
      LongPtr        =          ^LONGINT;

BEGIN
      myUserData     :=         LongH (GetWRefCon (theDialog))^^;
END;
```

`dialogID` is the resource ID for a dialog box (and for the corresponding dialog item list) that is to replace the standard look-up dialog box. All of the items in the replacement dialog item list must correspond to items in the standard dialog item list, although they can be moved around. *Table 7-1* lists standard items and their placement.

■ **Table 7-1** `TMAddSearch` search-area delimiters

Item number	Type	Rectangle (top, left, bottom, right)
1	OK button	{172, 240, 192, 310}
2	Cancel button	{172, 320, 192, 390}
3	Default highlight (`userItem`)	{168, 236, 196, 314}
4	Title (`staticText`)	{5, 15, 21, 210}
5	Item list (`userItem`)	{25, 15, 189, 210}
6	Zone list title (`staticText`)	{5, 240, 21, 391}
7	Zone list (`userItem`)	{25, 240, 147, 391}
8	Line (`userItem`)	{25, 225, 193, 226}
9	Version (`userItem`)	{197, 360, 207, 400}
10–13	Reserved	

`filterProc` is a modal dialog box filter procedure that `NuPLookup` calls after the standard `NuLookup` modal dialog box filter procedure. The format of the filter procedure is the same as that of a standard modal dialog box filter procedure. See Chapter 13 of *Inside Macintosh*, Volume I for more information about modal dialog filter procedures.

Hook and filter procedures

You can customize the operation of the network look-up dialog box for specific applications by using the filter procedures and the hook procedure. Filter procedures are used to filter zones from inclusion in the zone list, or to filter objects from the object list. The hook procedure is used to modify the behavior of items in the dialog box, and can also be used to call a background procedure.

Name filters

Before each item name is included in the network look-up dialog list, the item is passed to the name filter procedure for processing. Specify NIL if there is no filter procedure.

Function

```
MyNameFilter(theEntity: EntityName): INTEGER;
```

Description

This filter procedure is passed the network entity in theEntity, and returns an integer with one of the following values:

```
CONST
        nameInclude    =      1;
        nameDisable    =      2;
        nameReject     =      3;
```

nameInclude results in the inclusion of theEntity in the name list of the network look-up dialog box. nameDisable results in the inclusion of theEntity but disables it; the item in the list is visible but dimmed, and cannot be selected. nameReject causes theEntity not to appear in the list.

Zone filters

Before each zone item is included in the network look-up dialog list, the item is passed to the zone filter procedure for processing. Specify NIL if there is no filter procedure.

Function

```
MyZoneFilter(theZone: STR32): INTEGER;
```

Description

NuLookup and NuPLookup pass the name of an AppleTalk zone in theZone to the zone filter procedure, which returns an integer with one of the following values:

```
CONST
     zoneInclude    =      1;
     zoneDisable    =      2;
     zoneReject     =      3;
```

zoneInclude results in the inclusion of theZone in the zone list in the network look-up dialog box. zoneDisable results in the inclusion of theZone but disables it; the item in the zone list is visible but dimmed, and cannot be selected. zoneReject causes theZone not to appear in the zone list.

The hook procedure

NuLookup and NuPLookup call MyHookProc immediately after ModalDialog and before the standard hook procedure. ModalDialog returns a number that corresponds to the item clicked in the dialog box. NuLookup and NuPLookup employ a modal dialog box filter procedure that returns the item number for any physical items clicked in the dialog box, as well as the item numbers of any fake item clicked.

Function

```
MyHookProc(item: INTEGER; theDialog: DialogPtr): INTEGER;
```

Appropriate fake and real dialog box items are as follows:

```
CONST
{   real items in the dialog box item list   }
        hookOK              =       1;
        hookCancel          =       2;
        hookOutline         =       3;
        hookTitle           =       4;
        hookItemList        =       5;
        hookZoneTitle       =       6;
        hookZoneList        =       7;
        hookLine            =       8;
        hookVersion         =       9;
        hookReserved1       =       10;
        hookReserved2       =       11;
        hookReserved3       =       12;
        hookReserved4       =       13;

{   fake items in dialog box item list      }
        hookNull            =       100;
        hookItemRefresh     =       101;
        hookZoneRefresh     =       102;
        hookEject           =       103;
        hookPreflight       =       104;
        hookPostflight      =       105;
        hookKeyBase         =       1000;
```

The first 13 items correspond to physical items in the dialog box item list. The other items are fake items that correspond to certain actions that may need to be performed.

hookNull is a fake event that corresponds to a null event. The standard modal dialog box filter procedure returns hookNull in itemHit for null events.

hookItemRefresh causes the item list in the look-up dialog box to be discarded and regenerated.

hookZoneRefresh causes the zone list in the look-up dialog box to be discarded and regenerated. This value also causes a hookItemRefresh event to be generated.

hookEject causes all outstanding NBP lookups to be terminated and nLEject to be returned by NuLookup.

`hookPreflight` is processed after the zone and object lists are formed, but before the dialog box is displayed.

`hookPostflight` is processed before the dialog box is disposed of.

Any item greater than `hookKeyBase` is actually the ASCII value of the key that is pressed, offset by `hookKeyBase`. For example, an `itemHit` of 1032 decimal would correspond to a `keyDown` event generating a space (ASCII 32 decimal).

Quick reference

This section provides a reference to Communications Toolbox utilties. At the end of this section is a listing of routine selectors for programming in assembly language.

Routines

Communications Toolbox utilities	*See page*
AppendDITL(theDialog: DialogPtr; theDITL: Handle; method: DITLMethod);	*198*
CountDITL(theDialog: DialogPtr): INTEGER;	*201*
CTBGetCTBVersion: INTEGER	*192*
InitCTBUtilities: CTBUErr;	*192*
NuLookup(where: Point; prompt: STR255; numTypes: INTEGER; typeList: NLType; nameFilter: ProcPtr; zoneFilter: ProcPtr; hookProc: ProcPtr; VAR theReply: LookupReply): INTEGER;	*203*
NuPLookup(where: Point; prompt: STR255; numTypes: INTEGER; typeList: NLType; nameFilter: ProcPtr; zoneFilter: ProcPtr; hookProc: ProcPtr; userData: LONGINT; dialogID: INTEGER; filterProc: ProcPtr; VAR theReply: LookupReply): INTEGER;	*204*
ShortenDITL(theDialog: DialogPtr; numberItems: INTEGER);	*201*

Routines in your application	*See page*
MyNameFilter(theEntity: EntityName): INTEGER;	*206*
MyZoneFilter(theZone: STR32): INTEGER;	*207*
MyHookProc(item: INTEGER; theDialog: DialogPtr): INTEGER;	*208*

Constants and data types

```
TYPE
        NLType            =       ARRAY[0..3] OF RECORD
                hIcon     :       Handle;
                typeStr           Str32;
        END

        LookupReply       =       RECORD
                theEntity :       EntityName;
                theAddr   :       AddrBlock;
        END;

TYPE
        CTBUErr           =       OSErr;

CONST
        ctbuGenericError  =       -1;
        ctbuNoErr         =        0;


CONST

        curCTBUVersion    =        1;


        popupMenuCDEFproc =       1008;

        popupFixedWidth   =       $0001;
        popupUseCQD       =       $0002;
        popupUseAddResMenu =      $0004;
        popupUseWFont     =       $0008;

{menu title highlighting}
        popupTitleBold    =       $00000100;
        popupTitleItalic  =       $00000200;
        popupTitleUnderline =     $00000400;
        popupTitleOutline =       $00000800;
        popupTitleShadow  =       $00001000;
        popupTitleCondense =      $00002000;
        popupTitleExtend  =       $00004000;
        popupTitleNoStyle =       $00008000;
        popupLeftJust     =       $00000000;
        popupCenterJust   =       $00000001;
        popupRightJust    =       $000000FF;
```

```
        nlOk                    =        0;
        nlCancel                =        1;
        nlEject                 =        2;


{  values that name filterProc returns }
        nameInclude             =        1;
        nameDisable             =        2;
        nameReject              =        3;

{  values that zone filterProc returns }
        zoneInclude             =        1;
        zoneDisable             =        2;
        zoneReject              =        3;

{  dialog box items for hook procedure }
        hookOK                  =        1;
        hookCancel              =        2;
        hookOutline             =        3;
        hookTitle               =        4;
        hookItemList            =        5;
        hookZoneTitle           =        6;
        hookZoneList            =        7;
        hookLine                =        8;
        hookVersion             =        9;
        hookReserved1           =        10;
        hookReserved2           =        11;
        hookReserved3           =        12;
        hookReserved4           =        13;

{  fake items in dialog box item list }
        hookNull                =        100;
        hookItemRefresh         =        101;
        hookZoneRefresh         =        102;

        hookEject               =        103;

        hookPreflight           =        104;
        hookPostflight          =        105;

        hookKeyBase             =        1000;


TYPE
        DITLMethod              =        INTEGER

CONST
{  DITL manipulation constants  }
        overlayDITL             =        0;
        appendDITLRight         =        1;
        appendDITLBottom        =        2;
```

Pop-up menu control

Parameter	Before `NewControl`	After `NewControl`
`min`	ID of menu to use	1
`max`	width of pop-up title	number of menu items
`value`	pop-up title characteristics	currently selected item
`refCon`	resource type to append to menu using `AddResMenu` using pop-up `UseAddResMenu` variation code	available to application

Utility routine selectors

◆ *Assembly note:* Your application can access Communications Toolbox routines through a Macintosh Operating System trap. To call a routine, your application pushes the appropriate parameters onto the stack and invokes the trap macro that has the same name as the routine, preceded by an underscore. When expanded, these macros place the routine selector onto the stack, set A0 to point to the selector, and invoke the trap `_CommToolboxDispatch ($A08B)`. Upon returning from the trap, the trap macro pops the routine selector off the stack and places the return value into D0. It is your application's responsibility to clean up the stack by removing the parameters that were pushed onto the stack prior to invoking the trap macro.

AppendDITL	.EQU	1026	NuLookup	.EQU	1030
CountDITL	.EQU	1027	NuPLookup	.EQU	1031
CTBGetCTBVersion	.EQU	1029	ShortenDITL	.EQU	1028
InitCTBUtilities	.EQU	1025			

Chapter 8 Fundamentals of Writing Your Own Tools

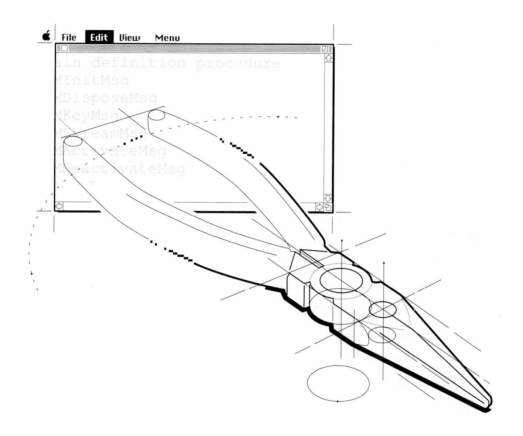

THIS CHAPTER provides general information about writing a connection tool, terminal emulation tool, or file transfer tool. You can find information specific to each kind of tool in Chapter 9, "Writing Connection Tools," Chapter 10, "Writing Terminal Tools," and Chapter 11, "Writing File Transfer Tools." Before writing a tool, you should read this chapter and the chapter about the type of tool you want to create.

This chapter discusses general concepts relevant to writing a tool. Then, it describes the six resources that are an essential part of any communications tool to be used with the Communications Toolbox. After that, the chapter provides example code to give you a better idea of what you need to do to write a tool. A "Quick Reference" at the end of the chapter shows you what you should name your six resources. It also lists the messages the File Transfer Manager sends to your tool, and the parameters that the File Transfer Manager passes with each message.

To write your own communications tool, you need to be familiar with the manager with which your tool will interface. See Chapter 3, "Connection Manager"; Chapter 4, "Terminal Manager"; or Chapter 5, "File Transfer Manager." You should also know about the Apple Computer, Inc. guidelines for communications tools, which are discussed in Appendix A.

You should also be familiar with the following topics:

- the Dialog Manager (described in *Inside Macintosh*, Volumes I, IV, V)

- the Script Manager (described in *Inside Macintosh*, Volume V)

- Creating stand-alone code (described in Macintosh Technical Note 110)

About writing a tool

The Communications Toolbox managers interact with an application in the same way that the Macintosh Toolbox managers do: the application calls a routine, which the appropriate manager handles by sending a message to a tool. For example, when an application requires a service, such as creating a new connection record, it calls the `CMNew` routine. The Connection Manager passes this request on by issuing a message, `cmInitMsg`, to the main code resource of the appropriate tool.

Most of the messages sent by one Communications Toolbox manager are similar to the messages sent by the other Communications Toolbox managers. This is because all of the managers have to handle similar tasks, such as tool selection, record validation, and string localization. For example, the initialization request messages are almost identical. The Connection Manager sends a `cmInitMsg`, the Terminal Manager sends a `tmInitMsg`, and the File Transfer Manager sends an `ftInitMsg`.

Because the majority of messages in one manager are similar to their counterparts in the others, this chapter shows you how to handle only Connection Manager messages. Even if you are not writing a connection tool, you can learn the basic concepts from the sample code that shows how a connection tool handles messages from the Connection Manager, and apply these concepts to writing a different kind of tool.

Descriptions of the routines associated with the various messages are given in Chapters 3, 4, and 5.

The six resources

You need to create six resources to make your own connection tool. All of these resources are described in this chapter, except the main code resource, which is described in detail in Chapter 9. (Resource descriptions for a terminal tool are provided in Chapter 10, and resource descriptions for a file transfer tool are provided in Chapter 11.)

There is one tool-related resource, which is optional:

`'cbnd'`   The bundle resource contains the name of the tool and information about what resources belong to the tool. For terminal emulation tools, this resource is of type `'tbnd'`; for file transfer tools, this resource is of type `'fbnd'`.

You also need to write five code resources, which *must* be part of your tool:

`'cdef'`   The main code resource performs the basic communications functions, such as `CMNew`, `CMRead`, and `CMWrite`. This resource is discussed in detail in Chapter 9. For terminal emulation tools, this resource is of type `'tdef'` and is discussed in Chapter 10; for file transfer tools, this resource is of type `'fdef'` and is discussed in Chapter 11.

`'cval'`   The validation resource validates connection records with `CMValidate`, and also fills in configuration record default values with `CMDefault`. For terminal emulation tools, this resource is of type `'tval'`; for file transfer tools, this resource is of type `'fval'`.

'cset'   The setup resource supports the custom tool-settings dialog box, which allows users to configure connection tools. For terminal emulation tools, this resource is of type 'tset'; for file transfer tools, this resource is of type 'fset'.

'cscr'   The scripting language interface resource handles the interface between a scripting language and the tool. For terminal emulation tools, this resource is of type 'tscr'; for file transfer tools, this resource is of type 'fscr'.

'cloc'   The localization resource handles localization of configuration strings. For terminal emulation tools, this resource is of type 'tloc'; for file transfer tools, this resource is of type 'floc'.

The bundle resource

The tool bundle contains the master list of resources that are associated with your connection tool. Besides the six standard resources, the tool bundle can contain references to any additional resources that your tool requires, such as dialog boxes or menus. Although your tool will work without a bundle resource, including one is a good programming practice. The bundle resource allows you to change resource IDs when conflicts arise without having to recompile your code.

Your connection tool can refer to resources with local IDs that the Communications Resource Manager can map to actual resource IDs (your tool should use the Communications Resource Manager routines CRMLocalToRealID and CRMRealToLocalID). The connection bundle resource, shown here, provides a data structure to accommodate this mapping.

```
type 'cbnd' {  /* or tbnd or fbnd */
        integer = $$CountOf(TypeArray) - 1;
        array TypeArray {
                literal longint;        /* Type */
                integer = $$CountOf(IDArray) - 1;
                wide array IDArray {
                        integer;        /* Local ID    */
                        integer;        /* Actual ID   */
                };
        };
};
```

The validation code resource

The validation code resource parses two possible messages from the manager—in the case of the Connection Manager, these are `cmValidateMsg` and `cmDefaultMsg`. An application or tool will request one of these services when it requires your tool to check the values in the connection record. For terminal tools, this record is called the *terminal record*; for file transfer tools, this record is called the *file transfer record*. An application or tool will request one of these services when it requires your tool to reset the connection record to its default values. Your connection tool should contain the default values for the connection record.

The validation code resource, an example of which is below, should be a resource of type `'cval'` for connection tools (`'tval'` for terminal tools and `'fval'` for file transfer tools). It should be able to accept the messages shown in this example:

```
FUNCTION cval(hConn: ConnHandle; msg: INTEGER; p1, p2, p3: LONGINT): LONGINT;
VAR
        pConfig:    ConfigPtr;


BEGIN
        CASE msg OF
        cmValidateMsg:         { hConn is valid here }
                BEGIN
                cval = DoValidate(hConn);
                END;
        cmDefaultMsg:  { hConn is not valid here }
                BEGIN          { p1 is a pointer to the configPtr }
                               { p2 is allocate or not }
                               { p3 is the procID of the tool }

                IF p2 = 1 THEN
                        BEGIN
                        pConfig := ConfigPtr(NewPtr(SIZEOF(ConfigRecord)));
                        ConfigHandle(p1)^ := pConfig;
                        { real programmers check errors here }
                        END
                ELSE
                        BEGIN
                        pConfig := ConfigHandle(p1)^;
                        END;
                DoDefault(pConfig);
                END;
        END; { case }
END;
```

The messages accepted by the validation code resource and their associated values are as follows:

```
CONST
{ validation code resource messages }
        cmValidateMsg          =       0;
        cmDefaultMsg           =       1;
```

For each of the messages defined here, `p1`, `p2`, and `p3` take on different meanings. These meanings are discussed in the message descriptions that follow. If your tool receives a message other than those shown, it should return `cmNotSupported`, `tmNotSupported`, or `ftNotSupported`.

cmValidateMsg

Your tool will receive `cmValidateMsg` when the application requires your tool to validate the fields in the connection record. Your tool should compare the values in this record with the values specified in your tool.

The example code on the following page shows how your tool can respond to `cmValidateMsg`.

After executing the code necessary to respond to `cmValidateMsg`, your code should pass back 0 if there were no errors, or 1 if the configuration record had to be rebuilt by your tool. `p1`, `p2`, and `p3` should be ignored.

```
{ perform validate here }
FUNCTION DoValidate(hConn: ConnHandle) : LONGINT;
VAR
        pPrivate:       PrivatePtr;
        pConfig:        ConfigPtr;


BEGIN
        DoValidate := 0;                { optimism reigns }
        pConfig := ConfigPtr(hConn^^.config);
        pPrivate := PrivatePtr(hConn^^.private);

        IF pConfig^.foobar = 0 THEN
                DoValidate := 0         { okey dokey }
        ELSE
                DoValidate := 1;        { uh-oh }
END;
```

cmDefaultMsg

Your tool will receive `cmDefaultMsg` when the application requires your tool to fill in the fields of a connection record. Default values should be specified in your tool. The example code shows how your tool can handle `cmDefaultMsg`.

After executing the code necessary to respond to `cmDefaultMsg`, `p1` should pass back a pointer to the configuration record pointer. If `p2` contained 1 when `CMDefault` was called, your tool should allocate the configuration record and return the pointer in `p1`. If `p2` was 0, then your tool should simply use the configuration pointer obtained by dereferencing `p1`.

```
PROCEDURE DoDefault(theConfig : ConfigPtr);

BEGIN
        WITH theConfig^ DO
                BEGIN
{ default is 9600 8 N 1  no handshaking }
```

```
                baudrate         := 9600;
                databits         := data8;
                stopbits         := stop10;
                paritybits       := noParity;

                WITH theConfig^.shaker DO
                BEGIN
                        fXOn     := 0;
                        fCTS     := 0;
                        xOn      := CHAR($11);
                        xOff     := CHAR($13);
                        errs     := 0;
                        evts     := 0;
                        fInX     := 0;
                        fDTR     := 0;
                END;

                portName := GetFirstSerial;

                flags := 0;
                END;

END;
```

The setup definition code resource

Applications can present users with a custom dialog box containing tool-specific items that allows them to configure their own connections or select a connection tool. The Connection Manager routines CMSetupPreflight, CMSetupSetup, CMSetupItem, CMSetupFilter, and CMSetupCleanup make this possible.

The connection tool setup code resource should be a function called 'cset' ('tset' for terminal tools and 'fset' for file transfer tools), and should be able to handle the following parameters:

```
{ main entry point for cset resource }
FUNCTION cset(pSetup: CMSetupPtr; msg: INTEGER;
        p1, p2, p3: LONGINT): LONGINT;
TYPE
        LocalHandle = ^LocalPtr;
        LocalPtr = ^LocalRecord;
        LocalRecord = RECORD  { private tool setup context }
         foobar: LONGINT;
        END;

        IntPtr = ^INTEGER;
        EventPtr = ^EventRecord;
```

```
BEGIN
    CASE msg OF
    cmSpreflightMsg:
        BEGIN
        theCookie := CookiePtr(NewPtr(SIZEOF(CookieRecord)));
        CookieHandle(p3)^ := theCookie;        { send back theCookie }
        cset := Preflight(pSetup, theCookie);
        END;
    cmSsetupMsg:
        BEGIN
        theCookie := CookieHandle(p3)^;               { get the magic cookie }
        Setup(pSetup);                                { do the setup }
        END;
    cmSitemMsg:
        BEGIN
        theCookie := CookieHandle(p3)^;               { get the magic cookie }
        Item(pSetup, theCookie, IntPtr(p1));          { process the items hit }
        END;

    cmSfilterMsg:
        BEGIN
        theCookie := CookieHandle(p3)^;               { get the magic cookie }
        cset := Filter(pSetup, theCookie, EventPtr(p1), IntPtr(p2));
        END;
    cmScleanupMsg:
        BEGIN
        theCookie := CookieHandle(p3)^;               { get the magic cookie }
        DisposPtr(Ptr(theCookie));                    { and get rid of it }
        END;
    END; { case }
END;
```

Valid values for `msg` are as follows:

```
CONST
        cmSpreflightMsg      =      0;
        cmSsetupMsg          =      1;
        cmSitemMsg           =      2;
        cmSfilterMsg         =      3;
        cmScleanupMsg        =      4;
```

For each of the messages just shown, `p1`, `p2`, and `p3` take on different meanings. These meanings are discussed in the message descriptions that follow. If your tool receives a message other than those shown, it should return `cmNotSupported`, `tmNotSupported`, or `ftNotSupported`. When your tool handles these routines, it will use a `CMSetupStruct` data structure.

```
TYPE
        CMSetupPtr              =       ^CMSetupStruct;
        CMSetupStruct           =       RECORD
                theDialog       :       DialogPtr;
                count           :       INTEGER; {dialog item number of first appended item}
                theConfig       :       Ptr;
                procID          :       INTEGER
        END;
```

cmSpreflightMsg

Your setup-definition code resource should perform a function similar to that shown in the
example code when it receives `cmSpreflightMsg` from the Connection Manager.

When passed to your connection tool, `p3` will be a pointer to a `LONGINT` that gets passed to
the other routines during setup definition. `p3` should serve as `magicCookie` if the setup
definition procedure requires some private context.

After executing the code necessary to respond to `cmSpreflightMsg`, your connection tool
should return a handle to a dialog item list. This handle should then be disposed of by the caller of
this function.

```
FUNCTION Preflight(pSetup: CMSetupPtr; theCookie: LocalPtr): LONGINT;
CONST
        localID = 1;                            { we want DITL local ID 1 }

VAR
        hDITL: Handle;
        theID: INTEGER;
        oldRF: INTEGER:

BEGIN
        theCookie^.foobar := 0;                 { setup theCookie }

        theID := CRMLocalToRealID(ClassCM, pSetup^.procID, 'DITL', localID);
        IF theID = -1 THEN
                Preflight := 0                  { no DITL found }
        ELSE
        BEGIN
                oldRF := CurResFile;
                UseResFile(pSetup^.procID);  { procID is the tool refnum }
                hDITL := Get1Resource('DITL', theID);
                UseResFile(oldRF);

                IF hDITL <> NIL THEN
                DetachResource(hDITL);                  { got it so detach it }

                Preflight := LONGINT(hDITL);
        END;
END;
```

cmSsetupMsg

Your setup-definition code resource should perform a function similar to that shown in the example code when it receives `cmSsetupMsg` from the Connection Manager.

When passed to your connection tool, `p3` will be a pointer to `magicCookie`, which is a `LONGINT`.

```
PROCEDURE Setup(pSetup: CMSetupPtr);
CONST
        myFirstItem = 1;
        mySecondItem = 2;

VAR
        first:  INTEGER;                  { first item appended (0-based) }
        pConfig:ConfigPtr;

BEGIN
        WITH pSetup^ DO
        BEGIN
                first := count - 1;             { count is 1-based }
                pConfig := ConfigPtr(theConfig);    { get the config ptr }

                GetDItem(theDialog, first+myFirstItem, itemKind, itemHandle,
                        itemRect);
                SetCtlValue(ControlHandle(itemHandle), pConfig^.foobar);


                GetDItem(theDialog, first+mySecondItem, itemKind, itemHandle,
                        itemRect);
                SetCtlValue(ControlHandle(itemHandle), 1-pConfig^.foobar);

        END; {with}
END;
```

cmSitemMsg

Your setup-definition code resource should perform a function similar to that shown in the example code when it receives `cmSitemMsg` from the Connection Manager.

When passed to your connection tool, `p1` points to an item that was selected from the dialog box item list, and `p3` contains a pointer to `magicCookie`. Your tool can change the selected item by modifying the item number to which `p1` points.

```
PROCEDURE Item(pSetup: CMSetupPtr; pItem: IntPtr);
CONST
        myFirstItem         =       1;
        mySecondItem        =       2;


VAR
        first               :       INTEGER;            { first item appended (0-based) }
        pConfig             :       ConfigPtr;
        value               :       INTEGER;
BEGIN
        WITH pSetup^ DO
        BEGIN
                first := count - 1;                     { count is 1-based }
                pConfig := ConfigPtr(theConfig);        { get the config ptr }

                CASE pItem^ -first OF
                myFirstItem:
                        BEGIN
                        GetDItem(theDialog,first+myFirstItem,itemKind,
                                itemHandle,itemRect);
                        value := GetCtlValue(ControlHandle(itemHandle))
                        value := 1 - value;
                        pConfig^.foobar := value;   { stick into config record }
                        SetCtlValue(ControlHandle(itemHandle), value); { update control }
                        END;
                mySecondItem:
                        BEGIN
                        SysBeep(5);
                        FlashMenuBar(0);
                        END;
                END; { case }
        END; { with }
END;
```

cmSfilterMsg

Your setup-definition code resource should perform a function similar to that shown in the
example code when it receives cmSfilterMsg from the Connection Manager.

When passed to your connection tool, p1 will contain a pointer to an event record, p2 will
contain a pointer to an item clicked in the dialog box list, and p3 will contain a pointer to
magicCookie.

If the event that was passed to this function was handled, your connection tool should return 1;
otherwise, it should return 0.

```
FUNCTION Filter(pSetup: CMSetupPtr; theCookie: LocalPtr;
                    pEvent: EventPtr;pItem: IntPtr): LONGINT;
BEGIN

     Filter := 0;                          { not hungry }


     IF pEvent^.what = keyDown THEN        { eat all keyDowns }
     BEGIN
          SysBeep(5);
          Filter := 1;                     { processed }
     END;
END;
```

cmScleanupMsg

Your setup-definition code resource should perform a function similar to the one shown in the
example code when it receives cmScleanupMsg from the Connection Manager.

When passed to your connection tool, p3 will contain a pointer to magicCookie.

```
PROCEDURE myCleanup(p3: LONGINT);
BEGIN
     DisposPtr( Ptr(p3) );                 { dispose of magicCookie }
     p3 := 0;
END;
```

The scripting language interface code resource

Your connection tool's scripting language interface code resource is responsible for handling the
interface between your tool and a scripting language. Also, it must provide complete configuration
information for saving and opening documents.

Your scripting interface code resource must handle two messages: cmMgetMsg and
cmMsetMsg. It should be a resource of type 'cscr' ('tscr' for terminal tools and 'fscr' for
file transfer tools) and be able to handle the parameters that are shown in this example:

```
FUNCTION cscr(hConn: ConnHandle; msg: INTEGER; p1, p2, p3: LONGINT):
LONGINT;
VAR
     pConfig:      ConfigPtr;

BEGIN

     cscr := 0;     { for now }

     CASE msg OF
     cmMgetMsg:
          cscr := LONGINT(GetConfig(hConn));
     cmMsetMsg:
          cscr := SetConfig(hConn, Ptr(p1));
     END; { case }
END;
```

Valid values for `msg` are as follows:

```
CONST
        cmMgetMsg       =       0;
        cmMsetMsg       =       1;
```

For each of the messages defined here, `p1`, `p2`, and `p3` take on different meanings. These meanings are discussed in the message descriptions that follow. If your tool receives a message other than those shown, it should return `cmNotSupported`, `tmNotSupported`, or `ftNotSupported`.

cmMgetMsg

Your tool will receive `cmMgetMsg` from the Connection Manager when the application requires a string that describes the connection record. The sample code shows how your application can handle `cmMgetMsg`.

After executing the code necessary to respond to `cmMgetMsg`, your connection tool should return `NIL` if there was a problem constructing the configuration string. Otherwise, it should return a pointer to a null-terminated string that contains American English tokens representing the configuration record pointed to by `config` in the connection record.

```
FUNCTION GetConfig(hConn: ConnHandle): Ptr;
VAR
        thePtr:         Ptr;
        pConfig:        ConfigPtr;
        theString,
        string2:        STR255;

BEGIN
        pConfig := ConfigPtr(hConn^^.config);       { get the config record }
        theString := 'FOOBAR ';                     { attribute name is FOOBAR }
        NumToString(pConfig^.foobar, string2);      { get the attribute value }
        theString := CONCAT(string, string2);       { make the config string }
        thePtr := NewPtr(SIZEOF(LENGTH(theString)+1));

        IF thePtr <> NIL THEN
        BEGIN
                BlockMove(Ptr(LONGINT(@theString)+1),
                thePtr, LENGTH(theString)); { copy it }
                Ptr(LONGINT(thePtr)+LENGTH(theString))^ := 0;      { 0 terminate it }
        END;

        GetConfig := thePtr;                { bye bye }
END;
```

cmMsetMsg

Your tool will receive `cmMsetMsg` from the Connection Manager when the application requires your tool to set the fields of the connection record to values that are specified in a string. The Connection Manager will pass a pointer to this string as a parameter to this call. The sample code shows how your tool can handle `cmMsetMsg`.

When passed to your connection tool's scripting interface code resource, `p1` will be a pointer to an American English null-terminated string that contains tokens representing a configuration record.

Your tool should return one of the following values: a number less than –1 to indicate an `OSErr`, –1 to indicate a generic error, 0 if there was no problem with the string, or a positive number to indicate the character position where parsing was stopped.

The Connection Manager automatically calls `CMValidate` after your tool has responded to `cmMsetMsg`.

```
FUNCTION SetConfig(hConn: ConnHandle; theSource: Ptr): INTEGER;

VAR

        pConfig         : ConfigPtr;           { tool specific config record }
        paramStr,
        valueStr        : Str255;              { parameter and value strings }
        outOfTokens     : BOOLEAN;             { end of the line? }
        returnVal       : INTEGER;             { what to return }

BEGIN

        { Init some stuff      }
        pConfig := ConfigPtr(hConn^^.config);
        returnVal := noErr;

        IF (theSource^ = CHR(0)) THEN
                outOfTokens := TRUE
        ELSE
                outOfTokens := FALSE;

        WHILE NOT outOfTokens DO BEGIN
                (* Build the first token and put it into paramStr *)


                IF (paramStr = 'FOOBAR') THEN BEGIN
                        (* Build the next token and put it into valueStr *)

                        pConfig^.foobar := valueStr;

                END
                ELSE BEGIN
                        (* returnVal = location of the paramStr *)
                        LEAVE;
                END;


                (* index to next token *)

        END; { while }

        SetConfig := returnVal;
END;
```

The localization code resource

Your connection tool's localization code resource is responsible for providing the services necessary to localize your tool. It must handle two messages, `cmL2English` and `cmL2Intl`.

Your localization code resource should be a resource of type `'cloc'`. It should be able to handle the parameters shown in the example code.

```
FUNCTION cloc(hConn: ConnHandle; msg: INTEGER; p1, p2, p3: LONGINT) : LONGINT;
```

Valid values for `msg` are as follows:

```
CONST
        cmL2English   =      0;
        cmL2Intl      =      1;
```

For each of the messages defined here, `p1`, `p2`, and `p3` take on different meanings. These meanings are discussed in the message descriptions that follow.

cmL2English and cmL2Intl

Your tool will receive `cmL2English` from the Connection Manager when the application requires your tool to localize a string to English. When the parameters `p1`, `p2`, and `p3` are passed to your tool, `p1` will contain a pointer to a localized null-terminated string that contains tokens representing a configuration record; `p2` will contain a pointer that points to a second pointer. Your tool will have to allocate space for this pointer (by calling `NewPtr`), which contains the American English null-terminated configuration string. `p3` will contain a language identifier, which is defined in the discussion of the Script Manager in *Inside Macintosh,* Volume V.

Your tool will receive `cmL2Intl` from the Connection Manager when the application requires your tool to localize a string to a language other than English. When the parameters `p1`, `p2`, and `p3` are passed to your tool, `p1` will contain a pointer to an American English null-terminated string that contains tokens representing a configuration record; `p2` will contain a pointer to a second pointer. Your tool will have to allocate space for this pointer, which contains the localized configuration string. `p3` will contain a language identifier, which is defined in the Script Manager in *Inside Macintosh,* Volume V. The next code example shows how your tool can handle both `cmL2English` and `cmL2Intl`.

After executing the code necessary to respond to `cmL2English` or `cmL2Intl`, your routine should return `NIL` if there was a Memory Manager error or if the language requested is not available. It should also return any appropriate error code in the status field of the connection record.

```
{ main entry point for cloc resource }
FUNCTION cloc(hConn: ConnHandle; msg: INTEGER; p1, p2, p3: LONGINT): LONGINT;
TYPE
        PtrPtr = ^Ptr;

VAR
        outPtr: Ptr;
        procID: INTEGER;
```

```
begin
        outPtr := PtrPtr(p2)^;                  { get output pointer }
        case msg of
                cmL2English:
                        cloc := Translate( Ptr(p1),outPtr,p3,verUS);
                cmL2Intl:
                        cloc := Translate( Ptr(p1),outPtr,verUS,p3);
        end; {case}
        PtrPtr(p2)^ := outPtr;                   { return output pointer }
end; { mytscrDEF }


{ Translates an input config string from one language to another }
{ returns 0 if no problem, non zero if there is a problem }
{ This routine needs to allocate outputStr. }
{ if language is not supported, return 0 but leave outputStr NIL }

function Translate( inputStr: Ptr; var outputStr: Ptr;
                        fromLanguage,toLanguage: longint): longint;
BEGIN
end; { Translate }
```

`config`: the configuration record

An application using your tool may save and restore the contents of a configuration record to set the state of the connection at any time. The configuration record, therefore, should be self-contained and should not contain any pointers or handles to other data structures. Your tool allocates this record in response to `cmDefaultMsg`. The Connection Manager, not the tool, deallocates the configuration record when the application calls `CMDispose`.

Quick reference

This section contains reference information for the data structures, definition procedures, and resource types that you need to write a terminal tool. A table at the end of this section lists messages the Connection Manager sends to connection tools, and what is passed in the parameters with each message.

Data structures

```
TYPE
        CMSetupPtr           =       ^CMSetupStruct;
        CMSetupStruct        =       RECORD
            theDialog        :       DialogPtr;
            count            :       INTEGER;
            theConfig        :       Ptr;
            procID           :       INTEGER
        END;
```

Definition procedures

```
FUNCTION    cdef(hConn:    ConnHandle; msg: INTEGER; p1, p2, p3: LONGINT) : LONGINT;

FUNCTION    cval(hConn:    ConnHandle; msg: INTEGER; p1, p2, p3: LONGINT) : LONGINT;

FUNCTION    cset(pSetup:   CMSetupPtr; msg: INTEGER; p1, p2, p3: LONGINT) : LONGINT;

FUNCTION    cscr(hConn:    ConnHandle; msg: INTEGER; p1, p2, p3: LONGINT) : LONGINT;

FUNCTION    cloc(hConn:    ConnHandle; msg: INTEGER; p1, p2, p3: LONGINT) : LONGINT;
```

Resource types

```
type 'cbnd' {
        integer = $$CountOf(TypeArray) - 1;
        array TypeArray {
                literal longint;       /* Type */
                integer = $$CountOf(IDArray) - 1;
                wide array IDArray {
                        integer;       /* Local ID */
                        integer;       /* Actual ID */
                };
        };
};
```

■ Table 8-1 Connection Manager messages and parameters

Constant	Parameter 1 p1	Parameter 2 p2	Parameter 3 p3
Validation code resource messages			
cmValidateMsg* 0	-	-	-
cmDefaultMsg 1	VAR cmConfigRec:Ptr	allocate:Boolean	procID:short
Setup code resource messages			
cmSpreflightMsg* 0	-	-	VAR magicCookie:LONGINT
cmSsetupMsg 1	-	-	VAR magicCookie:LONGINT
cmSitemMsg 2	VAR item:itemSelected	-	VAR magicCookie:LONGINT
cmSfilterMsg* 3	myEvent:EventRecord	VAR item:itemHit	VAR magicCookie:LONGINT
cmScleanupMsg 4	-	-	VAR magicCookie:LONGINT
Scripting code resource messages			
cmMgetMsg* 0	-	-	-
cmMsetMsg* 1	configPtr:Ptr	-	-
Localization code resource messages			
cmL2English* 0	inputPtr:Ptr	VAR outputPtr:Ptr	fromLanguage:integer
cmL2Intl* 1	inputPtr:Ptr	VAR outputPtr:Ptr	toLanguage:integer

* Indicates the routine is a function that returns a LONGINT.

Chapter 9 **Writing Connection Tools**

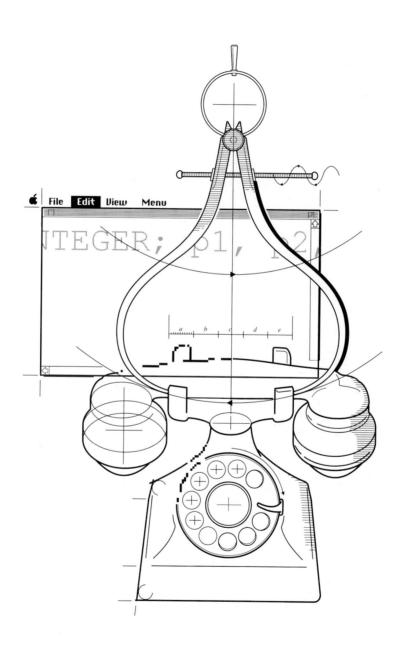

THIS CHAPTER tells you how to write the main code resource for a connection tool. There are at least five other code resources that you need to include as part of your tool; they are described in Chapter 8. You should read that chapter, as well as Chapter 3, before reading this chapter.

This chapter describes all the messages, parameters, and data structures that the Connection Manager passes to your tool's main code resource. Also in this chapter is sample code (with pseudocode mixed in) that will help you understand what your tool should do when it receives any of the messages. A "Quick Reference" at the end of the chapter shows you what you should name your six connection tool resources. It also lists the messages the Connection Manager sends to your tool, and the parameters that the Connection Manager passes with each message.

Your connection tool's main code resource

The purpose of the main code resource is to parse messages from the Connection Manager and then to branch to a routine that can handle each message. The main code resource should be a resource of type `'cdef'` and should be able to accept the parameters shown here.

```
FUNCTION  cdef(hConn: ConnHandle; msg: INTEGER; p1, p2, p3: LONGINT) : LONGINT;
```

The messages accepted by the main code resource, and their associated values, are as follows:

```
CONST
        cmInitMsg           =       0;
        cmDisposeMsg        =       1;
        cmSuspendMsg        =       2;
        cmResumeMsg         =       3;
        cmMenuMsg           =       4;
        cmEventMsg          =       5;
        cmActivateMsg       =       6;
        cmDeactivateMsg     =       7;
        cmIdleMsg           =       50;
        cmResetMsg          =       51;
        cmAbortMsg          =       52;
        cmReadMsg           =       100;
        cmWriteMsg          =       101;
        cmStatusMsg         =       102;
        cmListenMsg         =       103;
        cmAcceptMsg         =       104;
        cmCloseMsg          =       105;
        cmOpenMsg           =       106;
        cmBreakMsg          =       107;
        cmIOKillMsg         =       108;
        cmEnvironsMsg       =       109;
```

For each of the messages defined here, the three parameters `'cdef'` returns, namely p1, p2, and p3, take on different meanings. These parameters are described in the message descriptions that follow. Your tool can return an appropriate operating system error code, or `cmNotSupported` if it does not understand the message it received.

cmResetMsg

The Connection Manager will send `cmResetMsg` to your tool when the application requires your tool to reset the connection. The specific state to which your tool should reset the connection depends upon the connection protocol.

cmMenuMsg

The Connection Manager will send `cmMenuMsg` to your tool when a menu event has occurred in the application. When passed to your tool, `p1` will contain the menu ID, and `p2` will contain the menu item.

The sample code shows you a basic template into which you can code your tool's response to `cmMenuMsg`. When done, your tool should pass back 0 if the menu event was not handled, and 1 if it was.

```
FUNCTION myMenu(hConn : ConnHandle; mID : INTEGER; mItem: INTEGER) : LONGINT;
BEGIN
        myMenu := 0;
        { if mine then
                begin
                        myMenu := 1;
                        Process the menu command.
                end;
        }

END;
```

cmListenMsg

An application will call the `CMListen` routine when it requires your tool to wait for an incoming connection request. When passed to your tool, `p1` will contain the address of `CMCompletorRecord`, and `p2` will contain the timeout value in ticks.

Your tool uses a `CMCompletorRecord` structure when it receives a message to process asynchronously. This record contains a pointer to a completion routine your tool calls upon completion of the specified operation.

If the operation is to be performed asynchronously, the `async` field of the `CMCompletorRecord` is `TRUE` and the pointer to the completion routine is in the `completionRoutine` field. If the operation is to be performed synchronously, the `async` field of the `CMCompletorRecord` is `FALSE`. Your tool should ignore the `completionRoutine` field in this case.

The `CMCompletorRecord` is created in a local stack frame by the Connection Manager; therefore, your tool should copy the contents of the `CMCompletorRecrd` data structure if any information in it will be needed later.

```
TYPE
        CMCompletorPtr              =        ^CMCompletorRecord;
        CMCompletorRecord           =        RECORD
             async                  :        BOOLEAN;
             completionRoutine      :        ProcPtr;
        END;
```

The sample code shows you a basic template into which you can code your tool's response to `cmListenMsg`. When done, your tool should pass back an appropriate error code.

```
FUNCTION myListen(hConn : ConnHandle; completor : CMCompletorPtr;
                  timeout : LONGINT) : CMErr;
BEGIN
      { If connection is already open, return error condition }
      { Establish physical layer driver }
      { If completor^.async then
        begin
              Do async listen call.
              Set listen pending flag.
              Issue VBL task to terminate listen in specified timeout.
        end
        else
              Do sync listen call and return error when timeout.
      }
END;
```

cmIdleMsg

Your tool will receive `cmIdleMsg` when the application has idle time, such as when it needs your tool to check the status of an asynchronous routine. An application cannot call `CMIdle` from interrupt level.

cmEventMsg

The Connection Manager will pass `cmEventMsg` to your tool when an event occurred in a window associated with the connection tool. The sample code shows a template into which you can code your tool's response to `cmEventMsg`.

When passed to your tool, `p1` will be a pointer to the event record. The reference constant field of the window record will contain the connection handle.

```
PROCEDURE myEvent(hConn : ConnHandle; theEvent : EventRecord);
CONST
      CancelButton =   2;
VAR
      theDialog     :   DialogPtr;
      theItem       :   INTEGER;

BEGIN
      { Check if it is a dialog-related event }
      if IsDialogEvent(theEvent) then
      begin
            { get the item hit }
            if DialogSelect(theEvent,theDialog,theItem) then
            begin
                  if theItem = CancelButton then
                        { Cancel the connection }
            end;
      end
      else
            { Handle the keyDown, updateEvt, mouseDown and any other event here }
END;
```

cmAbortMsg

The Connection Manager will pass `cmAbortMsg` to your tool when the application has requested that a pending open or listen be aborted. The sample code shows a template into which you can code your tool's response to `cmAbortMsg`.

```
PROCEDURE myAbort(hConn : ConnHandle);
BEGIN
        { If no listen or open pending, return error condition. }
        { Terminate listen or open process. }
        { Close the physical layer driver. }
END;
```

cmAcceptMsg

The Connection Manager will pass `cmAcceptMsg` to your tool when the application has called the `cmAccept` routine. When passed to your tool, `p1` will contain 1 if your tool should accept the open request, or 0 if it should reject it.

Once your tool receives this message, it should clear the `cmStatusIncomingCallPresent` bit the next time it receives a `cmStatusMsg`.

The sample code shows a template into which you can code your tool's response to `cmAcceptMsg`. When finished, your tool should return an appropriate error code.

```
FUNCTION myAccept(hConn : ConnHandle; accept : INTEGER) : CMErr;
BEGIN
        { If the connection is already open, return error condition. }
        if accept <> cmAcceptOK then
        begin
                { Terminate the logical connection listen process. }
                { Close the physcial layer driver. }
        end
        else
                { set the open status bit }
END;
```

cmActivateMsg and cmDeactivateMsg

The Connection Manager will pass `cmActivateMsg` or `cmDeactivateMsg` to your tool when the application requires your tool to perform an action, such as installing or removing a menu from the menu bar in response to an activate or deactivate message.

cmSuspendMsg and cmResumeMsg

The Connection Manager will pass `cmSuspendMsg` or `cmResumeMsg` to your tool when the application requires your tool to perform an action, such as installing or removing a menu from the menu bar in response to a suspend or resume message.

cmInitMsg

The Connection Manager will pass `cmInitMsg` to your tool after the following sequence of events occurs. When a tool or application calls `CMNew`, the Connection Manager allocates space for the connection record. It then fills in some of the fields, based upon information that was passed in the parameters to the call. The Connection Manager fills in the `config` and `oldConfig` fields by calling `CMDefault`. Then, the Connection Manager passes `cmInitMsg` to your tool. After your tool has finished responding to `cmInitMsg`, the Connection Manager calls `CMValidate`.

If your tool allocates space for internal buffers in the `bufferArray` field of the connection record, applications and the Connection Manager must not manipulate the space. Also, your tool is responsible for freeing the space (in response to `cmDisposeMsg`). Connection tools are not required to use the `bufferArray` field.

The sample code shows how your tool can respond to `cmInitMsg`. After executing the code necessary to respond to `cmInitMsg`, your code should pass back an appropriate `OsErr` or `CMErr`.

```
FUNCTION        myInit(hConn: ConnHandle): CMErr;
VAR
        state: SignedByte;

BEGIN
        myInit := noErr;                          { optimism }
        state := HGetState(Handle(hConn));        { save handle state }
        HLock(Handle(hConn));                     { lock it down }

        WITH hConn^^ DO
        BEGIN
                flags := BOR(flags, cmData);          { yes we do data }
                IF BAND(flags, cmAttn) <> 0 THEN      { turn off attention }
                        flags := BXOR(flags, cmAttn);
                IF BAND(flags, cmCntl) <> 0 THEN      { turn off control }
                        flags := BXOR(flags, cmCntl);

                errCode := noErr;                     { optimism reigns }

                { need to check MemErr here }
                bufferArray[cmDataIn] := NewPtr(bufSizes[cmDataIn]);
                bufferArray[cmDataOut] := NewPtr(bufSizes[cmDataOut]);

                private := PrivatePtr(NewPtr(SIZEOF(PrivateData)));
                WITH private^ DO
                BEGIN
                { fill in private data structure here }
                END;
        END;

        HSetState(Handle(hConn), state);
END;
```

cmDisposeMsg

A tool or application will call CMDispose when it must dispose of a connection record and its associated data structures.

The Connection Manager passes cmDisposeMsg to your tool before disposing of the config and oldConfig fields of the connection record. Next, the Connection Manager disposes of the connection record.

To handle cmDisposeMsg, your tool should dispose of any buffers allocated in response to cmInitMsg and any private data storage (referenced off of cmPrivate in the connection record). Your tool must not attempt to dispose of either config or oldConfig in the connection record, or of the connection record itself. Doing so will cause a system crash.

The sample code shows how your tool can respond to cmDisposeMsg.

```
FUNCTION myDispose(hConn: ConnHandle): CMErr;
VAR
        pPrivate: PrivatePtr;                    { tool privates }

BEGIN
        myDispose := noErr;

{ if the connection is open then call CMClose on it }

        DisposPtr( Ptr(hConn^^.private) );
        DisposPtr( Ptr(hConn^^.bufferArray[cmDataIn]) );
        DisposPtr( Ptr(hConn^^.bufferArray[cmDataOut]) );
END;
```


cmReadMsg and **cmWriteMsg**

A tool or application will call CMRead when it requires your tool to read data from a remote entity. Likewise, a tool or application will call CMWrite when it requires your tool to write data to a remote entity. The Connection Manager will handle these calls by passing cmReadMsg or cmWriteMsg to the appropriate connection tool.

If a channel is requested that is not supported by your tool (for example, if a read is requested on the attention channel when the attention channel is not supported), your tool should return cmNotSupported.

After executing the code necessary to respond to cmReadMsg or cmWriteMsg, your tool should pass back an appropriate OSErr or CMErr.

When cmReadMsg or cmWriteMsg is passed to your tool, p1 points to the CMDataBuffer record, p2 points to the CMCompletorRecord record, and p3 contains the timeout value. The timeout value specifies a time period, in ticks, within which the read operation must be completed. If your tool does not complete the operation within the specified time, it should pass back a timeout error. An application passes -1 when it wants no timeout. If the application specifies 0, your connection tool should read as many bytes, up to toRead bytes, as it can in one read attempt.

Depending on the connection protocol your tool is supporting, your tool might ignore the timeout parameter.

The **CMDataBuffer** *record*

A `DataBuffer` record contains information about where the read or write buffer is located, how many bytes are supposed to be read or written, the channel that is to be used, and an end-of-message flag. Your tool should be able to accommodate the data structure defined here:

```
TYPE
        CMDataBufferPtr        =       ^CMDataBuffer;
        CMDataBuffer           =       RECORD
            thePtr             :       Ptr;
            count              :       LONGINT;
            channel            :       CMChannel;
            flags              :       CMFlags;
        END;
```

These are the valid values for `channel`:

```
CONST
        cmData         =       $00000001;
        cmCntl         =       $00000002;
        cmAttn         =       $00000004;
```

The **CMCompletorRecord** *record*

Your tool uses a `CMCompletorRecord` structure when it receives a message to process asynchronously. This record contains a pointer to a completion routine your tool calls upon completion of the specified operation.

If the operation is to be performed asynchronously, the `async` field of the `CMCompletorRecord` is `TRUE` and the pointer to the completion routine is in the `completionRoutine` field.

If the operation is to be performed synchronously, the `async` field of the `CMCompletorRecord` is `FALSE`. Your tool should ignore the `completionRoutine` field in this case.

The `CMCompletorRecord` is created in a local stack frame by the Connection Manager; therefore, your tool should copy the contents of the `CMCompletorRecord` data structure if any information in it will be needed later.

```
TYPE
        CMCompletorPtr                =       ^CMCompletorRecord;
        CMCompletorRecord             =       RECORD
            async                     :       BOOLEAN;
            completionRoutine         :       ProcPtr;
        END;
```

cmReadMsg

If your tool receives `cmReadMsg` with `timeout` 0, it should return immediately, even if it cannot read all the requested bytes. For example, if your tool receives a read request with `timeout` 0 for 512 bytes, and only 63 are available, your tool should read 63 bytes, put 63 in the `count` field of the `CMDataBuffer`, and return `noErr`.

```
FUNCTION myRead(hConn : ConnHandle; dp : CMDataBufferPtr;
                completor : CMCompletorPtr;timeout : LONGINT) : CMErr;
VAR
        pPrivate        : privateptr;
        err             : OSErr;

BEGIN

        dp^.flags := 0;         { set flags to zero, this tool does not support it }
        pPrivate := privateptr(hConn^^.cmPrivate);
        { is connection open ? }
        if (BAND(pPrivate^.status , cmStatusOpen) = 0) then
        begin
                myRead :=  cmNotOpen;
                EXIT(myRead);
        end;

        if ( dp^.channel <> cmData) then    { trying to do something we cannot support }
        begin
                dp^.count := 0;
                myRead :=  cmNotSupported;
                EXIT(myRead);
        end;

        { if async read then install VBL task to check timeout
          else check the available data to read in driver buffer }

        { do the read }
        err := PBRead( ParmBlkPtr(@pPrivate^.myRBlk.theParamBlk),
                    completor^.async );

        { handle err condition }
        if err <> noErr then
        begin
                dp^.count := 0;
                hConn^^.errCode := err;
                myRead :=  err;
                EXIT(myRead);
        end;

        { set the bytes read }
        if (pPrivate^.myRBlk.theParamBlk.ioActCount = 0) &
           ((completor <> nil) & completor^.async) then
        begin
                dp^.count := 0;
                hConn^^.asyncCount[cmDataIn] := 0;
        end
        else
```

```
        begin
                dp^.count := pPrivate^.myRBlk.theParamBlk.ioActCount;
                hConn^^.asyncCount[cmDataIn] :=
                                pPrivate^.myRBlk.theParamBlk.ioActCount;

        end;


        myRead :=  noErr;
END;
```

cmWriteMsg

If your tool receives a cmWriteMsg with timeout 0, it should return immediately, even if it cannot write all the requested bytes. For example, if your tool receives a write request with timeout 0 for 512 bytes, and only 63 can be written immediately, your tool should write 63 bytes, put 63 in the count field of the CMDataBuffer, and return noErr.

```
FUNCTION myWrite(hConn : ConnHandle; dp : CMDataBufferPtr;
                completor : CMCompletorPtr;timeout : LONGINT) : CMErr;
VAR
        pPrivate        : privateptr;
        err             : OSErr;

BEGIN
        pPrivate := privateptr(hConn^^.cmPrivate);

        { is connection open ? }
        if (BAND(pPrivate^.status , cmStatusOpen) = 0) then
        begin
                myWrite :=  cmNotOpen;
                EXIT(myWrite);
        end;

        if ( dp^.channel <> cmData) then
        { trying to do something we cannot support }
        begin
                dp^.count := 0;
                myWrite :=  cmNotSupported;
                EXIT(myWrite);
        end;

        { install VBL task to check timeout if async write }

        err := PBWrite( ParmBlkPtr(@pPrivate^.myWBlk.theParamBlk), completor^.async );
        { handle error condition }
        if err <> noErr then
        begin
                dp^.count := 0;
                hConn^^.errCode := err;
                myWrite :=  err;
                EXIT(myWrite);
        end;
```

```
{ set the bytes write }
{ ** Be sure to have the ShortCircuit compiler variable turned on ** }
if (pPrivate^.myWBlk.theParamBlk.ioActCount = 0)
    AND ((completor <> nil) AND completor^.async) then
begin
        dp^.count := 0;
        hConn^^.asyncCount[cmDataOut] := 0;
end
else
begin
        dp^.count := pPrivate^.myWBlk.theParamBlk.ioActCount;
        hConn^^.asyncCount[cmDataOut] := pPrivate^.myWBlk.theParamBlk.ioActCount;
end;

    myWrite := noErr;
END;
```

cmStatusMsg

The Connection Manager will send `cmStatusMsg` to your tool when an application requires your tool to send it information about a connection.

The sample code shows how your tool can respond to `cmStatusMsg`. After executing the code necessary to respond to `cmStatusMsg`, your code should pass back both an appropriate `OsErr` or `CMErr`. Also, `p1` should contain a pointer to `CMBufferSizes`, and `p2` should contain a pointer to a variable that returns the connection status flags.

Connection status flags are a bit field, with each bit corresponding to a particular status attribute. You can find a description of the status attributes in "`CMStatus` Getting Connection Status Information" in Chapter 3.

```
FUNCTION myStatus(hConn : ConnHandle; Var size : CMBufferSizes;
                  Var theflag : LONGINT) : CMErr;
VAR
    pPrivate        : privateptr;
    count           : LONGINT;
    err             : OSErr;

BEGIN
    pPrivate := privateptr(hConn^^.cmPrivate);
    theflag := 0;
    if (BAND(pPrivate^.status, cmStatusOpen) = 0) then       { is connection open ? }
            size[cmDataIn] := 0
    else
    begin
            err := SerGetBuf( pPrivate^.outrefnum, count );
            { Check output driver buffer }
            size[cmDataOut] := count;
            err := SerGetBuf( pPrivate^.inrefnum, count );
            { Check input driver buffer }
            size[cmDataIn] := count;
            if (count > 0) then
                    theflag := BOR(theflag, cmStatusDataAvail);
```

```
                          { Set data availabe bit }
                  theflag := BOR(theflag, cmStatusOpen);
                  { the connection is established }
          end;


      { set the other flags }
      if BAND(pPrivate^.status, cmStatusDRPend) = cmStatusDRPend
                  then theflag := BOR(theflag, cmStatusDRPend);
      if BAND(pPrivate^.status, cmStatusDWPend)  = cmStatusDWPend
                  then theflag := BOR(theflag, cmStatusDWPend);
      if BAND(pPrivate^.status, cmStatusBreakPending) = cmStatusBreakPending
                  then theflag := BOR(theflag, cmStatusBreakPending);
      if BAND(pPrivate^.status, cmStatusListenPend) = cmStatusListenPend
                  then theflag := BOR(theflag, cmStatusListenPend);
      myStatus := noErr;
END;
```

cmOpenMsg

Your tool's main code resource will receive `cmOpenMsg` from the Connection Manager when an
application or tool requires your tool to open a connection. When passed to your tool, `p1` contains
a pointer to `CMCompletorRecord`, and `p2` contains the timeout value in ticks.

The sample code shows a template into which you can code your tool's response to
`cmOpenMsg`. The Connection Manager, after the connection tool passes control back to it, disposes
of `CMCompletorRecord`. Therefore, your tool should copy `CMCompletorRecord` if it will need
any information the record contains.

After executing the code necessary to respond to `cmOpenMsg`, your code should pass back an
appropriate `OSErr` or `CMErr`.

```
FUNCTION myOpen(hConn : ConnHandle; completor : CMCompletorPtr;
                timeout : LONGINT) : CMErr;
VAR
      pPrivate       : privateptr;
      config         : configptr;
      err1,err2      : OSErr;
      theSerial      : CRMSerialPtr;
      savedState     : SignedByte;


BEGIN

      pPrivate := privateptr(hConn^^.cmPrivate);
      config := configptr(hConn^^.config);

      { get the CRM device info }
      theSerial := GetSerialPtr(config^.portName);

      { check if drivers are already open
        if drivers are open, warn the application }

      {      first open output driver, then input driver }
```

```
myOpen := noErr;
savedState := HGetState(Handle(theSerial^.outputDriverName));
HLock(Handle(theSerial^.outputDriverName));
err1 := OpenDriver(theSerial^.outputDriverName^^, pPrivate^.outrefnum);
HSetState(Handle(theSerial^.outputDriverName),savedState);
if (err1 = 0) then                              { output opened successfully }
begin
        savedState := HGetState(Handle(theSerial^.inputDriverName));
        HLock(Handle(theSerial^.inputDriverName));
        err2 := OpenDriver(theSerial^.inputDriverName^^, pPrivate^.inrefnum);
        HSetState(Handle(theSerial^.inputDriverName),savedState);
        if (err2 = 0) then                      { input opened successfully }
                pPrivate^.status := cmStatusOpen
        else                                    { input failed }
        begin
                myOpen := err2;
                err2 := CloseDriver(pPrivate^.outrefnum); { so close output }
        end;
end
else myOpen := err1;

{ call completor routine here if async is open }

END;
```

cmCloseMsg

Your tool's main code resource will receive `cmCloseMsg` from the Connection Manager when an application or tool requires your tool to close a connection.

The sample code shows how your tool can respond to `cmCloseMsg`. When passed to your tool, `p1` contains a pointer to `CMCompletorRecord`, and `p2` contains the timeout value in ticks. The Connection Manager, after the connection tool passes control back to it, disposes of `CMCompletorRecord`. Therefore, your tool should copy `CMCompletorRecord` if it will need any information the record contains.

After executing the code necessary to respond to a `cmCloseMsg`, your code should pass back an appropriate `OsErr` or `CMErr`.

```
FUNCTION myClose(hConn : ConnHandle; completor : CMCompletorPtr;
                 now : LONGINT) : CMErr;
VAR
        pPrivate        : privateptr;
        err             : OSErr;

BEGIN

        pPrivate := privateptr(hConn^^.cmPrivate);

        { is connection open ? }
        if (BAND(pPrivate^.status , cmStatusOpen) = 0) then
```

```
        begin
                myClose := cmNotOpen;
                EXIT(myClose);
        end;


        { if break pending, kill break VBL }

        { if now, kill pending reads and writes
          else wait for pending reads and writes to clear }

        { close input and output drivers }
        err := CloseDriver(pPrivate^.inrefnum);
        if err <> noErr then myClose := err;
        err := CloseDriver(pPrivate^.outrefnum);
        if err <> noErr then myClose := err;

        { call completor routine here if async is closed }

END;
```

cmBreakMsg

Your tool's main code resource will receive `cmBreakMsg` when an application or tool requires your tool to effect a break operation upon a connection.

When passed to your tool, `p1` contains `duration` in ticks, and `p2` contains a pointer to `CMCompletorRecord`.

The sample code shows how your tool can respond to `cmBreakMsg`. The Connection Manager, after the connection tool passes control back to it, disposes of `CMCompletorRecord`. Therefore, your tool should copy `CMCompletorRecord` if it will need any information the record contains.

```
FUNCTION        myBreak(hConn: ConnHandle; duration: LONGINT;
                        completor: CMCompletorPtr): CMErr;
VAR
        pPrivate        :       PrivatePtr;
        pConfig         :       ConfigPtr;
        err             :       OSErr;
        foo             :       LONGINT;

BEGIN
        myBreak         := noErr;                       {optimism}

        pPrivate        := PrivatePtr(hConn^^.private);
        pConfig         := ConfigPtr(hConn^^.config);

        if ( BAND(pPrivate^.status, cmStatusOpen) = 0 ) THEN    { not open }
        BEGIN
                myBreak :=      cmNotOpen;
                Exit(myBreak);
        END;
```

```
          IF (pPrivate^.breakPending) THEN      { break pending }
          BEGIN
                  myBreak :=      cmNoErr;
                  Exit(myBreak);
          END;


          IF completor^.async THEN
          BEGIN
                  { do it asynchronously }
                  { start the break }
                  { start a timer (VBL or such) when it finishes it will
                          turn off the break and then call the completion routine
                          if necessary }
          END
          ELSE
          BEGIN
                  { start the break }
                  Delay(duration, foo);
                  { end the break }
          END;
END;
```

cmIOKillMsg

Your tool's main code resource will receive `cmIOKillMsg` when a tool or application requires your tool to terminate a pending asynchronous input or output request. When passed to your tool, `p1` contains the channel that `cmIOKillMsg` should affect.

The sample code shows how your tool can respond to `cmIOKillMsg`.

```
FUNCTION myIOKill(hConn : ConnHandle; channel : INTEGER) : CMErr;
VAR
          pPrivate        :       privateptr;
          localBlk        :       HParamBlockRec;
          Err             :       OSErr;

BEGIN

          pPrivate := privateptr(hConn^^.cmPrivate);

          if (channel <> INTEGER(cmDataIn)) AND (channel <> INTEGER(cmDataOut)) then
          begin
                  myIOKill := cmNotSupported;
                  { can't cancel something I don't supPrivateort }
                  EXIT(myIOKill);
          end;

          localBlk.ioCompletion := nil;
          if (channel = INTEGER(cmDataIn))    then              { cancel read }
                  localBlk.ioRefNum := pPrivate^.myRBlk.theParamBlk.ioRefNum
          else                                                  { cancel write }
                  localBlk.ioRefNum := pPrivate^.myWBlk.theParamBlk.ioRefNum;
```

```
            Err := PBKillIO(ParmBlkPtr(@localBlk),false);

            if (Err <> noErr) then hConn^^.errCode := Err;

            myIOKill := Err;
END;
```

cmEnvironsMsg

The Connection Manager will send `cmEnvironsMsg` to your tool when an application requires
your tool to send it information about the connection environment. The `ConnEnvironRec`, which
contains this information, is shown here.

```
TYPE
        ConnEnvironRecPtr       =       ^ConnEnvironRec;
        ConnEnvironRec          =       PACKED RECORD;
            version             =       INTEGER;
            baudRate            =       LONGINT;
            dataBits            =       INTEGER;
            channels            =       CMChannel;
            swFlowControl       =       BOOLEAN;
            hwFlowControl       =       BOOLEAN;
            flags               =       CMFlags;
        END;

TYPE
        CMFlags         =       INTEGER;

CONST
        cmFlagsEOM      =       $0001;

CONST
        cmData          =       $00000001;
        cmCntl          =       $00000002;
        cmAttn          =       $00000004;

        cmDataClean     =       $00000100;
        cmCntlClean     =       $00000200;
        cmAttnClean     =       $00000400;

        cmNoMenus       =       $00010000;
        cmQuiet         =       $00020000;

TYPE
        CMChannel       :       INTEGER;
```

This sample code shows how your tool can respond to `cmEnvironsMsg`.

```
FUNCTION myEnvirons(hConn: ConnHandle; VAR theEnvirons: ConnEnvironRec): CMErr;
VAR
        pConfig:        ConfigPtr;
```

```
BEGIN
        pConfig := ConfigPtr(hConn^^.config);        { get the config handle }
        myEnvirons := noErr;                         { optimism }

        IF theEnvirons.version < curConnEnvRecVers THEN
                myEnvirons := envBadVers             { bad environment version }
        ELSE
        BEGIN

                IF theEnvirons.version > 1 THEN              { too advanced for me }
                        myEnvirons := envVersTooBig;        { but give it a whirl }

                WITH theEnvironsDO
                BEGIN
                        dataBits := pConfig^.dataBits;
                        baudrate := pConfig^.baudrate;
                        swFlowControl := ((pConfig^.shaker.fInX) AND
                        (pConfig^.shaker.fXOn));
                        hwFlowControl := ((pConfig^.shaker.fDTR) OR
                        (pConfig^.shaker.fCTS));
                        flags := 0;                  { no special flags supported }
                        channels := cmData;    { data channel only }
                END;
        END;
END;
```

Completion routines

When your connection tool calls `MyCompletion`, the `errCode` field of the connection record contains the appropriate error code. Because the `errCode` field of the connection record is used by all of the Connection Manager routines, the connection tool must first save the current value of the `errCode` field, and then set it to the appropriate code for the completion, call the **completion routine**, then restore the previously saved value. If your tool has multiple outstanding asynchronous operations, your tool should disable interrupts while the completion routine is executing.

When your tool calls the completion routine in response to the completion of an asynchronous read or write, the `asyncCount` field of the connection record contains the actual number of bytes read or written.

Quick reference

This section contains reference information for the data structures, resource names, and resource types that you need to write a connection tool. A table at the end of this section lists all the messages the Connection Manager sends to your tool, and what is passed in the parameters with each message.

Data structures

CMDataBuffer

```
TYPE
        CMDataBufferPtr        =        ^CMDataBuffer;
        CMDataBuffer           =        RECORD
            thePtr             :        Ptr;
            count              :        LONGINT;
            channel            :        CMChannel;
            flags              :        CMFlags;
        END;
```


CMCompletorRecord

```
TYPE
        CMCompletorPtr            =        ^CMCompletorRecord;
        CMCompletorRecord        =        RECORD
            async                :        BOOLEAN;
            completionRoutine    :        ProcPtr;
        END;
```


CMSetupStruct

```
        CMSetupPtr            =        ^CMSetupStruct;
        CMSetupStruct        =        RECORD
            theDialog        :        DialogPtr;
            count            :        INTEGER;
            theConfig        :        Ptr;
            procID           :        INTEGER
        END;
```

Resource names

```
FUNCTION        cdef(hConn: ConnHandle; msg: INTEGER; p1, p2, p3: LONGINT) : LONGINT;

FUNCTION        cval(hConn: ConnHandle; msg: INTEGER; p1, p2, p3: LONGINT) : LONGINT;

FUNCTION        cset(pSetup: CMSetupPtr; msg: INTEGER; p1, p2, p3: LONGINT) : LONGINT;

FUNCTION        cscr(hConn: ConnHandle; msg: INTEGER; p1, p2, p3: LONGINT) : LONGINT;

FUNCTION        cloc(hConn: ConnHandle; msg: INTEGER; p1, p2, p3: LONGINT) : LONGINT;
```

Resource types

```
type 'cbnd' {
        integer = $$CountOf(TypeArray) - 1;
        array TypeArray {
                literal longint;        /* Type  */
                integer = $$CountOf(IDArray) - 1;
                wide array IDArray {
                        integer;        /* Local ID  */
                        integer;        /* Actual ID */
                };
        };
};
```

■ **Table 9-1** Connection Manager messages and parameters

	Constant	Parameter 1 p1	Parameter 2 p2	Parameter 3 p3
Main code resource messages				
cmInitMsg*	0	–	–	–
cmDisposeMsg	1	–	–	–
cmSuspendMsg	2	–	–	–
cmResumeMsg	3	–	–	–
cmMenuMsg*	4	menuID:Integer	menuItem:Integer	–
cmEventMsg	5	myEvent:EventRecord	–	–
cmActivateMsg	6	–	–	–
cmDeactivateMsg	7	–	–	–
cmIdleMsg	50	–	–	–
cmResetMsg	51	–	–	–
cmAbortMsg*	52	–	–	–
cmReadMsg*	100	buffer:CMDataBufferPtr	timeout:LongInt	Completor:CompletorPtr
cmWriteMsg*	101	buffer:CMDataBufferPtr	timeout:LongInt	Completor:CompletorPtr
cmStatusMsg*	102	VAR size:CMBufferSizes	VAR flags:CMStatFlags	–
cmListenMsg*	103	Completor:CMCompletorPtr	timeout:LongInt	–
cmAcceptMsg*	104	accept:Boolean	–	–
cmCloseMsg*	105	Completor:CMCompletorPtr	timeout:LongInt	–
cmOpenMsg*	106	Completor:CMCompletorPtr	timeout:LongInt	–
cmBreakMsg	107	duration:LongInt	Completor:CMCompletorPtr	–
cmIOKillMsg*	108	which:INTEGER	–	–
cmEnvironsMsg*	109	VAR theEnvirons:ConnEnvironRec	–	–
Validation code resource messages				
cmValidateMsg*	0	–	–	–
cmDefaultMsg	1	VAR cmConfigRec:Ptr	allocate:Boolean	procID:short

* Indicates the routine is a function that returns a LONGINT.

■ **Table 9-1** Connection Manager messages and parameters (continued)

	Constant	Parameter 1 p1	Parameter 2 p2	Parameter 3 p3
Setup code resource messages				
cmSpreflightMsg*	0	-	-	VAR magicCookie:LONGINT
cmSsetupMsg	1	-	-	VAR magicCookie:LONGINT
cmSitemMsg	2	VAR item:itemSelected	-	VAR magicCookie:LONGINT
cmSfilterMsg*	3	myEvent:EventRecord	VAR item:itemHit	VAR magicCookie:LONGINT
cmScleanupMsg	4	-	-	VAR magicCookie:LONGINT
Scripting code resource messages				
cmMgetMsg*	0	-	-	-
cmMsetMsg*	1	configPtr:Ptr	-	-
Localization code resource messages				
cmL2English*	0	inputPtr:Ptr	VAR outputPtr:Ptr	fromLanguage:integer
cmL2Intl*	1	inputPtr:Ptr	VAR outputPtr:Ptr	toLanguage:integer

* Indicates the routine is a function that returns a LONGINT.

Chapter 10 **Writing Terminal Tools**

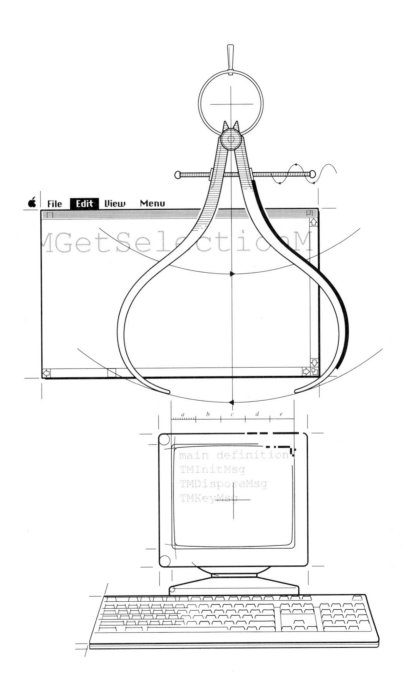

THIS CHAPTER tells you how to write the main code resource for a terminal tool. You will need to include six code resources in your tool; they are described in Chapter 8. You should read that chapter, as well as Chapter 4, before reading this chapter.

This chapter describes all the messages, parameters, and data structures that the Terminal Manager passes to your tool's main code resource. Also in this chapter is sample code (with pseudocode mixed in) that will help you understand what your tool should do when it receives any of the messages. A "Quick Reference" at the end of the chapter shows you what you should name your six terminal tool resources. It also lists the messages the Terminal Manager sends to your tool, and the parameters that the Terminal Manager passes with each message.

Your terminal tool's main code resource

The purpose of the main code resource is to parse messages from the Terminal Manager and then to branch to a routine that can handle each message. The main code resource should be a resource of type `'tdef'`, and should be able to accept the parameters shown here.

```
FUNCTION tdef(hTerm: TermHandle; msg: INTEGER; p1, p2, p3: LONGINT) : LONGINT;
```

The accepted messages are as follows:

```
CONST
        tmInitMsg             =        0;
        tmDisposeMsg          =        1;
        tmSuspendMsg          =        2;
        tmResumeMsg           =        3;
        tmMenuMsg             =        4;
        tmEventMsg            =        5;
        tmActivateMsg         =        6;
        tmDeactivateMsg       =        7;
        tmIdleMsg             =        50;
        tmResetMsg            =        51;
        tmKeyMsg              =        100;
        tmStreamMsg           =        101;
        tmResizeMsg           =        102;
        tmUpdateMsg           =        103;
        tmClickMsg            =        104;
        tmGetSelectionMsg     =        105;
        tmSetSelectionMsg     =        106;
        tmScrollMsg           =        107;
        tmClearMsg            =        108;
        tmGetLineMsg          =        109;
        tmPaintMsg            =        110;
        tmCursorMsg           =        111;
        tmGetEnvironsMsg      =        112;
        tmDoTermKeyMsg        =        113;
        tmCountTermKeysMsg    =        114;
        tmGetIndTermKeyMsg    =        115;
```

Your tool can return an appropriate operating system error code, or `tmNotSupported` if it does not understand the message it received.

tmInitMsg

The Terminal Manager will pass `tmInitMsg` to your tool after the following sequence of events occurs. When a tool or application calls `TMNew`, the Terminal Manager allocates space for the terminal record. It then fills in some of the fields, based upon information that was passed in the parameters to the call. The Terminal Manager fills in the `config` and `oldConfig` fields by calling `TMDefault`. Then the Terminal Manager passes `tmInitMsg` to your tool. After your tool has finished responding to `tmInitMsg`, the Terminal Manager calls `TMValidate`.

The following sample code shows how your tool can respond to `tmInitMsg`. After executing the code necessary to respond to `tmInitMsg`, your code should pass back an appropriate `OsErr` or `TMErr`:

```pascal
FUNCTION TermToolInit( hTerm : TermHandle ) : LongInt;
VAR
        privatePtr      :       TERMINALPrivatePtr;
        theState        :       SignedByte;
BEGIN
        theState := HGetState( Handle( hTerm));
        HLock( Handle( hTerm)) ;
        WITH hTerm^^ DO
        Begin
                { initialize TermToolInit to return no error }
                TermToolInit := TMNoErr ;

                { allocate space in the current heap for our private terminal tool record }
                privatePtr := TERMINALPrivatePtr( NewPtrClear( SIZEOF( TERMINALPrivateRecord)));

                IF privatePtr = NIL THEN
                BEGIN
                        {we have problem with allocating memory, return the error code and exit }
                        errCode := MemError;
                        TermToolInit := errCode;
                        Exit( TermToolInit );
                END
                ELSE
                BEGIN
                        { allocate terminal tool buffer space }
                        privatePtr^.tmprivatetermbuffer := NewPtrClear( MAXROW * MAXCOL );
                        IF (privatePtr^.tmprivatetermbuffer) = NIL THEN
                        BEGIN
                                { we have problem allocating the buffer space }
                                errCode := MemError;
                                TermToolInit := errCode;
                                { dispose the private terminal tool record }
                                DisposPtr( Ptr(privatePtr) );
                                Exit( TermToolInit );
                        END;

                        { get the terminal menu handle and menu ID and
                          assign it into out private tool record }

                END;
                { assign our terminal tool private record pointer to the terminal record }
                tmPrivate := Ptr( privatePtr );
        END;
        HSetState( Handle(hTerm), theState);
END;
```

`tmDisposeMsg`

A tool or application will call `TMDispose` when it must dispose of a terminal record and its associated data structures.

The Terminal Manager passes `tmDisposeMsg` to your tool before disposing of the `config` and `oldConfig` fields of the terminal record. Next, the Terminal Manager disposes of the terminal record.

To handle `tmDisposeMsg`, your tool should dispose of any buffers allocated in response to `tmInitMsg` and any private data storage (referenced off of `tmPrivate` in the terminal record). Your tool must not attempt to dispose of either `config` or `oldConfig` in the terminal record, or of the terminal record itself. Doing so will cause a system crash.

The sample code shows a template into which you can code your tool's response to `tmDisposeMsg`.

```
PROCEDURE TermToolDispose( hTerm:TermHandle );
VAR
        privatePtr      :       TERMINALPrivatePtr;
        theState        :       SignedByte;
BEGIN
        theState := HGetState( Handle( hTerm));
        HLock( Handle( hTerm) ) ;
        With hTerm^^ Do
        Begin
                privatePtr := TERMINALPrivatePtr( tmPrivate);

                { dispose the terminal buffer space }
                DisposPtr( privatePtr^.tmprivatetermbuffer );

                { dispose the terminal menu if there's any }
                { and it's not used by other tools }

                DisposPtr( Ptr(privatePtr) );
        END;
        HSetState( Handle(hTerm), theState);
END;
```

`tmKeyMsg`

Your tool will receive `tmKeyMsg` in response to a key-down, key-up, or autokey event in the application. The sample code shows how your tool can respond to these messages.

When passed to your tool, `p1` will point to the event record associated with the event. If the `keyCode` field of the event record contains –1, only `charCode` contains information.

```
PROCEDURE TermToolKey( hTerm:TermHandle; myEvent: EventRecord);
VAR
        theChar         :       CHAR;
        theKeyCode      :       CHAR;
        theModifier     :       INTEGER;
        theState        :       SignedByte;
```

```
BEGIN
        theChar := CHAR( BAND( myEvent.message, charCodeMask) );
        theKeyCode := CHAR( BAND( myEvent.message, keyCodeMask) );
        theModifier := myEvent.modifiers ;

        theState := HGetState( Handle( hTerm) ) ;
        HLock( Handle( hTerm) ) ;
        With hTerm^^ Do
        Begin
                { do special keyboard mapping if the keycode isn't -1 }
                { if keycode is -1, that is, fake keyDown event }

                { transmit data if the terminal is online }

                { echo data to the screen if online is off or localecho is true }
        END;
        HSetState( Handle(hTerm), theState);
END;
```

tmStreamMsg

The Terminal Manager will pass `tmStreamMsg` to your tool when the application has requested the `TMStream` routine. When passed to your tool, `p1` will point to the buffer of incoming data; `p2` will contain the length of the buffer in bytes; and `p3` will contain `flags`, which the application passed to `TMStream`. The sample code shows a template into which you can code your tool's response to `tmStreamMsg`.

After executing the code necessary to respond to a `tmStreamMsg`, your tool should return the number of characters it processed.

```
FUNCTION TermToolStream(hTerm: TermHandle; theBuffer: Ptr;
                        theBufferSize:LONGINT ; flag: CMFlags):LONGINT;
VAR
        theState        :       SignedByte;
        thePtr          :       Ptr;
        i               :       INTEGER;
        privatePtr      :       TERMINALPrivatePtr ;

BEGIN
        theState := HGetState( Handle( hTerm) ) ;
        HLock( Handle( hTerm) ) ;
        With hTerm^^ Do
        Begin
                { do special handling if flag is equal to EOM }

                privatePtr := TERMINALPrivatePtr( tmPrivate);
                With privatePtr^ Do
                BEGIN
                        thePtr  := tmprivatetermbuffer;
                        thePtr  := Ptr( Ord(thePtr) +
                                        tmprivatecurrentrow * tmprivatecurrentcol);
                        FOR i   := 1 TO theBufferSize DO
```

```
            BEGIN
                        { process data in theBuffer, such as moving the
                          cursor position, etc. }

                        { if data in theBuffer isn't a special escape sequence }
                        { assign data into our private terminal tool buffer }

                        thePtr := Ptr( LONGINT( theBuffer ) + i);
                        { advance tmprivatecurrentcol }
                        tmprivatecurrentcol := tmprivatecurrentcol + 1;
            END;

                    { return the number of chars we have processed }
                    TermToolStream := LONGINT( theBufferSize);
            END;
        END;
        HSetState( Handle(hTerm), theState);
END;
```

tmActivateMsg and tmResumeMsg

Your tool will receive tmActivateMsg when the application requires your tool to process an activate event (such as inserting menus into the menu bar, modifying a selection, or making the cursor blink) for a window that belongs to the Terminal Manager. The sample code shows a template into which you can code your tool's response to tmActivateMsg.

Your tool receives tmResumeMsg from the Terminal Manager when the application returns to the foreground in MultiFinder. Your tool can call the same routine in response to receiving tmResumeMsg as it calls in response to receiving tmActivateMsg.

```
PROCEDURE TermToolActivate( hTerm:TermHandle);
VAR
        privatePtr      :       TERMINALPrivatePtr;
        theState        :       SignedByte;
BEGIN
        theState := HGetState( Handle( hTerm));
        HLock( Handle( hTerm) );
        With hTerm^^ Do
        Begin
                privatePtr := TERMINALPrivatePtr( tmPrivate);

                { turn on the selection if there's any }
                IF NOT EmptyRect( selection.selRect ) THEN
                        HiliteSelection( hTerm);

                { put up my tool's menu if tmNoMenus isn't true }
                IF ( BAND( flags, tmNoMenus ) = 0 ) THEN
```

```
                    BEGIN
                            InsertMenu( privatePtr^.tmprivateMenuHandle, 0 );
                            DrawMenuBar;
                    END;
            END;
            HSetState( Handle(hTerm), theState );
    END;
```

tmDeactivateMsg and tmSuspendMsg

Your tool will receive tmDeactivateMsg when the application requires your tool to process a
deactivate event (such as removing a menu from the menu bar, modifying a selection, or making a
cursor stop blinking) for a window that belongs to the Terminal Manager. The sample code shows
how your tool can respond to tmDeactivateMsg.

Your tool receives tmSuspendMsg when the application goes to the background in
MultiFinder. Your tool can call the same routine in response to receiving tmSuspendMsg as it calls
in response to receiving tmDeactivateMsg.

```
PROCEDURE TermToolDeactivate( hTerm:TermHandle );
VAR
        theState        :       SignedByte;
        privatePtr      :       TERMINALPrivatePtr;
BEGIN
        theState := HGetState( Handle( hTerm) ) ;
        HLock( Handle( hTerm) ) ;
        With hTerm^^ Do
        Begin
                privatePtr := TERMINALPrivatePtr( tmPrivate);

                { turn on the selection if there's any }
                IF NOT EmptyRect( selection.selRect ) THEN
                        DeHiliteSelection( hTerm);
                { get rid of my tool's menu if tmNoMenus isn't true }
                IF ( BAND( flags, tmNoMenus ) = 0 ) THEN
                BEGIN
                        DeleteMenu( privatePtr^.tmprivateMenuID );
                        DrawMenuBar;
                END;
        END;
        HSetState( Handle(hTerm), theState );
END;
```

tmResizeMsg

Your tool will receive tmResizeMsg from the Terminal Manager when the application requires
your tool to resize the termRect. When passed to your tool, p1 points to the rectangle that
describes the new termRect. The code sample shows how your application can handle
tmResizeMsg.

```
PROCEDURE TermToolResize( hTerm:TermHandle; newtermRect: Rect );
VAR
        theState         :         SignedByte;
BEGIN
        theState := HGetState( Handle( hTerm) ) ;
        HLock( Handle( hTerm) ) ;
        With hTerm^^ Do
        Begin
                termRect := newtermRect ;
                { calculate new viewRect and visRect with the newtermRect }
                { redraw any newly exposed areas }
        End;
        HSetState( Handle(hTerm), theState);
END;
```

tmIdleMsg

Your tool will receive `tmIdleMsg` from the Terminal Manager when the application requires your tool to make the cursor blink. The sample code shows a template into which you can code your tool's response to `tmIdleMsg`.

```
PROCEDURE TermToolIdle( hTerm:TermHandle );
VAR
        theState         :         SignedByte;
BEGIN
        theState := HGetState( Handle( hTerm) ) ;
        HLock( Handle( hTerm) ) ;
        With hTerm^^ Do
        Begin
                { blink the cursor }
                InvertCursor( hTerm );
                { finish drawing any latent drawing that has yet to occur }
                DrawTermContent( hTerm );
                { search the terminal screen area for any searches that are going on... }
                IF mluField <> 0 Then
                        SearchTerm( hTerm );
        End;
        HSetState( Handle(hTerm), theState);

END;
```

tmUpdateMsg

Your tool will receive `tmUpdateMsg` from the Terminal Manager when the application requires your tool to update the terminal emulation window. When passed to your tool, `p1` will be a handle to the region that needs to be updated. The sample code shows a template into which you can code your tool's response to `tmUpdateMsg`.

```
PROCEDURE TermToolUpdate( hTerm:TermHandle ; visRgn:RgnHandle);
VAR
        theState        :       SignedByte;
BEGIN
        theState := HGetState( Handle( hTerm) ) ;
        HLock( Handle( hTerm) ) ;
        With hTerm^^ Do
        Begin
                { redraw the terminal area. The area to be drawn is specified by }
                { the region handle passed in. }
        End;
        HSetState( Handle(hTerm), theState);
END;
```

tmClickMsg

Your tool will receive tmClickMsg from the Terminal Manager when the application requires your
tool to handle a mouse-down event in the terminal emulation window; it should respond by calling
the application's click-loop procedure. Your tool should support placing and dragging the cursor.
When passed to your tool, p1 will contain a pointer to the event record.

The sample code shows a template into which you can code your tool's response to
tmClickMsg.

```
PROCEDURE TermToolClick( hTerm:TermHandle ; myEvent:Eventrecord);
VAR
        theState                :       SignedByte;
        clickInCachArea         :       Boolean;
BEGIN
        theState := HGetState( Handle( hTerm) ) ;
        HLock( Handle( hTerm) ) ;
        clickInCachArea := FALSE ;
        With hTerm^^ Do
        Begin
                { call the clickloop if there's any }
                if clikLoop <> NIL THEN
                BEGIN
                        clickInCachArea := CallclikLoop( refCon, clikLoop );
                END;
                if NOT clickInCachArea THEN
                BEGIN
                        { mouse click is in the terminal area, track mouse }
                END;
        End;
        HSetState( Handle(hTerm), theState);
END;
```

tmMenuMsg

Your tool will receive `tmMenuMsg` from the Terminal Manager when the user has chosen an item from a menu that belongs to your terminal tool. When passed to your tool, `p1` will contain the menu ID, and `p2` will contain the menu item. The sample code shows a template into which you can code your tool's response to `tmMenuMsg`.

After your tool has handled `tmMenuMsg`, it should return 0 if it did not handle the menu event, and 1 if it did.

```
FUNCTION TermToolMenu( hTerm:TermHandle ; menuID, menuItem:INTEGER ):LONGINT;
VAR
        theState        :       SignedByte;
        privatePtr      :       TERMINALPrivatePtr;
BEGIN
        theState := HGetState( Handle( hTerm) ) ;
        HLock( Handle( hTerm) ) ;
        With hTerm^^ Do
        BEGIN
                privatePtr := TERMINALPrivatePtr( tmPrivate );
                With privatePtr^ Do
                BEGIN
                        { does the menuID belong to the terminal? }
                        IF menuID = tmprivateMenuID THEN
                        BEGIN
                                { yes, it's one of ours, handle it based on the menuItem }

                                { unhilite the menu title }
                                HiliteMenu( tmprivateMenuID );
                                { if the menu belongs to the terminal tool, return 1 }
                                TermToolMenu := 1 ;
                        END
                        ELSE
                        { if the menu doesn't belong to the terminal tool, return 0 }
                                TermToolMenu := 0 ;
                END;
        END;
        HSetState( Handle(hTerm), theState);
END;
```

tmGetSelectionMsg

Your tool needs to be able to handle `tmGetSelectionMsg` to support cut and copy operations in the terminal emulation window. The sample code shows a template into which you can code your tool's response to `tmGetSelectionMsg`.

After responding to `tmGetSelectionMsg`, your tool should resize the data block (the passed-in handle) by calling `SetHandleSize` (p1, newSize), and a pointer to the scrap type (`ResType`) in p3. Your tool should also return an error code, if appropriate; 0 if there was no selection; or the size of the selected data.

```
FUNCTION TermToolGetSelection( hTerm:TermHandle ; DataHandle:Handle;
                              VAR selResType:ResType):LONGINT;
VAR
        theState        :       SignedByte;
        datasize        :       LONGINT;
BEGIN
        theState := HGetState( Handle( hTerm ) ) ;
        HLock( Handle( hTerm) ) ;
        With hTerm^^ Do
        BEGIN
                IF NOT EmptyRect( selection.selRect ) THEN
                BEGIN
                        { there's a selection }

                        { calculate the size of the selection }
                        datasize := GetSelectionSize( hTerm);
                        { grow DataHandle according to the size }
                        SetHandleSize(DataHandle, datasize );
                        { copy the data into DataHandle }

                        selResType := 'TEXT';
                        TermToolGetSelection := datasize ;
                END
                ELSE
                        { there's no selection }
                        TermToolGetSelection := 0 ;
        END;
        HSetState( Handle(hTerm), theState);
END;
```

tmSetSelectionMsg

An application will call TMSetSelection when it requires your tool to highlight an area of the
terminal emulation window. When passed to your tool, p1 will point to the field that needs to be
highlighted, and p2 will describe the type of selection. The example code shows a template into
which you can code your tool's response to tmSetSelectionMsg.

```
PROCEDURE TermToolSetSelection( hTerm:TermHandle ; mySelection:TMSelection;
                               myselType:LONGINT);
VAR
        theState        :       SignedByte;
BEGIN
        theState := HGetState( Handle( hTerm) ) ;
        HLock( Handle( hTerm) ) ;
        With hTerm^^ Do
        BEGIN
                IF NOT EmptyRect( selection.selRect ) THEN
                        { dehilite old selection if there's any }
                        DeHiliteSelection( hTerm);
                { assign new selection record to the terminal record }
                selection := mySelection ;
                selType := myselType;
```

```
                    HiliteSelection( hTerm );
        END;
        HSetState( Handle(hTerm), theState);
END;
```

tmScrollMsg

An application will call `tmScroll` when it requires your tool to scroll the terminal emulation region either horizontally or vertically. (The application is responsible for scrolling the cache area, if it supports one.) When passed to your tool, `p1` will contain the amount of horizontal scrolling, and `p2` will contain the amount of vertical scrolling. The example code shows a template into which you can code your tool's response to `tmScrollMsg`.

```
PROCEDURE TermToolScroll( hTerm:TermHandle; deltaH, deltaV:LONGINT );
VAR
        theState        :       SignedByte;
        updatergn       :       RgnHandle;
BEGIN
        theState := HGetState( Handle( hTerm) ) ;
        HLock( Handle( hTerm) ) ;
        With hTerm^^ Do
        BEGIN
                updatergn := NewRgn;
                ScrollRect( viewRect, deltaH, deltaV, updatergn );
                { update the newly scrolled in area }
                DisposeRgn( updatergn);
        END;
        HSetState( Handle(hTerm), theState);
END;
```

tmResetMsg

Your tool will receive `tmResetMsg` when the application requires your tool to reset the terminal emulation window. This reset operation should purge all local screen buffers, be a local operation, and call the cache procedure if `tmSaveBeforeClear` is set in the terminal record.

The code sample shows a template into which you can code your tool's response to `tmResetMsg`.

```
PROCEDURE TermToolReset( hTerm:TermHandle );
VAR
        theState        :       SignedByte;
        error           :       Boolean;
BEGIN
        theState := HGetState( Handle( hTerm) ) ;
        HLock( Handle( hTerm) ) ;
        With hTerm^^ Do
        BEGIN
                { clear the screen }
                TermToolClear( hTerm );
                { copy the saved configuration into the current configuration record }
                BlockMove( oldConfig, config, sizeof( ToolConfigRecord) );
                { call the validate routine to update my tool's private record }
```

```
                        error := TMValidate( hTerm);
                END;
                HSetState( Handle(hTerm), theState);
END;
```

tmClearMsg

Your tool will receive `tmClearMsg` when the application needs your tool to clear the terminal
emulation window. This clear operation should purge all local screen buffers, be a local operation,
and call the cache procedure if `tmSaveBeforeClear` is set in the terminal record.

    The code sample shows a template into which you can code your tool's response to
`tmClearMsg`.

```
PROCEDURE TermToolClear( hTerm:TermHandle );
VAR
        theState        :       SignedByte;
BEGIN
        theState := HGetState( Handle( hTerm) ) ;
        HLock( Handle( hTerm) ) ;
        With hTerm^^ Do
        BEGIN
                { erase the screen }
                EraseRect( viewRect );
                { clear up the terminal buffer }

        END;
        HSetState( Handle(hTerm), theState);
END;
```

tmGetLineMsg

An application will call `TMGetline` when it requires your tool to send it a `TermDataBlock`, which
contains the data, character attributes, and line attributes. For example, the application might
require the data in `TermDataBlock` to update its cache area for a specified line. When passed to
your tool, `p1` contains the line number, and `p2` points to the `TermDataBlock`, which your tool
should fill in.

    The sample code shows a template into which you can code your tool's response to
`tmGetLineMsg`. Your tool should fill the `TermDataBlock` with new information and resize the
`theTermData.theData` handle for the requested line.

```
PROCEDURE TermToolGetLine( hTerm:TermHandle ; lineNo:LONGINT ;
                           VAR myTermBlock:TermDataBlock);
VAR
        theState        :       SignedByte;
BEGIN
        theState := HGetState( Handle( hTerm) ) ;
        HLock( Handle( hTerm) ) ;
        With hTerm^^ Do
        BEGIN
                myTermBlock.flags := tmTextTerminal;        { this is a text terminal }
                myTermBlock.auxData := NIL;                 { no style information }
```

```
                { grow the datahandle size to fit a line of data }
                SetHandleSize( myTermBlock.theData, MAXCOL );
                { copy the terminal content into myTermBlock.theData }
        END;
        HSetState( Handle(hTerm), theState);
END;
```

tmPaintMsg

An application will call `TMPaint` when it requires your tool to display the contents of a
`TermDataBlock`. When passed to your tool, `p1` will point to the `TermDataBlock`, and `p2` will
point to the rectangle into which your tool is to display the line.

If `theTermData.theData` is a handle to plain text (not styled), your tool can calculate the
number of characters to paint by calling `GetHandleSize`. If your tool requires the data in
`theTermData` after it passes control back to the calling application, it must make a copy of this
data, since the application may change or destroy `TermDataBlock`.

The sample code shows a template into which you can code your tool's response to
tmPaintMsg.

```
PROCEDURE TermToolPaint( hTerm:TermHandle; theTermData:TermDataBlock; drawRect:Rect );
VAR
        theState        :       SignedByte;
BEGIN
        theState := HGetState( Handle( hTerm) ) ;
        HLock( Handle( hTerm) ) ;
        With hTerm^^ Do
        BEGIN
                { given the terminal data block, redraw those contents }
                { within the boundaries of the given rectangle }
        END;
        HSetState( Handle(hTerm), theState);
END;
```

tmCursorMsg

An application will call `TMCursor` when it requires your tool to pass it the current location of the
cursor. When passed to your tool, `p1` will specify the type of cursor.

The sample code shows a template into which you can code your tool's response to
tmCursorMsg. Your tool should return the current cursor position.

```
FUNCTION TermToolCursor( hTerm:TermHandle; cursorType: TMCursorTypes ):LONGINT;
VAR
        theState        :       SignedByte;
        privatePtr      :       TERMINALPrivatePtr;
BEGIN
        theState := HGetState( Handle( hTerm) ) ;
        HLock( Handle( hTerm) ) ;
        With hTerm^^ Do
        BEGIN
                privatePtr := TERMINALPrivatePtr( tmPrivate );
```

```
                { return row and col if cursorType is text cursor }
        IF cursorType = cursorText THEN
                TermToolCursor := LONGINT( privatePtr^.tmprivatecursor) ;
                { else return pixels if cursorType is graphic cursor }
        END;
        HSetState( Handle(hTerm), theState);
END;
```

tmGetEnvironsMsg

Your tool will receive `tmGetEnvironsMsg` when the application has called the `TMGetTermEnvirons`
routine. When passed to your tool, `p1` will point to the `TermEnvironRec`. Your tool should fill in this
record.

The sample code shows a template into which you can code your tool's response to `tmGetEnvironsMsg`.

```
FUNCTION TermToolGetEnvirons( hTerm:TermHandle ;
                                VAR myTermEnvRec:TermEnvironRec):LONGINT;
VAR
        theState      :       SignedByte;
        privatePtr    :       TERMINALPrivatePtr;
BEGIN
        theState := HGetState( Handle( hTerm) ) ;
        HLock( Handle( hTerm) ) ;
        With hTerm^^, myTermEnvRec Do
        BEGIN
                privatePtr := TERMINALPrivatePtr( tmPrivate );
                { return error if the given version number isn't the
                  same as the current version }
                IF version > curTermEnvRecVers THEN
                        TermToolGetEnvirons := envVersTooBig
                ELSE IF version < curTermEnvRecVers THEN
                        TermToolGetEnvirons := envBadVers
                ELSE BEGIN
                        termType := tmTextTerminal ;          { it's a text terminal }
                        textRows := MAXROW;
                        textCols := MAXCOL;
                        cellSize.h := privatePtr^.tmprivatecellsize.h;
                        cellSize.v := privatePtr^.tmprivatecellsize.v;
                        slop.h := THESLOP;
                        slop.v := THESLOP;
                        SetRect( graphicSize, 0, 0, 0, 0 );
                        SetRect( auxSpace, 0, 0, 0, 0 );
                        { return no error }
                        TermToolGetEnvirons := 0;
                END;
        END;
        HSetState( Handle(hTerm), theState);
END;
```

tmEventMsg

The Terminal Manager will pass `tmEventMsg` to your tool when an event occurs in a window associated with the terminal tool. The sample code shows a template into which you can code your tool's response to `tmEventMsg`. When passed to your tool, `p1` will be a pointer to the event record.

```
PROCEDURE TermToolEvent( hTerm:TermHandle ; myEventRecord:EventRecord);
VAR
        theState        :       SignedByte;
BEGIN
        theState := HGetState( Handle( hTerm) ) ;
        HLock( Handle( hTerm) ) ;
        With hTerm^^ Do
        BEGIN
                { an event has been received for a window or dialog box that was }
                { created by the terminal tool, process it accordingly. }
                CASE myEventRecord.what OF
                        mouseDown:
                                ;
                        keyDown, autoKey:
                                ;
                        updateEvt:
                                ;
                        activateEvt:
                                ;
                        END;
        END;
        HSetState( Handle(hTerm), theState);
END;
```

tmDoTermKeyMsg

Your tool will receive `tmDoTermKeyMsg` when the application has called the `TMDoTermKey` routine. When passed to your tool, `p1` will point to a string that corresponds to the key that was pressed. For example, if the user pressed the PF1 key, the string will be "PF1." If there is no key that corresponds to the string, your tool should do nothing.

The sample code shows a template into which you can code your tool's response to `tmDoTermKeyMsg`.

```
PROCEDURE TermToolDoTermKey( hTerm:TermHandle ; theStr: StringPtr );
VAR
        theState        :       SignedByte;
BEGIN
        theState := HGetState( Handle( hTerm) ) ;
        HLock( Handle( hTerm) ) ;
        With hTerm^^ Do
        BEGIN
                { perform the action determined by the special
                terminal key passed in, e.g HOME, PF1 etc.,
                and ignore theStr if it's not recognized by the terminal tool }
        END;
        HSetState( Handle(hTerm), theState);
END;
```

tmCountTermKeysMsg

Your tool will receive `tmCountTermKeysMsg` when the application requires your tool to pass it the number of special terminal key names that it supports.

The sample code shows how your tool can respond to `tmCountTermKeysMsg`.

```
FUNCTION TermToolCountTermKey( hTerm:TermHandle ):LONGINT;
VAR
        theState        :       SignedByte;
BEGIN
        theState := HGetState( Handle( hTerm) ) ;
        HLock( Handle( hTerm) ) ;
        With hTerm^^ Do
        BEGIN
                { return the number of special terminal keys
                  supported by the terminal tool }
        END;
        HSetState( Handle(hTerm), theState);
END;
```

tmGetIndTermKeyMsg

The Terminal Manager will pass `tmGetIndTermKeyMsg` to your tool when the application requires your tool to pass it the name of a special terminal key (for example, PF1, PA1, or DUP). When passed to your tool, `p1` contains the index (number) of the key.

The code sample shows a template into which you can code your tool's response to `tmGetIndTermKeyMsg`. When your tool is done, it should pass back a pointer to a Str255 return value that describes the key, or a pointer to an empty string if the index is invalid.

```
PROCEDURE TermToolGetIndTermKey(hTerm:TermHandle; index:INTEGER; VAR theStr:STR255);
VAR
        theState        :       SignedByte;
BEGIN
        theState := HGetState( Handle( hTerm) ) ;
        HLock( Handle( hTerm) ) ;
        With hTerm^^ Do
        BEGIN
                { return the terminal key supported by the terminal tool in theStr }
                { or return empty string if index is out of range }
        END;
        HSetState( Handle(hTerm), theState);
END;
```

Quick reference

This section contains reference information for the data structures, resource names, and resource types that you need to write a terminal tool. A table at the end of this section lists all the messages the Terminal Manager sends to your tool, and what is passed in the parameters with each message.

Data structures

TMSetupStruct

```
TYPE
        TMSetupPtr              =       ^TMSetupStruct;
        TMSetupStruct           =       RECORD
                theDialog       :       DialogPtr;
                count           :       INTEGER;
                theConfig       :       Ptr;
                procID          :       INTEGER
        END;
```

TMSearchBlock

```
TYPE
        TMSearchBlockPtr        =       ^TMSearchBlock;
        TMSearchBlock           =       RECORD;
                theString       :       StringHandle;
                where           :       Rect;
                searchType      :       TMSearchTypes;
                callBack        :       ProcPtr;
                refnum          :       INTEGER;
                next            :       TMSearchBlockPtr;
        END;
```

Resource names

```
FUNCTION       tdef(hTerm: TermHandle; msg: INTEGER; p1, p2, p3: LONGINT) : LONGINT;

FUNCTION       tval(hTerm: TermHandle; msg: INTEGER; p1, p2, p3: LONGINT) : LONGINT;

FUNCTION       tset(pSetup: SetupPtr; msg: INTEGER; p1, p2, p3: LONGINT) : LONGINT;

FUNCTION       tscr(hTerm: TermHandle; msg: INTEGER; p1, p2, p3: LONGINT) : LONGINT;

FUNCTION       tloc(hTerm: TermHandle; msg: INTEGER; p1, p2, p3: LONGINT) : LONGINT;
```

Resource Types

```
type 'tbnd' {
      integer = $$CountOf(TypeArray) - 1;
      array TypeArray {
            literal longint;              /* Type */
            integer = $$CountOf(IDArray) - 1;
            wide array IDArray {
                  integer;                /* Local ID  */
                  integer;                /* Actual ID    */
            };
      };
};

type 'tver' as 'vers';
```

■ Table 10-1 Terminal Manager messages and parameters

	Constant	Parameter 1 p1	Parameter 2 p2	Parameter 3 p3
Validation code resource messages				
tmValidateMsg*	0	–	–	–
tmDefaultMsg	1	VAR termConfigRec:Ptr	allocate:Boolean	procID:short
Setup code resource messages				
tmSpreflightMsg*	0	–	–	VAR magicCookie:LONGINT
tmSsetupMsg	1	–	–	VAR magicCookie:LONGINT
tmSitemMsg	2	VAR item:itemSelected	–	VAR magicCookie:LONGINT
tmSfilterMsg*	3	myEvent:EventRecord	VAR item:itemHit	VAR magicCookie:LONGINT
tmScleanupMsg	4	–	–	VAR magicCookie:LONGINT
Scripting code resource messages				
tmMgetMsg*	0	–	–	–
tmMsetMsg*	1	configPtr:Ptr	–	–
Localization code resource messages				
tmL2English*	0	inputPtr:Ptr	VAR outputPtr:Ptr	fromLanguage:integer
tmL2Intl*	1	inputPtr:Ptr	VAR outputPtr:Ptr	toLanguage:integer

* Indicates the routine is a function that returns a LONGINT.

■ **Table 10-1** Terminal Manager messages and parameters (continued)

	Constant	Parameter 1 p1	Parameter 2 p2	Parameter 3 p3
Main code resource messages				
tmInitMsg*	0	–	–	–
tmDisposeMsg	1	–	–	–
tmSuspendMsg	2	–	–	–
tmResumeMsg	3	–	–	–
tmMenuMsg*	4	menuID:Integer	menuItem:Integer	–
tmEventMsg	5	myEvent:EventRecord	–	–
tmActivateMsg	6	–	–	–
tmDeactivateMsg	7	–	–	–
tmIdleMsg	50	–	–	–
tmResetMsg	51	–	–	–
tmKeyMsg	100	myEvent:EventRecord	–	–
tmStreamMsg*	101	bufferPtr:Ptr	bufferSize:LontInt	flags:CMFlags
tmResizeMsg	102	newTermRect:Rect	–	–
tmUpdateMsg	103	visRgn:RgnHandle	–	–
tmClickMsg	104	myEvent:EventRecord	–	–
tmGetSelectionMsg*	105	dataHandle:Handle	VAR selTypes:TMSelTypes	–
tmSetSelectionMsg	106	theSelection:TMSelection	–	–
tmScrollMsg	107	deltaH:Integer	deltaV:Integer	–
tmClearMsg	108	–	–	–
tmGetLineMsg	109	lineNo:Integer	VAR myTermBlock:TermDataBlock	–
tmPaintMsg	110	myTermBlock:TermDataBlock	paintRect:Rect	–
tmCursorMsg*	111	cursorTypes:TMCursorTypes	–	–
tmGetEnvironsMsg*	112	VAR TermEnv:TermEnvironRec	–	–
tmDoTermKeyMsg*	113	termKey:Str255	–	–
tmCountTermKeysMsg*	114	–	–	–
tmGetIndTermKeyMsg	115	index:Integer	VAR termKey:Str255	–

* Indicates the routine is a function that returns a LONGINT.

Chapter 11 Writing File Transfer Tools

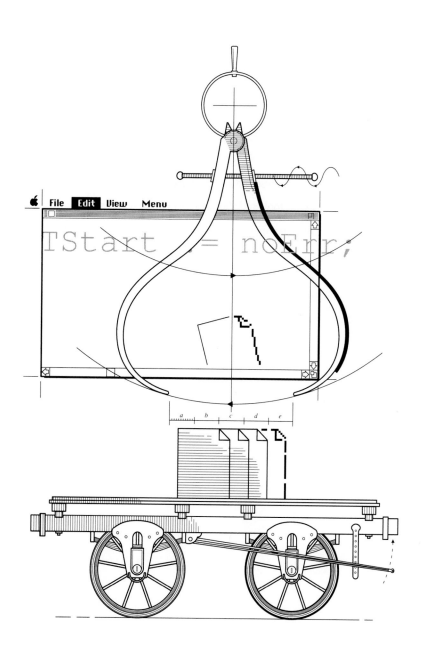

THIS CHAPTER tells you how to write the main code resource for a file transfer tool. You will need to include five other code resources as part of your tool; they are described in Chapter 8. You should also read that chapter, as well as Chapter 5, before reading this chapter.

This chapter describes all the messages, parameters, and data structures that the File Transfer Manager passes to your tool's main code resource. Also in this chapter is sample code (with pseudocode mixed in) that will help you understand what your tool should do when it receives any of the messages. A quick reference at the end of the chapter shows you what you should name your six file transfer tool resources. It also lists the messages the File Transfer Manager sends to your tool, and the parameters that the File Transfer Manager passes with each message.

Your file transfer tool's main code resource

The purpose of the main code resource is to parse messages from the File Transfer Manager and then to branch to a routine that can handle each message. The main code resource should be a resource of type `'fdef'` and should be able to accept the parameters shown here.

```
FUNCTION fdef(hTerm: TermHandle; msg: INTEGER; p1, p2, p3: LONGINT) : LONGINT;
```

The accepted messages are as follows:

```
CONST
        ftInitMsg           =       0;
        ftDisposeMsg        =       1;
        ftSuspendMsg        =       2;
        ftResumeMsg         =       3;
        ftMenuMsg           =       4;
        ftEventMsg          =       5;
        ftActivateMsg       =       6;
        ftDeactivateMsg     =       7;
        ftAbortMsg          =       52;
        ftStartMsg          =       100;
        ftExecMsg           =       102;
```

For each of the messages defined above, the three parameters that `'fdef'` returns, namely `p1`, `p2`, and `p3`, take on different meanings. These meanings are described in the message descriptions that follow. Your tool can return an appropriate operating system error code, or `ftNotSupported` if it does not understand the message it received.

ftInitMsg

The File Transfer Manager will pass `ftInitMsg` to your tool after the following sequence of events occurs. When a tool or application calls `FTNew`, the File Transfer Manager allocates space for the file transfer record. It then fills in some of the fields, based upon information that was passed in the parameters to the call. The File Transfer Manager fills in the `config` and `oldConfig` fields by calling `FTDefault`. Then the File Transfer Manager passes `ftInitMsg` to your tool. After your tool has finished responding to `ftInitMsg`, the File Transfer Manager calls `FTValidate`.

After executing the code necessary to respond to `ftInitMsg`, your code should pass back an appropriate `OsErr` or `FTErr`. Here's an example:

```
FUNCTION        myInit(hFT: FTHandle): CMErr;
VAR
        state   :       SignedByte;

BEGIN
        myInit := noErr;                                { optimism }
        state := HGetState(Handle(hFT));                { save handle state }
        HLock(Handle(hFT));                             { lock it down }

        WITH hFT^^ DO
```

```
        BEGIN
                errCode := noErr;                           { optimism reigns }

                private := PrivatePtr(NewPtr(SIZEOF(PrivateData)));
                WITH private^ DO
                BEGIN   { fill in private data structure here }
                END;
        END;

        HSetState(Handle(hFT), state);
END;
```

ftDisposeMsg

A tool or application will call `FTDispose` when it must dispose of a file transfer record and its associated data structures.

The File Transfer Manager passes `ftDisposeMsg` to your tool before disposing of the `config` and `oldConfig` fields of the file transfer record. Next, the File Transfer Manager disposes of the file transfer record.

To handle `ftDisposeMsg`, your tool should dispose of any buffers allocated in response to `ftInitMsg` and any private data storage (referenced off of `ftPrivate` in the file transfer record). Your tool must not attempt to dispose of either `config` or `oldConfig` in the file transfer record, or of the file transfer record itself. Doing so will cause a system crash.

The sample code shows a template into which you can code your tool's response to `ftDisposeMsg`.

```
PROCEDURE myDispose(hFT: FTHandle);
VAR
        err: FTErr;

BEGIN
        { abort FT in progress }
        { do cleanup }
        DisposPtr( Ptr(hFT^^.private) );
END;
```

ftStartMsg

Your tool will receive `ftStartMsg` from the File Transfer Manager when the application requires your tool to start a file transfer. The sample code shows a template into which you can code your tool's response to `ftStartMsg`.

Your tool should pass back the appropriate error message if unable to start the file transfer.

```
FUNCTION FTStartup(hFT: FTHandle): FTErr;
BEGIN
        FTStart := noErr;                                   { optimism }

        WITH hFT^^ DO
        BEGIN
                errCode := 0;
                flags := BOR(flags, ftIsFTMode);            { file transfer in progress }
```

```
        { initialize the variable }
        { open file }
        { prepare your I/O buffer }
        { draw the status dialog }

    END;

END;
```

ftExecMsg

An application calls `FTExec` to provide time for a file transfer in progress. Your tool should strive to be "MultiFinder-friendly" by minimizing the time it spends handling this message. When the file transfer is completed, your tool should close all files and dispose of any status dialog boxes.

```
PROCEDURE FTExec(hFT: FTHandle);
BEGIN
        { called when file transfer is in progress so do your
                stuff here...}
END;
```

ftAbortMsg

Your tool will receive `ftAbortMsg` from the File Transfer Manager when the application requires your tool to abort a file transfer. The sample code provides a template into which you can code your tool's response to `ftAbortMsg`.

If your tool is unable to abort successfully, it should pass back an appropriate error code.

```
FUNCTION FTAbort(hFT: FTHandle): FTErr;
BEGIN
        { abort the file transfer in progress here }
        { close the file }
        { dispose of the status dialog }
END;
```

ftActivateMsg and ftResumeMsg

Your tool will receive `ftActivateMsg` or `ftResumeMsg` when the application requires your tool to process an activate event (such as inserting menus into the menu bar). The sample code shows a template into which you can code your tool's response to `ftActivateMsg` or `ftResumeMsg`.

```
PROCEDURE myActivate(hFT: FTHandle);
BEGIN

END;
{
        p1, p2, p3 are ignored

        This routine may perform actions such as inserting a menu into the
        menu bar.
}
```

```
PROCEDURE myResume(hFT: FTHandle);
BEGIN

END;


{

        p1, p2, p3 are ignored

        This routine may perform the same actions as myActivate
}
```

ftDeactivateMsg and ftSuspendMsg

Your tool will receive `ftDeactivateMsg` or `ftSuspendMsg` when the application requires your tool to process a deactivate event (such as removing a menu from the menu bar) for a window that belongs to the File Transfer Manager.

ftMenuMsg

The File Transfer Manager will send `ftMenuMsg` to your tool when a menu event has occurred in the application. When passed to your tool, `p1` will contain the menu ID, and `p2` will contain the menu item.

The sample code shows a template into which you can code your tool's response to `ftMenuMsg`. When done, your tool should pass back 0 if the menu event was not handled, and 1 if it was.

```
FUNCTION myMenu(hFT: FTHandle; mID: INTEGER; mItem: INTEGER): LONGINT;
BEGIN
        myMenu := 0;                        { pessimism }
        { if mine then
                myMenu := 1;                { handle the menu event }
        }
END;
```

ftEventMsg

Your tool will receive `ftEventMsg` from the File Transfer Manager when an event has occurred in the application. When passed to your tool, `p1` will point to the event record, in which the reference constant field contains the file transfer handle.

Quick reference

This section contains reference information for the resource names and resource types that you need to write a file transfer tool. A table at the end of this section lists all the messages the File Transfer Manager sends to your tool, and what is passed in the parameters with each message.

Resource names

```
FUNCTION      fdef(hTerm: TermHandle; msg: INTEGER; p1, p2, p3: LONGINT) : LONGINT;

FUNCTION      fval(hTerm: TermHandle; msg: INTEGER; p1, p2, p3: LONGINT) : LONGINT;

FUNCTION      fset(pSetup: FTSetupPtr; msg: INTEGER; p1, p2, p3: LONGINT) : LONGINT;

FUNCTION      fscr(hTerm: TermHandle; msg: INTEGER; p1, p2, p3: LONGINT) : LONGINT;

FUNCTION      floc(hTerm: TermHandle; msg: INTEGER; p1, p2, p3: LONGINT) : LONGINT;
```

Resource types

```
type 'fbnd' {
      integer = $$CountOf(TypeArray) - 1;
      array TypeArray {
            literal longint;              /* Type */
            integer = $$CountOf(IDArray) - 1;
            wide array IDArray {
                  integer;                /* Local ID  */
                  integer;                /* Actual ID */
            };
      };
};
```

■ **Table 11-1** File Transfer Manager messages and parameters

	Constant	Parameter 1 p1	Parameter 2 p2	Parameter 3 p3
Main code resource messages				
ftInitMsg*	0	–	–	–
ftDisposeMsg	1	–	–	–
ftSuspendMsg	2	–	–	–
ftResumeMsg	3	–	–	–
ftMenuMsg*	4	menuID:Integer	menuItem:Integer	–
ftEventMsg	5	myEvent:EventRecord	–	–
ftActivateMsg	6	–	–	–
ftDeactivateMsg	7	–	–	–
ftAbortMsg*	52	–	–	–
ftStartMsg*	100	–	–	–
ftExecMsg	102	–	–	–
Validation code resource messages				
ftValidateMsg*	0	–	–	–
ftDefaultMsg	1	VAR ftConfigRec:Ptr	allocate:Boolean	procID:short
Setup code resource messages				
ftSpreflightMsg*	0	–	–	VAR magicCookie:LONGINT
ftSsetupMsg	1	–	–	VAR magicCookie:LONGINT
ftSitemMsg	2	VAR item:itemSelected	–	VAR magicCookie:LONGINT
ftSfilterMsg*	3	myEvent:EventRecord	VAR item:itemHit	VAR magicCookie:LONGINT
ftScleanupMsg	4	–	–	VAR magicCookie:LONGINT
Scripting code resource messages				
ftMgetMsg*	0	–	–	–
ftMsetMsg*	1	configPtr:Ptr	–	–
Localization code resource messages				
ftL2English*	0	inputPtr:Ptr	VAR outputPtr:Ptr	fromLanguage:integer
ftL2Intl*	1	inputPtr:Ptr	VAR outputPtr:Ptr	toLanguage:integer

* Indicates the routine is a function that returns a LONGINT.

Appendix A Guidelines for Communications Tools

THIS APPENDIX contains software design and human interface guidelines for communications tools. The guidelines presented in this appendix, while not hard-and-fast rules, will help ensure that your tool works with future releases of the Communications Toolbox, with other tools, and with applications that use the Communications Toolbox.

This appendix discusses the design goals your tool should implement. Then it discusses human interface considerations. Finally, the appendix describes hardware and software compatibility requirements.

To fully understand this appendix, you should first read Chapter 8, "Fundamentals of Writing Your Own Tool," and at least one of the following chapters: Chapter 9, "Writing Connection Tools"; Chapter 10, "Writing Terminal Tools"; or Chapter 11, "Writing File Transfer Tools."

Design goals

When you design your tool keep these goals in mind. Your tool should be

■ Self-contained: It should contain all the resources it needs in its bundle resource, and not need to make use of other tools or applications.

■ Task-specific: It should be a connection tool, a terminal tool, or a file transfer tool. It should respond to all the messages that the manager sends to it, but not to any messages that a Communications Toolbox manager intends a different tool to respond to. For instance, a terminal tool should not respond to Connection Manager messages and should not implement or maintain a data connection.

Keeping your tool self-contained

For users, installing a communications tool should be as simple as dragging the icon for that tool into the folder named *Communications Folder*. To achieve this level of simplicity, your tool must be self-contained; all the resources it needs for proper operation must be in the resource bundle.

There are, however, two exceptions to this principle. The first is when your tool uses a hardware interface that requires a driver to be loaded at INIT time, an unavoidable circumstance. The second exception is when your tool provides access to special data files (for example, a file of network addresses) that are kept on the user's system. Such data files provide your tool with a convenient way to store and distribute configuration information. In such a case, your tool should save all user settings in the session document; your tool must not require external files to reestablish a previously configured connection. Whenever your tool does require an external file to operate properly, it should check for the existence of that file and notify the user if the file is not present.

To prevent resource ID conflicts, your tool should use resource IDs that are out of the range of system resource IDs used by Apple Computer, Inc. Even when taking this precaution, font IDs may conflict. The only sure way to avoid this is to register your font IDs with Developer Technical Support. This problem arises because your tool's resource map gets linked into the resource chain, while your tool's code is executing, just below the system file's resource map.

Keeping your tool task-specific

The Communications Toolbox supports three kinds of communications tools: connection, terminal, and file transfer. Your tool should be one of these types and must not implement any services that another type of tool is intended to provide. For instance, if you are writing a terminal tool, it must not provide any connection services. Observing this principle helps ensure that tools will not interact with each other in unintended ways. Each type of tool is meant to provide specific services:

- Connection tools control the data path and its specifications. They can also alter the data path or strip high bits, as needed.

- Terminal tools control user input and output, including input from the mouse or keyboard, and output to the terminal emulation window.

- File transfer tools control sending and receiving disk files, or other encapsulated data entities. Only file transfer tools should manipulate disk files or the file system.

Tools written for the Communications Toolbox are meant to be used in a way that enables users to change one part of a communications configuration and still have the application work for them. For instance, a user running a VT100™ terminal emulation over a modem connection should be able to run the emulation over an X.25 connection and not notice any changes.

However, if a terminal or file transfer tool requires a specific type of connection (because of the protocol or standard being implemented) that is not in place, your tool should send an error to the application. A tool must never cause a system-level error when a user tries to use it in the "wrong" configuration. Rather, it should detect the presence or absence of a tool and send appropriate return codes to the application.

When writing a tool to implement an existing communications standard, you might find that the functions included in the standard require more than one type of tool for implementation. In cases like this, try to keep your tool task-specific by making use of the Macintosh interface. For example, if a connection protocol requires that your tool have status information constantly available, your tool can display this information in a separate window. You can also implement the standard by writing two task-specific tools that must be used together.

User interface considerations

This section describes the user interface considerations you should keep in mind when designing your tool. These considerations include:

- modeless tool operation
- the standard tool-settings dialog box
- windows and status dialog boxes
- error alerts
- menus
- handling errors
- using the right words

Modeless tool operation

Your tool should be modeless because the Communications Toolbox (and most applications that use it) allows for multiple simultaneous communications sessions; your session may not be the only one running (and your tool may be in use in more than one session at a time). Also keep in mind that even if the user is running a single session, he or she may be running that session under MultiFinder.

Although specific applications can present other user interfaces, the user will usually configure a tool from within an application by using the standard tool-settings dialog box, open or close the connection with menu items, and send or receive files with menu items. This dialog box and the menus are the basic aspects of the user interface.

The user will usually create a new document, configure it by using the standard tool-settings dialog box, and save it. Your tool should save all user settings in the session file, typically in a separate resource for each of the communications tool types (connection, terminal, and file transfer). The design of the Communications Toolbox assumes that the application will save settings in session documents so that a user can use a preconfigured document to open a connection. A user who uses several setting combinations is expected to prepare and use a separate document for each combination.

Users should not need to perform more configuration tasks when they open a connection or transfer a file; the only dialog boxes that should appear at this time are status dialog boxes. Therefore, your tool should fill in appropriate default settings when it is first selected in the standard tool-settings dialog box.

The standard tool-settings dialog box

Since users can use different tools inside the same application, the standard tool-settings dialog box for each tool ought to be visually compatible with those of other tools. This compatibility allows users to apply what they learn about configuring one type of tool to configuring a second type of tool. *Figure A-1* shows a sample tool-settings dialog box for a connection tool.

■ **Figure A-1** A sample tool-settings dialog box for a connection tool

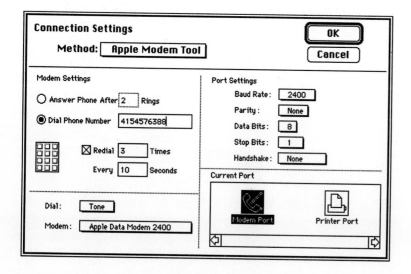

Many communications tools require more parameters set by the user than can be displayed attractively in a modal dialog box the size of the Macintosh Plus screen. Consider having your tool use 9-point Geneva for tool controls, instead of 12-point Chicago.

If your tool is complex and requires more controls than can fit in a modal dialog box even when using 9-point Geneva, it can divide these controls among two or more dialog boxes. The controls should be grouped according to function. Your tool should place the controls a user is most likely to select in the first dialog box displayed when the standard tool-settings dialog box comes up; it should place "power user" controls in subsequent dialog boxes.

Since the standard tool-settings dialog box is modal, your tool should not use additional modal dialog boxes that pop up on top of the standard tool-settings dialog box. If your tool requires a cascading dialog box, it should use dialog boxes like SFGetFile, which controls settings that do not usually need to be changed. Your tool should never display more than two layers of modal dialog boxes on the screen at the same time.

Windows and status dialog boxes

The terminal window is the only window that any of the communications tools displays during normal operation. But a connection or file transfer tool might need to pass information to the user. Since these tools should not place text in the terminal window, such a tool should display its own window or modeless dialog box.

Display of status dialog boxes is the most common method tools use to request input or display output. When a tool performs an operation that will take a long time—for example, transferring a file or establishing a complex connection—the tool should post a status dialog box. This status dialog box should have the following characteristics:

- It should be modeless.

- It should contain a Cancel button to allow the user to stop the operation. Use of the Command-period key combination for cancellation is problematic because multiple sessions may be running; users could inadvertently cancel dialog boxes other than the one they intend to cancel by pressing the Command-period key combination several times.

Figure A-2 shows an example of a file transfer tool status dialog box.

- **Figure A-2** Example file transfer tool status dialog box

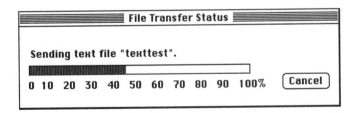

A tool might also put up its own window for user input and output during a session. For example, a connection tool might provide a command window that allows users to type in commands directly to control the connection. Your tool should either display this kind of window when the application initially selects your tool, or install a custom menu item that toggles in a manner similar to Hide Clipboard/Show Clipboard. Keep in mind that all command functions should be available through standard Macintosh controls, such as menu items and configuration dialog box settings. If your tool displays a command-line mode for compatibility with an existing standard, the command-line mode should supplement the standard Macintosh interface rather than replacing it.

Error alerts

Your tool is responsible for informing users of significant error conditions if the `cmQuiet` or `ftQuiet` bit is not set in the connection record or file transfer record. For instance, a connection tool should provide the user with status information when opening or closing a connection, and a file transfer tool should report the success or failure of a file transfer. However, a tool should not report less critical information, for example, showing a message when reading or writing data.

Menus

Your tool can place a menu of its own in the menu bar of the application. However, it should avoid displaying such menus, because the menu bar has limited available space, and application designers tend to assume that they can use the entire menu bar. Also, since up to three tools can be active at once, up to three tool menus might be displayed in addition to the menus owned by the application. If you do choose to implement a menu for your tool, choose a menu name that is as short as possible to avoid overflowing the menu bar.

Tool-specific menus are placed to the right of application menus. This means that if the menu items of your tool have Command-key equivalents, they will override any conflicting Command-key equivalents for application menus. If two tool menus are displayed at the same time, the rightmost menu will override the other in a similar fashion. Also, your application should not have any Command-key equivalents for non-ADB (Apple Desktop Bus™) keyboards; conflicts can arise out of the need to use the Control key as a Command key.

Handling errors

Your tool should allow users to set up any communications configuration, even ones that are unusable. This allows a system administrator to configure and save a session document for another person, who uses a different configuration from that on the system administrator's machine. In such cases, your tool should return an error only if the user attempts to open a connection, start terminal emulation, or initiate a file transfer using a setup that won't work.

Using the right words

Macintosh developers normally use terms that are intuitive and easy to learn, even for naïve users. However, this practice sometimes conflicts with the need to use established industry-standard terms, which may be difficult for the novice to understand. Since communications software developers often implement pre-existing industry standards, this problem is especially common for developers of communications tools.

Where standard terms for a function already exist and are widely accepted in the industry, you can use the standard terms. This convention is meant to ensure both that your tool properly implements the standard, and that experienced communications users who are familiar with the standard terms are not confused. However, you should attempt to make these terms as easily understandable as possible for inexperienced users. You can do this in several ways. Alternate standard terms are sometimes available. For example, the term *Show Controls* and its less intuitive counterpart *Transparent Mode* are used by Digital Equipment Corporation for the same VT102 terminal setting. You might also be able to embed the standard term in a longer description, or use small graphics in the tool-settings dialog box to make meanings clearer.

Compatibility requirements

The Communications Toolbox can run on all Macintosh computers that have:

- at least 1 MB of RAM

- Macintosh Plus (128K) ROM, or later versions

- system software version 6.0.4, or a later version

In order to be compatible with future releases of system software, it is important that your tool be 32-bit clean. Your tool may have additional requirements or restrictions.

Keyboard considerations

Terminal tools should support all Macintosh keyboards, including the original Macintosh keyboards with and without the detachable keypad. If arrow keys, function keys, the Control key, or other keys are required by your tool but are not on all keyboards, your tool should provide an alternative means of accessing them. Your tool could provide a keypad menu, or allow the user to use the Command key as a Control key.

Appendix B Communications Tools Scripting Interfaces

THE MACINTOSH Communications Toolbox provides a scripting interface that allows applications to configure tools by sending and receiving configuration strings. Configuration strings comprise keyword/value token pairs and enable applications to control all the fields in a tool's configuration record, including the elements in the tool's settings dialog box.

This appendix defines and describes the keywords and values supported by each of the tools in the Basic Connectivity Set. You should read relevant sections earlier in this book to understand how this information fits into the model already presented.

In the tables that follow, valid tokens appear in `Courier` typeface. Value tokens printed in *italics* are variables. Unless otherwise noted, value tokens can be set by applications (by calling `CMSetConfig`), by users (through the user interface), or by tools.

Six rules for configuration strings

Be sure your application follows these rules when using the scripting interface with communications tools.

1. Your application can set as few as none and as many as all of the fields in a configuration record with each call to `xxSetConfig`.

2. If a string contains more than one keyword/value token pair, separate each pair with a blank space.

3. The first item in a keyword/value token pair must be a keyword and the second must be the value your application assigns to the keyword.

4. Do not be concerned with case sensitivity; communications tools should check for case.

5. If either a keyword token or value token contains a space, enclose the token in double quotes ("").

6. Precede double quote and backslash characters that are part of the token with a backslash. (Double quotes that enclose a space need not be preceded with a backslash.)

ADSP Tool scripting interface

Keyword token names for the ADSP Tool are compatible with those used by the TCP Tool and the TGA Tool.

The variables used in NBP names should abide by the character restrictions of NBP. In particular, do not use the equals, "=", approximately equals, "≈", colon, ":", at-sign, "@", and asterisk, "*", characters. The ADSP tool does not enforce these restrictions to allow compatibility with future versions of NBP.

NBP names, AppleTalk addresses, and socket numbers must be quoted. To avoid potential problems, have your application put quotes around all tokens.

Keyword token	Value token*	Description	Example
LocalAddress	*string*	NBP form of local address. It is the concatenation of `LocalADSPName` and `LocalADSPType` in "name:type@zone" format. If your application passes `LocalAddress` into `CMSetConfig`, the tool ignores both the keyword token and its value. Only the ADSP Tool can set this value.	"Mike's Macintosh: Terminal Server@Stevens Creek 1"
LocalADSPName	*string*	Name to use, when combined with `LocalADSPType`, for registering local connection end's NBP name. The default value is taken from the Chooser name. If there is no Chooser name, `"Local User"` is the default. Only applications and users can set this value.	"Mike's Macintosh"
LocalADSPType	*string*	NBP type to use with `LocalADSPName` to register local connection end's NBP name. The default value is `"ADSP"`. Only applications and users can set this value.	"Terminal Server"
LocalSocket	*string*	NBP type to use with `LocalADSPName` to register local connection end's NBP name. The default value is `"ADSP"`. Only the ADSP Tool can set this value.	"Terminal Server"

(continued) ➡

* Valid tokens appear in `Courier` typeface. Value tokens printed in *italics* are variables.

Keyword token	Value token*	Description	Example
OurSocketNumber	*number*	When non-zero, socket number to be used for a connection. If `RegisterName` is zero and the application may call `CMListen`, `OurSocketNumber` must be non-zero. The socket is in hexadecimal format and must be quoted. The default is `0`. Only applications can set this value.	`"A7"`
RegisterName	*number*	If `0`, no name is registered.	`"2"`
		If `1`, and `LocalADSPName` and `LocalADSPType` are valid, then an NBP name is registered whenever the application calls `CMListen`. If the name exists already, an error is returned from `CMListen`. The default is `1`.	
		If `2`, it is not an error to issue a `CMListen` using the same name. In this case, the second `CMListen` uses the same AppleTalk socket as the first one. Only applications can set this value.	
RemoteAddrBlock	*number*	AppleTalk address (in hexadecimal format WWWWNNSS, where WWWW is the network number, NN is the node ID, and SS is the socket number) of remote connection end. If this field is non-zero, the remote name, type, and zone variables are ignored, and NBP is not used to determine the remote end's AppleTalk address when the application calls `CMOpen`. The address must be quoted. The default is `0`. Only applications can set this value.	`"a7f96cfc"`
RemoteAddress	*string*	NBP form of remote connection end's name. `RemoteAddress` is the concatenation of `RemoteADSPName`, `RemoteADSPType`, and `RemoteADSPZone` in the form `"name:type@zone"`. If your application passes `Remote0 Address` into `CMSetConfig`, the tool ignores both the keyword token and its value. Only the ADSP Tool can set this value.	`"Mega vax: Terminal Server@Vaxland"`

Keyword token	Value token*	Description	Example
RemoteADSPName	*string*	When opening a connection, name part of the full NBP name used to determine remote end's AppleTalk address. If this string is empty, `RemoteAddrBlock` must be non-zero, otherwise `CMOpen` fails immediately. The default is `Remote User`. Only applications and users can set this value.	`"Mega vax"`
RemoteADSPType	*string*	When opening a connection, type part of full NBP name used to determine remote end's AppleTalk address. If this string is empty, then `RemoteAddrBlock` must be non-zero, otherwise `CMOpen` fails immediately. The default is `ADSP`. Only applications and users can set this value.	`"Terminal Server"`
RemoteADSPZone	*string*	When opening a connection, zone part of full NBP name used to determine remote end's AppleTalk address. If this string is empty, `RemoteAddrBlock` must be non-zero, otherwise `CMOpen` fails immediately. The default is `""`. Only applications and users can set this value.	`"Vaxland"`
RemoteSocket	*string*	Concatenation of `RemoteADSPName` and `RemoteADSPType` in the form `"name:type"`. If `RemoteSocket` appears in a script, the tool generates an error. Only the ADSP Tool can set this value.	`"Mega vax:Terminal Server"`
RoundTripTime	*number*	Estimate of time (in seconds) for a packet to go from local machine to remote machine and back. `RoundTripTime` is used to set retry intervals for NBP and ADSP. The current version of ADSP uses 30 seconds as the probe timer, so don't set this variable to a larger value. Future versions of ADSP will not have this restriction, so no error-checking is performed. The default is 1. Only applications can set this value.	`"1"`

(continued) ➡

* Valid tokens appear in `Courier` typeface. Value tokens printed in *italics* are variables.

ADSP Tool scripting interface *(continued)*

Keyword token	Value token*	Description	Example
UseChooserName	*number*	If 1, Chooser name is used as name registered on network when a listen operation is made, regardless of any setting made by LocalName. If set, CMGetConfig also reports the Chooser name. The default is 0, and is automatically reset to 0 if the user modifies the local name when the human interface is displayed. Only applications can set this value.	"1"

* Valid tokens appear in Courier typeface. Value tokens printed in *italics* are variables.

Apple Modem Tool scripting interface

Keyword token	Value token*	Description	Example
Baud	*number*	Baud rate of modem. The default is 2400.	"2400"
DataBits	5|6|7|8	Number of data bits to use. The default is 8.	"5"
Dial	TONE|PULSE|MIXED	Dialing method. The default is tone.	"Tone"
Handshake	none|XON/XOFF	Type of handshaking on connection. The default is none.	"None"
HoldConnection	TRUE|FALSE	When true, tool does not drop DTR while closing connection. The default is false.	"True"
ModemType	*"A Modem Type"*	Type of modem to which computer is connected. The default is Hayes-Compatible Modem.	"Apple Data Modem 2400"
Parity	None|Even|Odd	Type of parity on connection. The default is none.	"None"
PhoneNumber	*"the phone number"*	Phone number to dial. The tool passes commas, parentheses, and dashes to the modem. Commas typically generate pauses. Parentheses and dashes are typically ignored. The default is "".	"4154576388"
Port	"Modem Port"|"Printer Port"|*other*	Current port for sending and receiving data. The default is Modem Port.	"Modem Port"
RemindDisconnect	TRUE|FALSE	When true and HoldConnection is true, tool reminds user it is holding DTR high. The default is false.	"True"
Retry	TRUE|FALSE	Specifies whether tool should retry number when remote modem does not pickup. The default is 3.	"True"

* Valid tokens appear in Courier typeface. Value tokens printed in *italics* are variables.

Apple Modem Tool scripting interface *(continued)*

Keyword token	Value token*	Description	Example
RetryInterval	*number*	Number of seconds between retries. The default is 10.	"1"
RetryTimes	*number*	Number of times to retry. The default is 3.	"3"
StopBits	1|1.5|2	Number of stop bits on connection. The default is 1.	"1"
TypeOfCall	Originate| Answer	Specifies whether originating or answering a call. The default is originate.	"Originate"
WaitRings	*number*	Number of rings to wait before answering incoming call. The default is 2.	"2"

* Valid tokens appear in Courier typeface. Value tokens printed in *italics* are variables.

LAT Tool scripting interface

Keyword token	Value token*	Description	Example
HostAddress	*string*	Ethernet address of LAT host. This token is 12 characters long and in hex format. If less than 12 characters are supplied, the characters are right-justified and leading zeros are placed in the string. If this field is used, HostName must contain a name ("" is not acceptable). The default value is x'000000000000'. This keyword token is used only when SelectHost is 1. Only applications can set this value.	"AA0004000504"
HostName	*string*	Name of host offering LAT service. The maximum length is 16 characters. The default is "". HostName is used only when SelectHost is 1. Only applications can set this value.	"MAYTAG"
LocalPort	*string*	Name of local port for LAT Driver. The maximum length of this string is 16 characters. This keyword token cannot be set to "". The default is Port0. Only applications can set this value.	"Port0"
PortName	*string*	Name of port on host offering LAT service. The maximum length is 16 characters. The default is "". PortName is used only when SelectHost is 1. Only applications can set this value.	""
SelectHost	*number*	Specifies which method of host selection is desired. The default is 0, which means use the best host available; 1 means specify a host. Only applications can set this value.	"0"
ServiceName	*string*	Name of terminal service offered by LAT host. The maximum length is 16 characters. The default is "". Only applications and users can set this value.	"MAYTAG"

* Valid tokens appear in Courier typeface. Value tokens printed in *italics* are variables.

Serial Tool and Serial NB Tool scripting interface

Keyword token	Value token*	Description	Example
Baud	*number*	Baud rate of modem. The default is `9600`.	`"2400"`
DataBits	5|6|7|8	Number of data bits. The default is `8`.	`"5"`
Handshake	None| XON/XOFF| DTR&CTS| DTROnly| CTSOnly	Specifies type of handshaking on connection. The default is `none`.	`"None"`
HoldConnection	TRUE|FALSE	When true, tool does not drop DTR while closing connection. The default is `false`.	`"True"`
Parity	None|Odd| Even	Type of parity on connection. The default is `none`.	`"None"`
Port	`"Modem Port"`| `"Printer Port"`|*other*	Current port for sending and receiving data. The default is `Modem Port`.	`"Modem Port"`
RemindDisconnect	TRUE|FALSE	When true and `HoldConnection` is true, tool reminds user it is holding DTR high. The default is `false`.	`"True"`
StopBits	1|1.5|2	Number of stop bits on connection. The default is 1.	`"1"`

* Valid tokens appear in `Courier` typeface. Value tokens printed in *italics* are variables.

Text Tool scripting interface

Keyword token	Value token*	Description	Example
CharPerLine	*number*	Specifies number of characters per line. The default is 80.	"80"
DelayPerChar	*number*	Specifies delay in 1/60 seconds between characters sent. The default is 0.	"1"
DelayPerLine	*number*	Specifies delay in 1/60 seconds between lines sent. The default is 0.	"1"
Ending	CR|LF|CR&LF	Specifies control characters for the end of a line of outgoing text. The default is CR.	"CR&LF"
WordWrap	TRUE|FALSE	Specifies whether tool wraps data, which would otherwise extend past right margin, to a new line. The default is false.	"True"

* Valid tokens appear in `Courier` typeface. Value tokens printed in *italics* are variables.

TTY Tool scripting interface

Keyword token	Value token*	Description	Example
AutoRepeat	TRUE|FALSE	Specifies whether Tab, Return, Backspace, Enter, Escape, and noncontrol keys repeat when held down. The default is `true`.	"True"
AutoWrap	TRUE|FALSE	Specifies whether text automatically wraps to next line when it reaches the right margin. The default is `false`.	"True"
Cursor	Block|Underline	Specifies either a block cursor or underline cursor. The default is `underline`.	"Block"
FontSize	9|12	Size of display font. The default is `9`.	"9"
LocalEcho	TRUE|FALSE	Specifies whether tool echoes keystrokes to local computer. The default is `false`.	"True"
NewLine	TRUE|FALSE	When true, specifies that the tool sends both a line feed and carriage return when user presses the Return key. When false, specifies that the tool sends only a carriage return. The default is `false`.	"True"
Online	TRUE|FALSE	Specifies whether keystrokes are sent to remote computer. The default is `true`.	"True"
RepeatControls	TRUE|FALSE	Specifies whether tool repeats control characters when the control key is held down. The default is `false`.	"True"
Scroll	JUMP|SMOOTH	Specifies method for scrolling the screen. The default is `jump`.	"Smooth"
ShowControls	TRUE|FALSE	When true, tool displays control characters instead of executing them. The default is `false`.	"True"
SwapBackspaceDelete	TRUE|FALSE	When true, tool swaps functionality of Backspace and Delete keys. The default is `false`.	"True"
Width	80|132	Number of display columns. The default is 80.	"80"

* Valid tokens appear in `Courier` typeface. Value tokens printed in *italics* are variables.

VT102 Tool scripting interface

Keyword token	Value token*	Description	Example
ActiveCharSet	G0|G1	Specifies active character set. The default is G0.	"G0"
AnswerBack	*string*	Specifies string returned to remote computer when answerback character is detected in incoming data stream. The default is "".	"VT102"
AutoRepeat	TRUE|FALSE	Specifies whether Tab, Return, Backspace, Enter, Escape, and noncontrol keys repeat when held down. The default is true.	"True"
AutoWrap	TRUE|FALSE	Specifies whether text automatically wraps to next line when it reaches the right margin. The default is false.	"True"
Cursor	block|underline	Specifies either a block cursor or underline cursor. The default is underline.	"Block"
CursorKey	ANSI|Application	Specifies characters transmitted when Cursor (arrow) keys are pressed. The default is ANSI. ·	"ANSI"
FontSize	9|12	Size of display font. The default is 9.	"12"
G0	USASCII|Graphic|International[†]	Specifies G0 character set. The default is USASCII.	"USASCII"
G1	USASCII|Graphic|International[†]	Specifies G1 character set. The default is USASCII.	"International"

(continued) ➡

* Valid tokens appear in Courier typeface. Value tokens printed in *italics* are variables.

[†] NRCSet must be set to a value other than "USASCII" before G0, G1, G2, or G3 can be set to "International".

Keyword token	Value token*	Description	Example
G2	USASCII|Graphic| International[†]	Specifies G2 character set. The default is USASCII.	"International"
G3	USASCII|Graphic| International[†]	Specifies G3 character set. The default is USASCII.	"International"
InsertChar	TRUE|FALSE	Specifies whether characters are inserted between or written over existing text. The default is false.	"True"
InverseVideo	TRUE|FALSE	When true, specifies data is displayed on the Macintosh as white text on a black background. The default is false.	"True"
KeyboardLocked	TRUE|FALSE	Specifies whether keyboard is locked. The default is false.	"True"
KeyClick	TRUE|FALSE	Specifies whether an audible clicking sound is made when a key is pressed. The default is false.	"True"
Keypad	Numeric| Application	Specifies whether keys on the keypad generate numeric characters or control characters. The default is numeric.	"Numeric"
LocalEcho	TRUE|FALSE	Specifies whether tool echoes keystrokes to local computer. The default is false.	"True"
NewLine	TRUE|FALSE	When true, specifies that tool sends both a line feed and carriage return when user presses the Return key. When false, specifies that the tool sends only a carriage return. The default is false.	"True"

Keyword token	Value token*	Description	Example
NRCSet	*string*	Specifies National Replacement Character Set[†]. The default is USASCII.	"Finnish"
Online	TRUE | FALSE	Specifies whether keystrokes are sent to remote computer. The default is true.	"True"
OriginAtMargin	TRUE | FALSE	Specifies whether cursor can move outside of scrolling region. Also determines whether screen addressing is based on the complete screen or is relative to the scrolling margin. The default is false.	"True"
RepeatControls	TRUE | FALSE	Specifies whether control keys repeat when held down. The default is false.	"True"
Scroll	Jump | Smooth	Specifies method for scrolling the screen. The default is Jump.	"Smooth"
ShowControls	TRUE | FALSE	When true, tool displays control characters instead of executing them. The default is false.	"True"
ShowStatusBar	TRUE | FALSE	Specifies whether tool shows status bar The default is false.	"True"
ShowTabRuler	TRUE | FALSE	Specifies whether tool shows tab ruler. The default is false.	"True"
SwapBackspaceDelete	TRUE | FALSE	When true, tool swaps functionality of Backspace and Delete keys. The default is false.	"True"

(continued) ➡

* Valid tokens appear in Courier typeface. Value tokens printed in *italics* are variables.

[†] NRCSet must be set to a value other than "USASCII" before G0, G1, G2, or G3 can be set to "International".

VT102 Tool scripting interface *(continued)*

Keyword token	Value token*	Description	Example
TerminalMode	ANSI/VT102|VT52	Specifies terminal to emulate: VT100™ or VT52™. The default is ANSI/VT102.	"VT52"
Width	80|132	Number of display columns. The default is 80.	"80"

* Valid tokens appear in Courier typeface. Value tokens printed in *italics* are variables.

† NRCSet must be set to a value other than "USASCII" before G0, G1, G2, or G3 can be set to "International".

VT320 Tool scripting interface

Keyword token	Value token*	Description	Example
AnswerBack	*string*	Specifies string returned to remote computer when answerback character is detected in incoming data stream. The default is `""`.	`"VT320"`
AutoRepeat	TRUE|FALSE	Specifies whether Tab, Return, Backspace, Enter, Escape, and noncontrol keys repeat when held down. The default is `true`.	`"True"`
AutoWrap	TRUE|FALSE	Specifies whether text automatically wraps to next line when it reaches the right margin. The default is `false`.	`"True"`
Cursor	block| underline	Specifies either a block cursor or underline cursor. The default is `underline`.	`"Block"`
CursorKey	ANSI| Application	Specifies characters transmitted when Cursor (arrow) keys are pressed. The default is `ANSI`.	`"ANSI"`
FontSize	9|12	Size of display font. The default is `9`.	`"12"`
G0	USASCII| Graphics| ISOLatin| DECSupplemental| UserPreferred| SoftCharacterSet| International[†]	Specifies `G0` character set. The default is `USASCII`.	`"USASCII"`
G1	USASCII| Graphics| ISOLatin| DECSupplemental| UserPreferred| SoftCharacterSet| International[†]	Specifies `G1` character set. The default is `USASCII`.	`"International"`

(continued) ➡

* Valid tokens appear in `Courier` typeface. Value tokens printed in *italics* are variables.

† NRCSet must be set to a value other than `"USASCII"` before G0, G1, G2, or G3 can be set to `"International"`.

VT320 Tool scripting interface *(continued)*

Keyword token	Value token*	Description	Example
G2	USASCII| Graphics| ISOLatin| DECSupplemental| UserPreferred| SoftCharacterSet| International[†]	Specifies G2 character set. The default is UserPreferred.	"International"
G3	USASCII| Graphics| ISOLatin| DECSupplemental| UserPreferred| SoftCharacterSet| International[†]	Specifies G3 character set. The default is UserPreferred.	"International"
GL	G0|G1|G2|G3	Specifies GL character set. The default is G0.	"G0"
GR	G1|G2|G3	Specifies GR character set. The default is G2.	"G2"
InsertChar	TRUE|FALSE	Specifies whether characters are inserted between or written over existing text. The default is false.	"True"
InverseVideo	TRUE|FALSE	When true, specifies data is displayed on the Macintosh as white text on a black background. The default is false.	"True"
KeyboardLocked	TRUE|FALSE	Specifies whether keyboard is locked. The default is false.	"True"
KeyClick	TRUE|FALSE	Specifies whether an audible clicking sound is made when a key is pressed. The default is false.	"True"
Keypad	Numeric| Application	Specifies whether keys on the keypad generate numeric characters or control characters. The default is numeric.	"Numeric"

Keyword token	Value token*	Description	Example
LocalEcho	TRUE | FALSE	Specifies whether tool echoes keystrokes to local computer. The default is `false`.	"True"
NewLine	TRUE | FALSE	When true, specifies that tool sends both a line feed and carriage return when the user presses the Return key. When false, specifies that the tool sends only a carriage return. The default is `false`.	"True"
NRCSet	*string*	Specifies National Replacement Character set. The default is USASCII.	"French"
Online	TRUE | FALSE	Specifies whether keystrokes are sent to remote computer. The default is `true`.	"True"
OriginAtMargin	TRUE | FALSE	Specifies whether the cursor can move outside of scrolling region. Also determines whether screen addressing is based on the complete screen or is relative to the scrolling margin. The default is `false`.	"True"
PreferredSet	DecSupplement | ISOLatin	Specifies DECSupplemental set or ISOLATIN set. DECSupplemental is the default.	"ISOLATIN "
RepeatControls	TRUE | FALSE	Specifies whether control keys repeat when held down. The default is `false`.	"True"
Scroll	Jump | Smooth	Specifies method for scrolling screen. The default is `Jump`.	"Smooth"
ShowControls	TRUE | FALSE	When true, tool displays control characters instead of executing them. The default is `false`.	"True"

(continued) ➡

* Valid tokens appear in `Courier` typeface. Value tokens printed in *italics* are variables.

† NRCSet must be set to a value other than "USASCII" before G0, G1, G2, or G3 can be set to "International".

VT320 Tool scripting interface *(continued)*

Keyword token	Value token*	Description	Example
ShowStatusBar	TRUE|FALSE	Specifies whether tool shows status bar. The default is `false`.	"True"
ShowTabRuler	TRUE|FALSE	Specifies whether tool shows tab ruler. The default is `false`.	"True"
StatusLine	invisible| visible| hostwriteable	Specifies whether the status bar is visible. When `hostwriteable`, the host can change settings on the status bar. `hostwriteable` implies the status bar is visible. The default is `invisible`.	"Visible"
SwapBackspaceDelete	TRUE|FALSE	When true, tool swaps functionality of Backspace and Delete keys. The default is `true`.	"True"
TerminalID	VT320ID|VT100ID| VT101ID|VT102ID| VT220ID	Specifies terminal ID. The default is VT320ID.	"VT320"
TerminalMode	VT300-7|VT300-8| ANSI/VT100|VT52	Specifies terminal to emulate. The default is VT300-7.	"VT100"
UserFeaturesLocked	TRUE|FALSE	Specifies whether host can change user settings. The default is `false`.	"True"
UserKeysLocked	TRUE|FALSE	Specifies whether user-defined keys can be changed by host system. The default is `false`.	"True"
Width	80|132	Number of display columns. The default is 80.	"80"

* Valid tokens appear in `Courier` typeface. Value tokens printed in *italics* are variables.

† NRCSet must be set to a value other than "USASCII" before G0, G1, G2, or G3 can be set to "International".

XMODEM Tool scripting interface

Keyword token	Value token*	Description	Example
Creator	*string*	Specifies four-byte creator field for received text files. Only valid for `StraightXMODEM` and `XMODEMText` methods. The default is `ttxt`, which indicates the received file is a TeachText document.	`"MPS"`
MacBinaryAutoReceive	TRUE|FALSE	Enables MacBinary files to be received automatically. The default is `false`.	`"True"`
Method	MacBinary| MacTerminal| StraightXMODEM| XMODEMText	Specifies type of file handling for XMODEM file transfers. The default is `MacBinary`.	`"MacBinary"`
Option	Standard|CRC| 1KBlocks|CleanLink	Specifies type of block handling. The default is `standard`.	`"Standard"`
Retry	*number*	Specifies number of times to retry sending block. The default is `10`.	`"20"`
TimeOut	*number*	Specifies time, in seconds, in which the next packet must be received. The default is `10`.	`"5"`
UseRemoteName	TRUE|FALSE	For MacBinary and MacTerminal® methods, specifies whether incoming file should be named using host-supplied file name. The default is `true`.	`"True"`

* Valid tokens appear in `Courier` typeface. Value tokens printed in *italics* are variables.

Appendix C **Useful Code Samples**

THIS APPENDIX shows you solutions to common programming
problems:

- implementing effective idle loops

- determining events that need to be handled by one of the Communications
  Toolbox managers

- customizing the tool-settings dialog box

- determining whether the Communications Toolbox managers are installed

- using the scripting interface

Using FTExec and TMIdle effectively

The following code sample shows when your application needs to call FTExec and TMIdle during a file transfer.

```
PROCEDURE DoIdle;
VAR
        theWindow       : WindowPtr;          { The target to idle }
        doFT            : BOOLEAN;            { route data to FT Tool }
        doTM            : BOOLEAN;            { route data to Term Tool }
        savedPort       : GrafPtr;            { for later reset }

BEGIN
        GetPort(savedPort);                   { Save for later }
        theWindow := FrontWindow;             { Gimme the first one }

        { Give idle time for the window    }
        WHILE (theWindow <> NIL) DO BEGIN
                (*
                Make sure the window belongs to the application
                *)

                SetPort(theWindow);           { Focus on it }

                IF gConn <> NIL THEN          { Give time to the connection }
                        CMIdle(gConn);

                doFT := FALSE;                { Send data to FT tool }
                doTM := TRUE;                 { Send data to terminal tool }

                IF gFT <> NIL THEN BEGIN
                        { Is there a file transfer in progress ?? }
                        IF BAND(gFT^^.flags, ftIsFTMode) <> 0 THEN BEGIN
                                doFT := TRUE;
                                gWasFT := TRUE;

                                { If the FT tool uses my connection then }
                                { don't route data to the terminal tool }

                                IF BAND(gFT^^.attributes, ftSameCircuit) <> 0 THEN
                                        doTM := FALSE;
                        END     { In progress }

                ELSE BEGIN
                        IF gWasFT THEN BEGIN
                                { FT no longer in progress }
                                gWasFT := FALSE;

                                { if it failed, alert }
                                IF BAND(gFT^^.flags, FTSucc) = 0 THEN
                                        ; { Handle error }

                                (*
                                Re-add the file transfer auto-receive string
                                that was removed at FTStart()
                                *)

                        END;

                        { AutoReceive string was received? }
                        IF gStartFT THEN
                                DoReceive;
```

```
                        END; { No FT in progress }

                        IF doFT THEN                          { Give time to FT tool }
                              FTExec(gFT);

                  END; { Good FT Handle }

                  IF gTerm <> NIL THEN BEGIN
                        { Send data to terminal }
                        IF doTM THEN BEGIN
                              TMIdle(gTerm);           { So it can blink its cursor, etc }

                              TermRecvProc;            { Send Data to the terminal }
                        END; { Send data to terminal }

                  END; { Good Terminal }

                  { Try the next window }
                  theWindow := WindowPtr(WindowPeek(theWindow)^.nextWindow);

            END; { while each window }

            SetPort(savedPort);                       { Back to the way it was }

END; { DoIdle }

PROCEDURE TermRecvProc;
VAR
      theErr      : CMErr;                            { Any errors }
      status      : CMStatFlags;                      { For the conn tool }
      sizes       : BufferSizes;
      flags       : INTEGER;

BEGIN
      IF (gConn <> NIL) AND (gTerm <> NIL) THEN BEGIN

            { Get the state of the connection    }
            theErr := CMStatus(gConn, sizes, status);

            IF (theErr = noErr) THEN  BEGIN

                  { Route the data if we have any }
                  IF (BAND(status, cmStatusDataAvail) <> 0) AND
                     (sizes[cmDataIn] <> 0) THEN BEGIN

                        { Don't overflow my buffer }
                        IF sizes[cmDataIn] > kBufferSize THEN
                              sizes[cmDataIn] := kBufferSize;

                        { Tell the tool to get the data      }
                        theErr := CMRead(gConn, gBuffer, sizes[cmDataIn],
                                          cmData, FALSE,NIL,0,flags);

                        { Send data to the terminal }
                        IF (theErr = noErr) THEN
                              sizes[cmDataIn] := TMStream(gTerm,gBuffer,
                                                      sizes[cmDataIn],flags);

                  END; { sizes <> 0 }

            END; { Good Status }
```

```
        IF (theErr <> noErr) THEN
                AlertUser('Couldn''t send data to terminal',FALSE);

    END; { Good term & conn }

END; { TermRecvProc }
```

Determining events for Communications Toolbox managers

The following routines show how an application can determine if an event needs to be handled by one of the Communications Toolbox Manager event-processing routines.

```
FUNCTION        IsFTWindow(theWindow: WindowPtr): BOOLEAN;
VAR
        pWindow:        WindowPtr;
        tempFT:         FTHandle;
        hFT:            FTHandle;

BEGIN
        IsFTWindow := FALSE;

        IF WindowPeek(theWindow)^.windowKind <> dialogKind THEN
                Exit(IsFTWindow);

        tempFT := FTHandle(GetWRefCon(theWindow));

        pWindow := FrontWindow;

        WHILE pWindow <> NIL DO
                BEGIN
                hFT := GethFT(pWindow);
                IF hFT <> NIL THEN
                        BEGIN
                        IF LONGINT(hFT) = LONGINT(tempFT) THEN
                                BEGIN
                                IsFTWindow := TRUE;
                                Exit(IsFTWindow);
                                END;
                        END;
                pWindow := WindowPtr(WindowPeek(pWindow)^.nextWindow);
                END;
END;


FUNCTION IsFTEvent(theEvent: EventRecord): FTHandle;
VAR
        theWindow       : WindowPtr;
        hFT             : FTHandle;

BEGIN
        IsFTEvent := NIL;
        theWindow := NIL;

        CASE theEvent.what OF
                autoKey, keyDown:       { no Command-key equivalents on a Macintosh Plus }
                        BEGIN
                        theWindow := FrontWindow;
                        END;
                mouseDown:
                        BEGIN
                        IF FindWindow(theEvent.where, theWindow)=0 THEN
                                ;
                        END;
                updateEvt:
                        BEGIN
                        theWindow := WindowPtr(theEvent.message);
                        END;
                activateEvt:
                        BEGIN
```

```
                              theWindow := WindowPtr(theEvent.message);
                           END;
                 END; {case}


       IF theWindow <> NIL THEN
              BEGIN
              IF IsFTWindow(theWindow) THEN
                     BEGIN
                     hFT := FTHandle(GetWRefCon(theWindow));
                     IsFTEvent := hFT;
                     END
              ELSE
                     BEGIN
                     hFT := GethFT(theWindow);
                     IF hFT <> NIL THEN
                            BEGIN
                            IF BAND(hFT^^.flags, FTIsFTMode) <> 0 THEN
                                   IF BAND(hFT^^.attributes,
                                     FTSameCircuit) <> 0 THEN
                                          IF theEvent.what IN
                                     [autoKey, keyDown] THEN
                                                 IsFTEvent := hFT;
                            END;
                     END;
              END;
END;


{$S EventSeg}
FUNCTION IsConnEvent(theEvent: EventRecord): ConnHandle;
VAR
       theWindow       : WindowPtr;
       hConn           : ConnHandle;

BEGIN
       IsConnEvent := NIL;
       theWindow := NIL;

       CASE theEvent.what OF
              autoKey, keyDown:      { no Command-key equivalents on a Macintosh Plus }
                     BEGIN
                     theWindow := FrontWindow;

                     END;
              mouseDown:
                     BEGIN
                     IF FindWindow(theEvent.where, theWindow)=0 THEN
                             ;
                     END;
              updateEvt:
                     BEGIN
                     theWindow := WindowPtr(theEvent.message);
                     END;
              activateEvt:
                     BEGIN
                     theWindow := WindowPtr(theEvent.message);
                     END;
              END; {case}

       IF theWindow <> NIL THEN
              BEGIN
              IF IsConnWindow(theWindow) THEN
                     BEGIN
```

```
                         hConn := ConnHandle(GetWRefCon(theWindow));
                         IsConnEvent := hConn;
                         END;
               END;
END;


{$S EventSeg}
FUNCTION IsTermEvent(theEvent: EventRecord): TermHandle;
VAR
        theWindow       : WindowPtr;
        hTerm           : TermHandle;

BEGIN
        IsTermEvent := NIL;
        theWindow := NIL;

        CASE theEvent.what OF
                autoKey, keyDown:        { no Command-key equivalents on a Macintosh Plus }
                        BEGIN
                        theWindow := FrontWindow;
                        END;
                mouseDown:
                        BEGIN
                        IF FindWindow(theEvent.where, theWindow)=0 THEN
                                ;
                        END;
                updateEvt:
                        BEGIN
                        theWindow := WindowPtr(theEvent.message);
                        END;

                activateEvt:
                        BEGIN
                        theWindow := WindowPtr(theEvent.message);
                        END;
                END; {case}

        IF theWindow <> NIL THEN
                BEGIN
                IF IsTermWindow(theWindow) THEN
                        BEGIN
                        hTerm := TermHandle(GetWRefCon(theWindow));
                        IsTermEvent := hTerm;
                        END;
                END;
END;


PROCEDURE MainLoop;
VAR
        theEvent        : EventRecord;
        theWindow       : WindowPtr;
        theWindowPeek   : WindowPeek;
        theControl      : ControlHandle;
        savedPort       : GrafPtr;
        theKey          : CHAR;

        processed       : BOOLEAN;
        result          : LONGINT;
        hFT             : FTHandle;
```

```
BEGIN
        WHILE NOT done DO
                BEGIN
                SystemTask;

                DoIdle;                              { application idle loop procedure }
                IF WaitNextEvent(everyEvent,theEvent, 0, NIL) THEN
                        BEGIN
                        hFT := IsFTEvent(theEvent);
                        IF hFT <> NIL THEN
                                FTEvent(hFT, theEvent)
                        ELSE
                                BEGIN
                                CASE theEvent.what OF
                                        autoKey, keyDown:
                                                DoKey(theEvent);
                                        mouseDown:
                                                DoClick(theEvent);
                                        updateEvt:
                                                DoUpdate(theEvent);

                                        app4Evt:
                                                DoResume(theEvent);
                                        activateEvt:
                                                DoActivate(theEvent);
                                        END; { case }
                                END;
                        END; { gne }
                END; { if done }
        END;
```

The custom tool-settings dialog box

The sample code that follows shows how your application can use Connection Manager routines to present the user with a custom tool-settings dialog box.

Choose.p

This performs the standard dialog box for configuration and selection of a Connection tool.

```
CONST
        ChooseItemOK            =       1;              { Location of Dialog Box Items }
        ChooseItemCancel        =       2;
        ChooseItemPopup         =       5;
        ChooseResourceBase      =       256;

TYPE
        dialogInfoP             =       ^dialogInfo; { storage private to the
                                                       configuration dialog box}
        dialogInfo              =       RECORD
            tempProcID          :       INTEGER;        { MUST be the first item in record }
            magicCookie         :       LONGINT;        { MUST be the second item in
                                                          the record }

            tempConfig          :       Ptr;            { configuration record being used -
                                                          these are needed by the filter
                                                          procedure }
            count               :       INTEGER;
        END;

FUNCTION        ChooseEntry(VAR theHandle: ConnHandle; where: Point): INTEGER;
{ theHandle is the current connection handle.
  where is the upper-left corner of the selection dialog box? }

VAR
        maxExtent :     Rect;           { max size of dialog box in global coordinates }
        oldSize :       Point;          { old size of dialog box before resizing }

        savedPort :     GrafPtr;        { saved port }
        theWindow :     WindowPtr;      { for invalidating after DisposDialog }
        theDialog :     DialogPtr;      { the choose dialog box}
        infoP :         dialogInfoP;    { pointer to dialog data }

        tempTool :      Str255;         { currently selected tool name }
        oldName :       Str255;         { initially selected tool name }

        theControl :    ControlHandle;{ Pop-up Control }
        hMenu :         MenuHandle;     { handle to pop-up menu control's menu }
        theItem :       INTEGER;        { for manipulating dialog box items }
        itemKind :      INTEGER;
        itemHandle :    Handle;
        itemRect :      Rect;

        thePtr :        Ptr;            { ptr to temporary configuration record }
        configSize :    LONGINT;        { Size of the configuration record }

        oldVal :        INTEGER;        { old pop-up menu value }
        newVal :        INTEGER;        { current pop-up menu value }

        hDITL :         Handle;         { handle to DITL to append }
```

```
        theErr :        OSErr;          { for building list of tools }
Label
        1;                              { Cleanup }


BEGIN
        ChooseEntry := ChooseFailed;                            { pessimistic }
        InitCursor;                                             { reset to arrow }
        GetPort(savedPort);

        theDialog := nil;
        infoP := nil;

        theDialog := GetNewDialog(chooseResourceBase, NIL, POINTER(-1));
        IF theDialog = NIL THEN                                 { unsuccessful }
                Goto 1;                                         { Go Cleanup }


        SetPort(theDialog);
        infoP := dialogInfoP(NewPtr(SIZEOF(dialogInfo)));  { internal data space }
        IF infoP = NIL THEN                                     { no memory }
                Goto 1;                                         { Go Cleanup }
        SetWRefCon(theDialog, LONGINT(infoP));                  { set the refcon to infoP }
        WITH infoP^ DO
        BEGIN
                count := CountDITL(theDialog);                  { # items in DITL }

                tempProcID := theHandle^^.procID;               { get the tool procID }
                CMGetToolName(tempProcID, tempTool);            { get the toolname }
                oldName := tempTool;                            { save the toolname }

                thePtr := theHandle^^.config;                   { get the configuration
                                                                field }
                configSize := GetPtrSize(thePtr);               { get size of configuration
                                                                record }
                IF MemError <> noErr THEN                       { memory problem }
                        Goto 1;                                 { Go Cleanup }

                tempConfig := NewPtr(configSize);               { copy it if possible... }
                IF tempConfig = NIL THEN                        { didn't get it }
                        Goto 1;                                 { Go Cleanup }

                BlockMove(thePtr, tempConfig, configSize); { copy it }

                { set up pop-up menu }
                theControl := GetNewControl(chooseResourceBase, theDialog);
                IF theControl = NIL THEN
                        Goto 1;                                 { Go Cleanup }

                hMenu := GetMHandle(chooseResourceBase);
                IF hMenu = NIL THEN
                        Goto 1;                                 { Go Cleanup }

        { Enter all of the connection tools into the pop-up menu }
                theItem := 1;
                theErr := noErr;
                WHILE theErr = noErr DO                          { while no problems }
                BEGIN
                        theErr := CRMGetIndToolName( ClassCM, theItem, tempTool);

                        IF theErr = noErr THEN                   { no problems ociffer }
                        BEGIN
                                IF tempTool <> '' THEN          { got one! }
```

```
                BEGIN
                        { Orig. tool? Case INsensitive? Diacrit
                        sensitive? }
                        IF EqualString(tempTool, oldName, FALSE, TRUE)
                                THEN oldVal := theItem;
                        AppendMenu(hMenu, 'X');
                        { this is to prevent problems with special
                        menu characters, like /}
                        SetItem(hMenu, theItem, tempTool);
                        { get the next one please }
                        theItem := theItem + 1;
                END;
        END;
END; {while}


theItem := theItem - 1;                         { One too many above }

IF oldVal = 0 THEN                              { Current tool not in menu }
BEGIN
        { The user has moved the file out of the communications
          directory. We can show the name, but this menu item
          needs to be disabled }
        theItem := theItem + 1;                 { Update these counts }
        oldVal := 1;
        InsMenuItem(hMenu, 'X', 0);
        SetItem(hMenu,oldVal,oldName);
        DisableItem(hMenu, oldVal);             { disable it }
END;


SetCtlMax(theControl, theItem);                 { max of ctl = num tools}

{ fix rectangle size in case of control resize }
GetDItem(theDialog, ChooseItemPopup, itemKind, itemHandle, itemRect);
itemRect := theControl^^.contrlRect;
SetDItem(theDialog, ChooseItemPopup, itemKind, itemHandle, itemRect);

oldSize := theDialog^.portRect.botRight;    { old size of dialog box}

newVal := oldVal;
SetCtlValue(theControl, oldVal);                { set up pop-up value }

                                                { get DITL to append }
hDITL := CMSetupPreflight(tempProcID, magicCookie);

{
  Set the dialog box's text info based on
  the tool's finf resource
}

AppendDITL(theDialog, hDITL, appendDITLBottom); { append it }
IF hDITL <> NIL THEN                 { done with the DITL }
        DisposHandle(hDITL);

                                                { set up the items }
CMSetupSetup(tempProcID, tempConfig, count+1, theDialog, magicCookie);

MoveWindow(theDialog, where.h, where.v, TRUE);  { move dialog box }
ShowWindow(theDialog);

                                                {Get dialog box size}
maxExtent := WindowPeek(theDialog)^.strucRgn^^.rgnBBox;
```

```
theItem := 0;
WHILE (theItem <> ChooseItemOK) AND (theItem <> ChooseItemCancel) DO
BEGIN
        ModalDialog(@ChooseFilter, theItem);{ modal dialog box}
        IF theItem = ChooseItemPopup THEN    { did pop-up get hit? }
        BEGIN
                                                  { what is new value? }
                    newVal := GetCtlValue(theControl);
                    IF newVal <> oldVal THEN
                    { it has changed! }
                    BEGIN
                            { cleanup the setup  }
                            CMSetupCleanup(tempProcID, tempConfig, count+1,
                                            theDialog, magicCookie);
                            ShortenDITL(theDialog,
                                        CountDITL(theDialog) - count);
                            { done with tool }
                            CMSetupPostflight(tempProcID);
                            { reset size }
                            SizeWindow(theDialog, oldSize.h,
                                        oldSize.v, TRUE);

                            { get new tool name }
                            GetItem(hMenu, newVal, tempTool);
                            { get procID }
                            tempProcID := CMGetProcID(tempTool);

                            hDITL := CMSetupPreflight(tempProcID,
                                                        magicCookie);
                            { new DITL }

                    {
                            Set the dialog box's text info based on
                            the tool's finf resource
                    }


                        { append it }
                    AppendDITL(theDialog, hDITL, appendDITLBottom);
                    IF hDITL <> NIL THEN
                                { get rid of it }
                                DisposHandle(hDITL);

                        { get rid of old config }
                        DisposPtr(tempConfig);
                        tempConfig := NIL;    { pessimistic }
                        { and get a new one }
                        CMDefault(tempConfig, tempProcID, TRUE);
                        if tempConfig = NIL               { Clean up from error}
                        BEGIN
                                ShortenDITL(theDialog,
                                            CountDITL(theDialog) - count);
                                CMSetupPostflight(tempProcID);
                                { Out of memory }
                                chooseEntry := chooseFailed;
                                Goto 1;           { Finish clean up }
                        END;

                        CMSetupSetup(tempProcID, tempConfig, count+1,
                                        { set up the items }
                                        theDialog, magicCookie);

                        oldVal := newVal;      { Now the old tool }
```

```
                            UnionRect(maxExtent,
                            WindowPeek(theDialog)^.strucRgn^^.rgnBBox,
                            maxExtent);                 {grow max size}
                    END;
            END; {item = count }

            IF theItem > count THEN               { tool's item hit }
                    CMSetupItem(tempProcID, tempConfig, count+1, theDialog,
                            theItem, magicCookie);
    END;                                     {while theItem NOT OK or Cancel}

    HideWindow(theDialog);                        { hide the dialog box }
    newVal := GetCtlValue(theControl);            { check name change}
    GetItem(hMenu, newVal, tempTool);             { get the new name }
    tempProcID := CMGetProcID(tempTool);

    { Clean out the old tool }
    CMSetupCleanup(tempProcID, tempConfig, count+1, theDialog, magicCookie);
    ShortenDITL(theDialog, CountDITL(theDialog) - count);
    CMSetupPostflight(tempProcID);

    IF theItem = ChooseItemOK THEN
    BEGIN                                      { has the name of tool changed? }
            IF NOT EqualString(oldName, tempTool, FALSE, TRUE) THEN
            BEGIN
                    ChooseEntry := ChooseOKMajor;
                    tempProcID := CMGetProcID(tempTool);

                    IF NOT DoNewConn(ConnHandle(theHandle), tempProcID,
                                    tempConfig) THEN
                            ChooseEntry := ChooseAborted;

                    IF theHandle = NIL THEN      { disaster! }
                            ChooseEntry := ChooseDisaster
                    ELSE
                    BEGIN
                            configSize := GetPtrSize(tempConfig);
                            BlockMove(tempConfig,
                                    theHandle^^.config, configSize);
                            { validate for kicks }
                            IF CMValidate(theHandle) THEN
                            END;
            END
            ELSE
            BEGIN                                { same tool, so validate }
                    ChooseEntry := ChooseOKMinor;
                    configSize := GetPtrSize(tempConfig);
                    BlockMove(tempConfig, theHandle^^.config, configSize);
                    IF CMValidate(theHandle) THEN
                            ;
            END;
    END
    ELSE                                         { user hit CANCEL }
            ChooseEntry := ChooseCancel;

{Now we need to go through the window list and update all areas that were ever covered
up by the configuration dialog box which has grown, and potentially shrunk, too. We
have kept track of the largest size of the dialog box. We will now convert it to local
coordinates and invalrect everybody in the window list. }
            theWindow := FrontWindow;
            WHILE theWindow <> NIL DO
            BEGIN
```

```
                        SetPort(theWindow);
                        itemRect := maxExtent;
                        { get max extent in local coordinates }
                        GlobalToLocal(itemRect.topLeft);
                        GlobalToLocal(itemRect.botRight);
                        InvalRect(itemRect);

                        theWindow := WindowPtr( WindowPeek(theWindow)^.nextWindow );
                END;

        END;    { with }
1: { Clean everything up }
        IF theDialog <> nil THEN DisposDialog(theDialog);
        IF infoP <> nil THEN
        BEGIN
                IF infoP^.tempConfig <> nil THEN DisposPtr(infoP^.tempConfig);
                DisposPtr(Ptr(infoP));
        END;
        SetPort(savedPort);                             { back to original port }
END;


{ change from one connection type to another }
FUNCTION DoNewConn(VAR hConn:ConnHandle; tempProcID:INTEGER;
                   tempConfig:Ptr): BOOLEAN;
VAR
        savedDesiredSizes    :          BufferSizes;
        savedRefCon          :          LONGINT;
        savedUserData        :          LONGINT;
        savedFlags           :          LONGINT;
        savedReserved0       :          LONGINT;
        savedReserved1       :          LONGINT;
        savedReserved2       :          LONGINT;

        status               :          LONGINT;
        sizes                :          BufferSizes;
        theErr               :          CMErr;

BEGIN
        theErr := CMStatus(hConn, sizes, status);       { get conn status }
        IF theErr = noErr THEN                          { OK }
                IF BAnd(status, CMStatusOpen+CMStatusOpening) <> 0 THEN
                        ;
{The connection is open. Confirm whether the user really wants to close the connection,
setting result to FALSE if user aborts}

        WITH hConn^^ DO                                 { save all desired parameters }
        BEGIN
                savedFlags := flags;
                savedDesiredSizes := BufSizes;
                savedRefCon := refcon;
                savedUserData := userData;
                savedReserved0 := reserved0;
                savedReserved1 := reserved1;
                savedReserved2 := reserved2;
        END;

        CMDispose(hConn);                               { get rid of old conn }

        hConn := CMNew(tempProcID, savedFlags, savedDesiredSizes, savedRefCon,
                       savedUserData);
        IF hConn <> NIL THEN
                WITH hConn^^ DO BEGIN                    { Restore other fields }
```

```
                      reserved0 := savedReserved0;
                      reserved1 := savedReserved1;
                      reserved2 := savedReserved2;
              END;
        DoNewConn := TRUE;
END;


{ Choose dialog box filter procedure }
FUNCTION ChooseFilter(theDialog : DialogPtr; VAR theEvent:EventRecord;
                      VAR theItem:INTEGER) : BOOLEAN;
VAR
        theControl    :     ControlHandle;
        where         :     Point;
        result        :     BOOLEAN;
        theKey        :     CHAR;

        savedPort     :     GrafPtr;
        theWindow     :     WindowPtr;             { for event processing }

        pDialogInfo   :     DialogInfoP;           { dialog box private data }

BEGIN
        theItem := 0;                              { nothing initially }
        result := FALSE;                           { for now… }

        pDialogInfo := DialogInfoP(GetWRefCon(theDialog));  { get the dlog data }
        WITH pDialogInfo^ DO
        BEGIN
                result := CMSetupFilter(tempProcID, tempConfig, count+1, theDialog,
                                    theEvent, theItem, magicCookie);

                ChooseFilter := result;            { TRUE or FALSE }
                IF result THEN                     { it WAS processed }
                        Exit(ChooseFilter);        { so exit }
        END;

        CASE theEvent.what OF                      { process the event }
                updateEvt:
                BEGIN
                        GetPort(savedPort);                 { get the port }
                        theWindow := WindowPtr(theEvent.message);
                                                            { get the update owner }
                        SetPort(theWindow);
                        BeginUpdate(theWindow);
                        EraseRect(theWindow^.portRect);     { erase }

                        IF theWindow = theDialog THEN       { process if ours }
                                UpdtDialog(theDialog, theWindow^.visRgn);

                        EndUpdate(theWindow);               { otherwise eat it }
                        SetPort(savedPort);
                        result := TRUE;                     { We regenerate updates when
                                                              we have finished choosing }

                END;
                mouseDown:
                BEGIN
                        where := theEvent.where;   { where was the mouse-down }
                        GlobalToLocal(where);      { convert to local coordinates }

                        IF FindControl(where, theDialog, theControl) <> 0 THEN
                                                            {Click in control?}
                        BEGIN
```

```
                        IF TrackControl(theControl,
                                     where, POINTER(-1)) <> 0 THEN
                                            { track it }
                        BEGIN
                               result := TRUE;        { we got the event }
                               theItem := FindDItem(theDialog, where) + 1;
                                            { so item hit }
                        END
                        ELSE BEGIN                  { tracked out of it }
                               result := TRUE;
                               theItem := 0;        { so no item hit }
                        END;
               END;
        END;
        keyDown:                                  { keyDown }
        BEGIN
               {Standard return/enter/cmd '.' processing }
        END;
        otherwise
        BEGIN
        END;
    END; { case }
    ChooseFilter := result;
END;
```

Choose.r

```
#define ChooseResourceBase  256

resource 'DLOG' (ChooseResourceBase, "setup dialog") {
       {0, 0, 70, 450}, dBoxProc, invisible, noGoAway, 0x0, ChooseResourceBase,
       "Setup Dialog Box"
};
resource 'CNTL' (ChooseResourceBase, "Tools control ") {
       {30, 5, 50, 300},
       popupRightJust,        /* right just */
       visible,
       90,                    /* width of title */
       ChooseResourceBase,    /* menu associated */
       popupMenuCDEFproc,     /* no options CDEF 63 = 16 * 63 + variation code */
       0,                     /* reference menu 11000, pop-up title width 50 */
       "Method:"              /* Title */
};
resource 'DITL' (ChooseResourceBase, "Basic configuration DITL") {
       {   /* array DITLarray: 5 elements */
              {32, 370, 52, 440},
              Button {
                     enabled, "OK"         /* [1] */
              },
              {5, 370, 25, 440},            /* [2] */
              Button {
                     enabled, "Cancel"
              },
              {28, 366, 56, 444},          /* [3] outline of OK button */
              UserItem {
                     enabled
              },
              {5, 5, 21, 200},             /* [4] title */
              StaticText {
                     disabled, "Connection Configuration"
              },
```

```
                {30, 5, 50, 300},              /* [5] select tool popup menu user item */
                UserItem {
                        enabled
                }
        }
};
resource 'MENU' (ChooseResourceBase, "Popup Menu") {
        ChooseResourceBase, textMenuProc, allEnabled, enabled, "Choose Menu",
        { /* Items are added to this menu at execution time */
        }
};
```

Determining whether the managers are installed

This sample code shows how your application can determine whether the Communications Toolbox managers are installed.

```
FUNCTION Installed : BOOLEAN;
CONST
        CommToolboxTrap = $8B;
        UnimplementedTrapNumber = $9F;

BEGIN
        Installed := TRUE;
        IF NGetTrapAddress(UnimplementedTrapNumber, OSTrap) =
           NGetTrapAddress(CommToolboxTrap, OSTrap) THEN
        BEGIN
                Installed := FALSE;
        END;
END;
```

Using the scripting interface

This sample code shows how your application can save the settings of a communications tool by using the Communications Toolbox scripting interface. After initialization, the code shown first checks if a preferences folder, which contains tool settings written in preference files, already exists. If so, the application uses the settings in this file. Otherwise, the code generates a new preferences file.

```
/*
** Constants and Variables
*/

#define             kCreatorType         'ACTB'
#define             kPrefType            'PCTB'
#define             kPreferenceFileName  "\pMyPreferences"

OSErr               osErr                = noErr;
SysEnvRec           theWorld;
CInfoPBPtr          infoPB               = NewPtrClear(sizeof(*infoPB));
WDPBPtr             wdPB                 = NewPtrClear(sizeof(*wdPB));
HParmBlkPtr         dirPB                = NewPtrClear(sizeof(*dirPB));

short               prefVRefNum;
long                prefDirID;
Str63               prefFileName         = kPreferenceFileName;
short               prefRefNum;
ConnHandle          prefConn;

ConnHandle          docConn;
CMBufferSizes sizes                      = { 0, 0, 0, 0, 0, 0, 0, 0 };
Point               where                = { 75, 75 };
Str63               toolName;
short               procID;
Handle              h;
Ptr                 p;




/*
** Initialization
*/

InitGraf((Ptr) &qd.thePort);
InitFonts();
InitWindows();
InitMenus();
TEInit();
InitDialogs(nil);
InitCursor();

osErr = InitCTBUtilities();
osErr = InitCRM();
osErr = InitCM();

/* find the system folder's volume reference number and directory ID */
osErr = SysEnvirons(curSysEnvVers, &theWorld);
(*wdPB).ioVRefNum = theWorld.sysVRefNum;
if (noErr == (osErr = PBGetWDInfo(wdPB, false))) {
        /* create the preferences folder */
        (*dirPB).fileParam.ioVRefNum      = (*wdPB).ioWDVRefNum;
```

```
(*dirPB).fileParam.ioDirID        = (*wdPB).ioWDDirID;
(*dirPB).fileParam.ioNamePtr      = "\pPreferences";
osErr = PBDirCreate(dirPB, false);
if (dupFNErr == osErr)
      osErr = noErr;
if (noErr == osErr) {
      /* does the preference file exist? */
      prefVRefNum   = (*dirPB).fileParam.ioVRefNum;
      prefDirID     = (*dirPB).fileParam.ioDirID;
      (*infoPB).hFileInfo.ioFDirIndex   = 0;
      (*infoPB).hFileInfo.ioVRefNum     = prefVRefNum;
      (*infoPB).hFileInfo.ioDirID       = prefDirID;
      (*infoPB).hFileInfo.ioNamePtr     = prefFileName;
      osErr = PBGetCatInfo(infoPB, false);
      if (fnfErr == osErr) {
            /* no, so create a new preference file */
            if (noErr == (osErr = HCreate(prefVRefNum, prefDirID,
                  prefFileName, kCreatorType, kPrefType))) {
                  HCreateResFile(prefVRefNum, prefDirID, prefFileName);
                  if (noErr == (osErr = ResError())) {
                        /* open the preference file */
                        prefRefNum = HOpenResFile(prefVRefNum, prefDirID,
                                    prefFileName, fsRdWrPerm);
                        if (-1 == prefRefNum) {
                              osErr = ResError();
                        } else {
                              /* create a default connection */
                              osErr = CRMGetIndToolName(classCM, 1,
                                          toolName);
                              if (noErr == osErr) {
                                    prefConn =
                                          CMNew(CMGetProcID(toolName),
                                          cmData, sizes, 0, 0);
                                    /* allow the user to select a
                                    prefered tool and configuration */
                                    osErr = CMChoose(&prefConn,
                                          where, nil);
                                    /* write the prefered tool name to
                                    the preference file */
                                    HLock((Handle) prefConn);
                                    CMGetToolName((**prefConn).procID,
                                          toolName);
                                    HUnlock((Handle) prefConn);
                                    h = NewHandle(1 + toolName[0]);
                                    HLock(h);
                                    BlockMove(toolName, *h,
                                          GetHandleSize(h));
                                    HUnlock(h);
                                    AddResource(h, 'pTXT', 0, "");
                                    ReleaseResource(h);
                                    /* write the prefered configuration
                                    to the preference file */
                                    p = CMGetConfig(prefConn);
                                    h = NewHandle(GetPtrSize(p));
                                    HLock(h);
                                    BlockMove(p, *h, GetHandleSize(h));
                                    HUnlock(h);
                                    AddResource(h, 'cTXT', 0, "");
                                    ReleaseResource(h);
                                    DisposPtr(p);
                                    /* dispose of the connection */
                                    CMDispose(prefConn);
```

```
                                   }
                                   /* close the file so that it can be used
                                   in a shared environment */
                                   CloseResFile(prefRefNum);
                           }
                   }
               }
           }
       }
}




/*
** New Document
*/

/* focus on the preference file */
prefRefNum = HOpenResFile(prefVRefNum, prefDirID, prefFileName, fsRdWrPerm);
if (-1 != prefRefNum) {
       /* get the prefered tool name */
       h = Get1Resource('pTXT', 0);
       HLock(h);
       procID=CMGetProcID(*h);
       HUnlock(h);
       ReleaseResource(h);
       if (-1 != procID) {
               /* create a new connection */
               docConn = CMNew(procID, cmData, sizes, 0, 0);
               /* set the prefered configuration */
               h = Get1Resource('cTXT', 0);
               HLock(h);
               osErr = CMSetConfig(docConn, *h);
               HUnlock(h);
               ReleaseResource(h);
       } else {
               /* the prefered tool could not be found so … */
               osErr = CRMGetIndToolName(classCM, 1, toolName);
               docConn = CMNew(CMGetProcID(toolName), cmData, sizes, 0, 0);
               osErr = CMChoose(&docConn, where, nil);
       }
       CloseResFile(prefRefNum);
}
```

Glossary

background procedure A procedure that runs while the user is using another application.

cache region The area in the terminal emulation window in which information is displayed that has scrolled out of the terminal emulation region.

channel A logical line of communication that exists on a connection.

Communications Resource Manager The Communications Toolbox manager that makes it easier for your application to register and keep track of communications resources.

communications resource record A Communications Resource Manager data structure that contains information such as the type of device the record represents, and whether the device is available for use.

Communications Toolbox utilities A Communications Toolbox manager that contains useful routines, most of which are not specific to programming networking or communications applications.

completion routine Any application-defined code to be executed when an asynchronous call to a routine is completed.

connection A logical line of communication between two entities.

Connection Manager The Communications Toolbox manager that makes it easier for you to implement and maintain data connections.

connection record A Connection Manager data structure containing information that describes one instance of a connection tool.

connection tool A self-contained collection of resources that implements a specific connection protocol.

control definition procedure A procedure called by the Control Manager when it needs to implement the functions of a specific type of control.

entity A task or process running on a computer. Two entities can coexist on the same computer if the computer is multitasking, such as when applications are running in a MultiFinder environment.

File Transfer Manager The Communications Toolbox manager that makes it easier for you to implement file transfers.

file transfer record A File Transfer Manager data structure that contains all the specifics about a file transfer. For example, the file transfer record might show that the File Transfer Manager should use the XMODEM tool to perform file transfers, and that the tool should not display any custom menus while transferring files.

file transfer tool A self-contained collection of resources that implements a specific file transfer protocol.

filter procedure A routine that `ModalDialog`, `NuLookup`, and `NuPLookup` call to filter or modify events that occur in a dialog box.

Macintosh Toolbox The software in the Macintosh ROM that helps you implement the standard Macintosh user interface in your application.

Name Binding Protocol (NBP) The AppleTalk transport-level protocol that translates a character string name into the internet address of the corresponding socket client. NBP enables AppleTalk protocols to understand user-defined zones and device names by providing and maintaining translation tables that map these names to corresponding socket addresses.

routine A function or procedure.

terminal emulation The process of making a computer emulate the characteristics of a terminal.

terminal emulation buffer The area in memory that contains the data displayed in the terminal emulation region.

terminal emulation region The area in the terminal emulation window in which your application writes the output of its terminal emulation. This region is the same size (number of rows and columns, or pixels) as the screen of the terminal your application is emulating.

terminal emulation window The window in which your application displays a terminal emulation region and cache region.

terminal environment record A Terminal Manager data structure that reflects the internal conditions of a terminal tool.

Terminal Manager The Communications Toolbox Manager that makes it easier for you to implement terminal emulation.

terminal record A Terminal Manager data structure that contains the specifics of a terminal emulation. For example, the terminal record might show that your application is emulating a VT320 terminal, and that the Terminal Manager should try to cache the terminal window before clearing it.

terminal tool A self-contained collection of resources that implements the characteristics of a specific terminal.

zone An arbitrary subset of the networks within an internet.

Index

A

Activate events
  in Connection Manager 61
  in File Transfer Manager 151
  procedure to 20
  in Terminal Manager 105
ADSP Tool scripting interface
  295-298
APDA xiv
AppendDITL routine
  description of 198-200
  sample used in code 200, 325, 326
Apple Communications Library xiv
Apple Developer Programs xv
Apple Modem Tool scripting
  interface 299-300
Apple SuperDrive 5
AppleTalk 190, 202-205
Apple Technical Library xiv
application-provided routines
  for Connection Manager 69
  for File Transfer Manager 156-160
  for Terminal Manager 114-118
Assembly language
  calling Connection Manager 73
  calling Communications Resource
    Manager 187
  calling File Transfer Manager
    165-166
  calling Terminal Manager 124-125
  calling Utilities 214
autoRec string 135
AutoRecCallback procedure
  sample used in code 18

B

breakProc procedure
  in terminal record 83
bundle resource 217-218
byte stream 29

C

cacheProc routine
  in terminal record 83
cache region 78 (fig.), 79
caching lines 116-117
'cdef' code resource 217
channel 29-30
Choose.p sample code 323-330
Choose.r sample code 330-331
clean-up operations
  Connection Manager 45
  File Transfer Manager 146
  Terminal Manager 96
'cloc' code resource 218
CMAbort routine 49
cmAbortMsg message 238
CMAccept routine 52
cmAcceptMsg message 238
CMActivate routine
  description of 61
  sample used in code 20
cmActivateMsg message 238
CMAddSearch routine
  description of 59
  sample used in code 18
CMBreak routine
  description of 53
  sample used in code 115
cmBreakMsg message 247-248
CMChoose routine
  description of 41-42
  sample used in code 14
CMClearSearch routine 60
CMClose routine
  description of 49
  sample used in code 12
cmCloseMsg message 246-247
CMCompletorRecord record 241
CMDataBuffer record 241
cmDeactivateMsg message 238
CMDefault routine
  description of 40
  sample used in code 326

CMDefaultMsg message 217, 220-221
CMDispose routine
  description of 50
  sample used in code 19, 328
cmDisposeMsg message 240
CMEnglishToIntl routine 63
cmEnvironsMsg message 249-250
CMEvent routine 62
cmEventMsg message 237
CMGetCMVersion routine 65
CMGetConfig routine 47
CMGetConnEnvirons routine
  description of 54-55
  sample used in code 118, 160
CMGetIndToolName routine
  sample used in code 17
CMGetProcID routine
  description of 37
  sample used in code 17, 326
CMGetRefCon routine 64
CMGetToolName routine
  description of 64
  sample used in code 324
CMGetUserData routine 65
CMGetVersion routine 65
CMIdle routine
  description of 50
  sample used in code 316
cmIdleMsg message 237
cmInitMsg message 217, 239
CMIntlToEnglish routine 63
CMIOKill routine 52
cmIOKillMsg message 248-249
cmL2English message 229-230
cmL2Intl code resource 229-230
CMListen routine 50
cmListenMsg message 236-237
CMMenu routine
  description of 61
  sample used in code 10
cmMenuMsg message 236
cmMgetMsg message 227
cmMsetMsg message 226, 228

CMNew routine
    description of 38-39
    sample used in code 17, 328
CMOpen routine
    description of 48
    sample used in code 11
cmOpenMsg message 245-246
CMRead routine
    description of 56-57
    sample used in code 158, 317
cmReadMsg message 240, 241-242
CMRemoveSearch routine
    description of 60
    sample used in code 13, 18
CMReset routine 53
cmResetMsg message 235
CMResume routine
    description of 61
    sample used in code 21
cmResumeMsg message 238
cmScleanupMsg message 226
CMSetConfig routine 47
CMSetRefCon routine 64
CMSetupCleanup routine
    description of 45
    sample used in code 326, 327
CMSetupFilter routine
    description of 44
    sample used in code 329
CMSetupItem routine
    description of 45
    sample used in code 327
CMSetupPostflight routine
    description of 46
    sample used in code 326, 327
CMSetupPreflight routine
    description of 43
    sample used in code 325, 326
CMSetupSetup routine
    description of 44
    sample used in code 325, 326
CMSetUserData routine 65
cmSfilterMsg message 225-226
cmSitemMsg message 224-225
cmSpreflightMsg message 223
cmSsetupMsg message 224
CMStatus routine
    description of 51
    sample used in code 11, 317, 328
cmStatusMsg message 244-245
cmSuspendMsg message 238

CMValidate routine
    description of 40
    sample used in code 40, 327
cmValidateMsg message 219-220
CMWrite routine
    description of 58-59
    sample used in code 115, 157
cmWriteMsg message 240,
        243-244
code resources 217-218
code samples
    events for Communications
        Toolbox managers,
            determining 319-322
    idle loops, implementing
        effective 316-318
    Macintosh Communications
        Toolbox managers, checking
        for installation 322
    tool-settings dialog box,
        customizing 323-331
Communications Folder 5
Communications Resource
        Manager. See also
        communications resource
        record; specific routines
    data flow of 169 (fig.), 170
    devices 174-175, 182-184
    function of 169-170
    head of queue of 176
    ID 180-181
    initializing 179
    resources 177-179
    routines
        application of 3, 169-170
        list of 173
        quick reference to 185-187
        resource mapping 180-181
        selectors 187
    version number 176
communications resource
        record 170-172
Communications Toolbox. See
        Macintosh Communications
        Toolbox
compatibility guidelines for
        communications tools 285
completion routines 34
    for Connection Manager routines
        66
_CommToolboxDispatch trap
        macro 73, 124, 165, 187, 214

configuration
    of connection 14
    of connection tool 41-42
        custom 43-46
    of file transfer 15
    of file transfer tool 142-143
        custom 144-147
    of terminal emulation 14-15
    of terminal tool 92-93
        custom 94-97
configuration record
    in writing own tool 230
configuration string
    in Connection Manager 47, 63
    in File Transfer Manager 148, 153
    localizing 63
    in Terminal Manager 98, 108
connection
    aborting 49
    break procedure 115
    breaks, sending 53
    closing 49
    configuring 14
    initiating 11
    opening 36-42, 48
    resetting 53
    sending data along 114-115
    status information 51
    terminating 11-12
    using 48-55
connection environment 54-55
Connection Manager. See also
        connection record; specific
        routines
    calling from assembler 73
    channels 29-30
    clean-up operations 45
    closing connection 49
    closing tool file 46
    configuration record
        initializing 40
        sample used in code 40
        validating 40
    configuration string in 47, 63
    connection record for 69
    custom configuration of
        connection tool 43-46
    data flow of 29 (fig.), 30
    data streams 59-60
    and File Transfer Manager 128
    function of 29-30
    handling events 61-62

initializing 36
interfacing with scripting
    language 47
opening connection 36-42, 48
reading data 56-57
routines
    application of 3-4, 29
    completion 66
    list of 35
    miscellaneous 64-65
    quick reference to 67-72
    selectors 73
and terminal tools 76
using connection 48-55
version number 65
writing data 58-59
connection record
for Connection Manager 69
creating 38-39
data structure 31-34
disposing of 50
features of 30
function of 31
reference constant of 64
saving the state of 333
connection requests 50, 52
connection tool
completion routines 250
configuration of 41-42
and Connection Manager 4
custom configuration of 43-46
main code resource for
    function of 235
    messages accepted by 235-250
    quick reference to 251-254
name of 64
writing own
    bundle resource for 217-218
    configuration record 230
    function of 217
    initialization request
        message 217
    localization code resource
        229-230
    quick reference to 231-232
    scripting language interface
        code resource 226-228
    setup definition code
        resource 221-226
    validation code resource
        219-221

constants and data types
    for Communications Resource
        Manager 186-187
    for Connection Manager 70-72
    for File Transfer Manager 164-165
    for Terminal Manager 122-124
    for utilities 212-213
control definition procedure
    193-197
Control Manager 190
conventions, in manual xv
CountDITL routine
    description of 201
    sample used in code 326, 327
CRMGet1IndResource
    routine 177
CRMGet1NamedResource
    routine 178
CRMGet1Resource routine 177
CRMGetCRMVersion routine 176
CRMGetHeader routine 176
CRMGetIndex routine 178
CRMGetIndResource
    routine 177
CRMGetIndToolName routine
    description of 179
    sample used in code 17, 18
CRMGetNamedResource
    routine 178
CRMGetResource routine 177
CRMInstall routine 174
CRMLocalToRealID routine
    description of 181
    sample used in code 223
CRMRealToLocalID routine 180
CRMReleaseResource
    routine 178
CRMRemove routine 175
CRMSearch routine
    description of 175
    sample used in code 184
CRMSerialRecord data
    structure 182
'cscr' code resource 218
'cset' code resource 218
CTBGetCTBVersion routine 192
cursor position 111
custom tool-settings dialog box
    in Connection Manager 43-45
    in Terminal Manager 94-96
'cval' code resource 217

D
DataBuffer record 241
data flow
    in Communications Resource
        Manager 169 (fig.), 170
    in Connection Manager 29 (fig.),
        30
    in File Transfer Manager 129 (fig.),
        130
    in Terminal Manager 77 (fig.), 78
data stream search
    in Connection Manager 59-60
    in Terminal Manager 102-103
data structures
    communications resource
        record 171-172
    connection record 31-34
    file transfer record 130
    terminal record 80-86
device management 170
Device Manager 28, 168
devices
    installing 174
    registering 182
    removing 175
    searching for 175
    and serial port, searching for 184
dialog item lists (DITLs)
    appending 198-200
    counting 201
    shortening 201
Dialog Manager 76, 190, 216
Digital Equipment Corporation 291
DITLs. See Dialog item lists
DoActivate procedure 20
DoClick procedure 23
DoCommand procedure 10
DoConnectionConfig
    procedure 14
DoFileTransferConfig
    procedure 15
DoInitiate procedure 11
DoKey procedure 22-23
DoKill procedure 11-12
DoReceive procedure 13
DoResume procedure 20-21
DoSend procedure 12-13
DoTerminalConfig
    procedure 14-15
DoUpdate procedure 21-22

E

emulating a terminal
   see Terminal Manager 75
   see Writing Terminal Tools 255
English, translating to and from
   in Connection Manager 63
   in File Transfer Manager 153
   in Terminal Manager 108
entity 30
`environsProc` routine
   in file transfer record 133
   in terminal record 82
Event handling
   sample used in code 10
Event Manager 76

F

file
   receiving, starting 13
   sending, starting 12-13
file transfer
   configuring 15
   preparing 138-143
   processing data 150
   starting 149-150
   stopping 150
File Transfer Manager. *See also* File
      transfer record; specific
      routines
   calling from Assembler 165
   clean-up operations 146
   configuration string in 148, 153
   custom configuration of file
      transfer tool 144-147
   data flow in 129 (fig.), 130
   function of 129-130
   handling events 151-152
   initializing 138
   interfacing with scripting
      language 148
   preparing file transfers 138-143
   routines
      application of 3, 129-130
      list of 137
      miscellaneous 154-155
      provided by application
         156-160
      quick reference to 161-166
      selectors 165-166
   transferring files 149-150
   version number 155

file transfer record
   creating 139-140
   data structure of 131-136
   disposing 150
   features of 130
   function of 130
   initializing 141
   saving the state of 333
   validating 141
file transfer tool
   configuring 142-143
   custom configuration of 144-147
   function of 129
   main code resource for
      function of 279
      messages accepted by 279-282
      quick reference to 283-284
   name of 154
   writing own
      bundle resource for 217-218
      configuration record 230
      function of 217
      initialization request
         message 217
      localization code resource
         229-230
      quick reference to 231-232
      scripting language interface
         code resource 226-228
      setup definition code
         resource 221-226
      validation code resource
         219-221
filter procedure
   in configuring connection tool 42
   definition of 206
   name 206
   zone 207
`FindSerialPorts`
      procedure 184
`FTAbort` routine 150
`ftAbortMsg` message 281
`FTActivate` routine
   description of 151
   sample used in code 20
`ftActivateMsg` message 281-282
`FTChoose` routine
   description of 142-143
   sample used in code 15
`ftDeactivateMsg` message 282
`FTDefault` routine 141

`FTDispose` routine
   description of 150
   sample used in code 19
`ftDisposeMsg` message 280
`FTEnglishToIntl` routine 153
`FTEvent` routine 152
`ftEventMsg` message 282
`FTExec` routine
   description of 150
   sample used in code 317-318
   using 31
`ftExecMsg` message 281
`FTGetConfig` routine 148
`FTGetFTVersion` routine 155
`FTGetProcID` routine
   description of 139
   sample used in code 18
`FTGetRefCon` routine 154
`FTGetToolName` routine 154
`FTGetUserData` routine 155
`FTGetVersion` routine 155
`ftInitMsg` message 217, 279-280
`FTIntlToEnglish` routine 153
`FTMenu` routine
   description of 152
   sample used in code 10
`ftMenuMsg` message 282
`FTNew` routine
   description of 139-140
   sample used in code 18
`ftOpenDataFork` 156
`ftOpenRsrcFork` 156
`ftPrivate` 133
`ftReadAbort` 156, 157
`ftReadComplete` 156, 157
`ftReadDataFork` 156, 157
`ftReadOpenFile` 156
`ftReadRsrcFork` 156, 157
`FTResume` routine
   description of 151
   sample used in code 21
`ftResumeMsg` message 281-282
`FTSetConfig` routine 148
`FTSetRefCon` routine 154
`FTSetupCleanup` routine 146
`FTSetupFilter` routine 145
`FTSetupItem` routine 146
`FTSetupPostflight`
      routine 147
`FTSetupPreflight` routine 144
`FTSetupSetUp` routine 145

FTSetUserData routine 155
FTStart routine
 description of 149
 sample used in code 13, 18
ftStartMsg message 280-281
ftSuspendMsg message 282
FTValidate routine
 description of 141
 sample used in code 141
ftWriteAbort 159, 160
ftWriteComplete 159, 160
ftWriteDataFork 159
ftWriteFileInfo 159, 160
ftWriteOpenFile 159
ftWriteRsrcFork 159

G
globals 9

H
hard disk 5
hardware 5
hook procedure 206-209

I, J
ID
 mapping to Local ID 180
 mapping to Real ID 181
InitCM routine 36
InitCRM routine 174
InitCTBUtilities routine 192
InitFT routine 138
InitTM routine 88
installation of tools 5
installation, checking for
  Communications Toolbox
  managers sample code 332
installing devices 174
interfacing
 between Macintosh
  Communications Toolbox
  applications and tools 4,
  5 (fig.)
 scripting language code
  resource 226-228
 user interface considerations
  287-291
 with scripting language 47, 98, 148
IsConnEvent function 320-321

IsFTEvent function 319-320
IsFTWindow function 319-320
IsTermEvent function 321-322

K
Keyboard events
 procedures for 22-23
 in Terminal Manager 106

L
LAT Tool scripting interface 301
localization code resource 229-230

M
Macintosh Communications
  Toolbox. *See also* specific
  managers
 contents of 3-4
 function of 8
 globals used in 9
 installation of 5
 interface between application and
  tools 4, 5 (fig.)
 managers in 3-4
 reference manual for xiv
 requirements for 5
 sample application of 8-25
 sections of 9
Macintosh computers 5, 291
Macintosh Operating System trap 73,
  124, 165, 187, 214
Main program loop in sample
  code 24-25, 321-322
MakeNew procedure in sample
  code 16-18
Memory Manager 168
menu choices, handling 10
Menu events
 closing session document 19
 configuring connection 14
 configuring file transfer 15
 configuring terminal
  emulation 14-15
 in Connection Manager 61
 in File Transfer Manager 152
 handling menu choices 10
 initiating connection 11
 making new session
  document 16-18
 receiving file 13

 sending file 12-13
 in Terminal Manager 105
 terminating connection 11-13
modeless tools 288
Modem Tool scripting interface See
  Apple Modem Tool scripting
  interface
Mouse events
 clikLoop 118
 procedure for 23
 in Terminal Manager 106
MultiFinder 5, 168
MyBreakProc routine 115
MyCacheProc routine 116-117
MyCallBack routine 117
MyClikLoop routine 118
MyCompletion routine 66
MyEnvironsProc routine
  118, 160
MyHookProc routine 208-209
MyNameFilter routine 206
MyReadProc routine 156-157
MyRecvProc routine 158
MySearchCallBack routine 60
MySendProc routine 114, 157
MyWriteProc routine 159-160
MyZoneFilter routine 207

N
name filters 206
network look-up utilities 202 (fig.),
  203-205
NewControl routine 193
NuLookup routine 202-204
NuPLookup routine 202, 204-205

O
Operating System Utilities 168

P
pop-up menu control definition
  procedure 193-197
PopUpMenuSelect function 193
popupUseAddResMenu variation
  code constant 195
popupUseCQD variation code
  constant 195
popupUseWfont variation code
  constant 195

programming problems
  custom tool-settings dialog
    box 323-331
  events needed to be handled by
    Macintosh Communications
    Toolbox managers 319-322
  idle loops 316-318
  installation of Macintosh
    Communications Toolbox
    managers, checking for 332

Q

QuickDraw 76

R

regions in terminal window
  terminal emulation region 84
  scroll-back region 84
removing devices 175
Resource management 170
Resource Manager
  and Communications Resource
    Manager 168
  and Connection Manager 28
  and File Transfer Manager 128
  and Terminal Manager 76
  and utilities 190
resource-mapping routines 180
resources
  getting usage index for 178
  loading 177-178
  loading indexed 177
  loading named 178
  releasing 178
Resume events
  in Connection Manager 61
  in File Transfer Manager 151
  procedure for 20-21
  in Terminal Manager 105
routines. *See also* specific names of
  Communications Resource
    Manager
    application of 3, 169-170
    description of 177-179
    list of 173
    quick reference to 185-187
    resource mapping 180-181
    selectors 187
  Connection Manager
    application of 3-4, 29

completion 66
  list of 35
  miscellaneous 64-65
  quick reference to 67-72
  selectors 73
File Transfer Manager
  application of 3, 129-130
  list of 137
  miscellaneous 154-155
  provided by application
    156-160
  quick reference to 161-165
  selectors 165-166
Terminal Manager
  application of 3-4, 77-78
  list of 87
  miscellaneous 109-113
  provided by application
    114-118
  quick reference to 119-124
  selectors 124-125
  terminal emulation 99-101
and tools 4
utilities
  list of 191
  quick reference to 211-214
  selectors 214
routine selectors
  Communications Resource
    Manager 187
  Connection Manager 73
  File Transfer Manager 165-166
  Terminal Manager 124-125
  utilities 214

S

Sample code
  Application shell
    Handling events that belong to
    Communications Toolbox
    Managers
      IsConnEvent 320
      IsFTEvent 319
      IsFTWindow 319, 320
      IsTermEvent 321
    DoActivate 20
    DoClick 23
    DoCommand 10
    DoConnectionConfig 14
    DoFileTransferConfig 15
    DoInitiate 11

DoKey 22
DoKill 11
DoReceive 13
DoResume 20
DoSend 12
DoTerminalConfig 14
DoUpdate 21
Tool-settings dialog box,
  customizing
  Choose.p 323-330
  Choose.r 330-331
Using the scripting interface 293,
  294
Scrap Manager 76
scripting interface
  for communications tools 293
scripting language, interfacing with
  code resource 226-228
  in Connection Manager 47
  in File Transfer Manager 148
  in Terminal Manager 98
  sample code 333
Script Manager 216
Scroll-back cache 78 (fig.), 79
search call-back procedure 103, 117
searching for devices 175
searching
  with CMAddSearch 35
  with TMAddSearch 87
sendProc routine
  in file transfer record 134
  in terminal record 83
Serial Tool scripting interface 302
Serial NB Tool scripting interface 302
session document
  closing 19
  making new 16-18
setup definition code resource
  221-226
ShortenDITL routine
  description of 201
  sample used in code 326, 327
Show Controls 291
Standard File Package 128
Superdrive 5
status dialog boxes 289 (fig.), 290
System Folder 5

T

TermDataBlock data structure 79

terminal emulation
  configuring 14-15
  preparing 88-93
  routines 99-101
  window 78 (fig.), 79
terminal emulation buffer 79,
    102-103
terminal emulation region 78 (fig.),
    79, 99-101, 116
terminal emulation tool
  writing own
    bundle resource for 217-218
    configuration record 230
    function of 217
    initialization request
      message 217
    localization code resource
      229-230
    quick reference to 231-232
    scripting language interface
      code resource 226-228
    setup definition code
      resource 221-226
    validation code resource
      219-221
terminal keys 111-112
Terminal Manager. *See also*
    Terminal emulation;
    Terminal record; specific
    routines
  calling from Assembler 124
  clean-up operations 96
  closing tool file 97
  configuration string in 98, 108
  custom configuration of terminal
    tool 94-97
  data flow in 77 (fig.), 78
  data stream search in 102-103
  function of 77-78
  handling events 105-107
  initializing 88
  interfacing with scripting
    language 98
  manipulating selections 104
  preparing for terminal
    emulation 88-93
  routines
    application of 3-4, 77-78
    list of 87
    miscellaneous 109-113
    provided by application
      114-118

quick reference to 119-124
selectors 124-125
terminal emulation 99-101
searching terminal emulation
  buffer 102-103
terminal emulation routines
  99-101
terminal record for 121-122
version number 110
terminal record
  creating 89-90
  data structure 80-86
  disposing of 101
  features of 78
  fields in 80
  function of 77, 80
  initializing 81
  resetting 101
  resizing 101
  saving the state of 333
  validating 91
terminal tool
  configuring 92-93
  custom configuration of 94-97
  information 112-113
  keyboards for 291
  list of 76
  main code resource for
    function of 257
    messages accepted by 257-272
    quick reference to 273-276
  name of 109
  reference constant 109
  search of terminal emulation
    buffer 102
termRect 83
Text Tool scripting interface 303
TMActivate routine
  description of 105
  sample used in code 20
tmActivateMsg message 261-262
TMAddSearch routine 102-103
TMChoose routine 92-93
TMClear routine 100
tmClearMsg message 268
TMClearSearch routine 103
TMClick routine 106
  sample used in code 23
tmClickMsg message 264
TMCountTermKeys routine 112
tmCountTermKeysMsg
  message 272

tmCursorMsg message 269-270
tmDeactivateMsg message 262
TMDefault routine 91
TMDispose routine
  description of 101
  sample used in code 19
tmDisposeMsg message 259
TMDoTermKey routine
  description of 111
  sample used in code 111
tmDoTermKeyMsg message 271
TMEnglishToIntl routine 108
TMEvent routine
  description of 107
  sample used in code 24
tmEventMsg message 271
TMGetConfig routine 98
TMGetCursor routine 111
tmGetEnvironsMsg message 270
TMGetIndTermKey routine 112
tmGetIndTermKeyMsg
  message 272
TMGetLine routine 100
tmGetLineMsg message 268-269
TMGetProcID routine
  description of 88
  sample used in code 17
TMGetRefCon routine 109
TMGetSelect routine 104
tmGetSelectionMsg
  message 265-266
TMGetTermEnvirons
  routine 112-113
TMGetTMVersion routine 110
TMGetToolName routine 109
TMGetUserData routine 110
TMGetVersion routine 110
TMIdle routine
  description of 99
  sample used in code 317-318
  using 316
tmIdleMsg message 263
tmInitMsg message 217, 257-258
TMIntlToEnglish routine 108
TMKey routine
  description of 106
  sample used in code 23
  and Terminal Manager 77
tmKeyMsg message 259-260
TMMenu routine
  description of 105
  sample used in code 10

tmMenuMsg message 265
TMNew routine
  description of 89-90
  sample used in code 17
TMPaint routine 99
tmPaintMsg message 269
tmPrivate 83
TMRemoveSearch routine 103
TMReset routine 101
tmResetMsg message 267-268
TMResize routine
  description of 101
  sample used in code 23
tmResizeMsg message 262-263
TMResume routine
  description of 105
  sample used in code 21
tmResumeMsg message 261-262
TMScroll routine
  description of 100
  sample used in code 23
tmScrollMsg message 267
TMSetConfig routine 98
TMSetRefCon routine 109
TMSetSelection routine 104
tmSetSelectionMsg
      message 266-267
TMSetupCleanup routine 96
TMSetupFilter routine 95
TMSetupItem routine 96
TMSetupPostflight routine 97
TMSetupPreflight routine 94
TMSetupSetup routine 95
TMSetUserData routine 110
TMStream routine
  description of 99
  sample used in code 317
tmStreamMsg message 260-261
tmSuspendMsg message 262
TMUpdate routine 106
tmUpdateMsg message 263-264
TMValidate routine
  description of 91
  sample used in code 91
tool file, closing
  in Connection Manager 46
  in File Transfer Manager 147
  in Terminal Manager 97
tools. See also Macintosh
      Communications Toolbox;
      specific tools
  compatibility requirements 291

design goals of 286-287
function of 4
modeless operation 288
name of 179
and routines 4
self-contained 286
task-specific 286-287
user interface considerations
  error alerts 290
  handling errors 290
  menus 290
  modeless tool operation
      287-288
  right words 291
  standard tool-settings dialog
      box 288 (fig.)-289
  windows and status dialog
      boxes 289-290 (fig.)
tool-settings dialog box
  customizing 323-331
  in File Transfer Manager 144-147
  standard 288 (fig.), 289
transferring files
  preparing for 138-141
  processing data 150
  starting 149
  stopping 150
Transparent Mode 291
TTY Tool scripting interface 304

U

Update events
  procedures for 21-22
  in Terminal Manager 106
Update procedure
  sample used in code 21-22
utilities
  and AppleTalk 202-205
  DITLs 198-201
  initializing 192
  pop-up menu control definition
      procedure 193-197
  routines
    list of 191
    quick reference to 211-214
    selectors 214
  version number 192

V

validation code resource 219-221

variation codes 194
version number
  Communications Resource
      Manager 176
  Connection Manager 65
  File Transfer Manager 155
  Terminal Manager 110
  utilities 192
viewRect 84
visRect 84
VT102 terminal setting 291
VT102 Tool scripting interface
      305-308
VT320 Tool scripting interface
      309-312

W, X, Y, Z

XMODEM Tool 129
XMODEM Tool scripting
      interface 313
zone filters 207